W9-BVI-516

FAST FORWARD

DESTINATIONS

EDITOR

S.D. ROBINSON

AUTHORS

A. ELCHUK
W. EWART
P. GRAY
W. GREENWAY
C. HENDERSON
M. LYONS
D. VERHULST

LANGUAGE ▲ LITERATURE ▲ MEDIA

PRENTICE-HALL CANADA, INC.

Canadian Cataloguing in Publication Data
Robinson, Sam, date
Fast forward

(Destinations)
ISBN 0-13-202391-1

1. English language – Composition and exercises.
2. Communication – Problems, exercises, etc.
I. Title. II. Series: Destinations (Scarborough, Ont.).

P91.2.R623 1989 808'.042 C89-095321-X

Prentice-Hall, Inc., Englewood Cliffs, New Jersey
Prentice-Hall International, Inc., London
Prentice-Hall of Australia, Pty., Ltd., Sydney
Prentice-Hall of India Pvt., Ltd., New Delhi
Prentice-Hall of Japan, Inc., Tokyo
Prentice-Hall of Southeast Asia (PTE) Ltd., Singapore
Editora Prentice-Hall do Brasil Ltda., Rio de Janeiro
Prentice-Hall Hispanoamericana, S.A., Mexico

ISBN 0-13-202391-1
Third Printing

Project Editors: Mary Beth Leatherdale and Lavinia Inbar
Production Editor: Elise Levine
Manufacturing: Lois Enns and Crystale Sheehan
Design: Derek Chung Tiam Fook
Photo Research: Suzette Chan
Cover Photo: Masterfile

Printed and bound in Canada by Friesen Printers
3 4 5 6 FP 94 93 92

DESTINATIONS

Destinations is an English/Language Arts program developed for use in senior high school English courses. Each level consists of a student text, accompanying anthology, and a teacher resource book.

LANGUAGE LITERATURE ▲ MEDIA	STORIES ▲ ARTICLES POEMS ▲ PLAYS
FAST FORWARD STUDENT TEXT + TEACHER RESOURCE BOOK	**ACCELERATE** ANTHOLOGY
STRAIGHT AHEAD STUDENT TEXT + TEACHER RESOURCE BOOK	**OVERDRIVE** ANTHOLOGY
IN FLIGHT STUDENT TEXT + TEACHER RESOURCE BOOK	**GLIDE PATH** ANTHOLOGY

ANNOTATED TABLE OF CONTENTS

TABLE OF CONTENTS

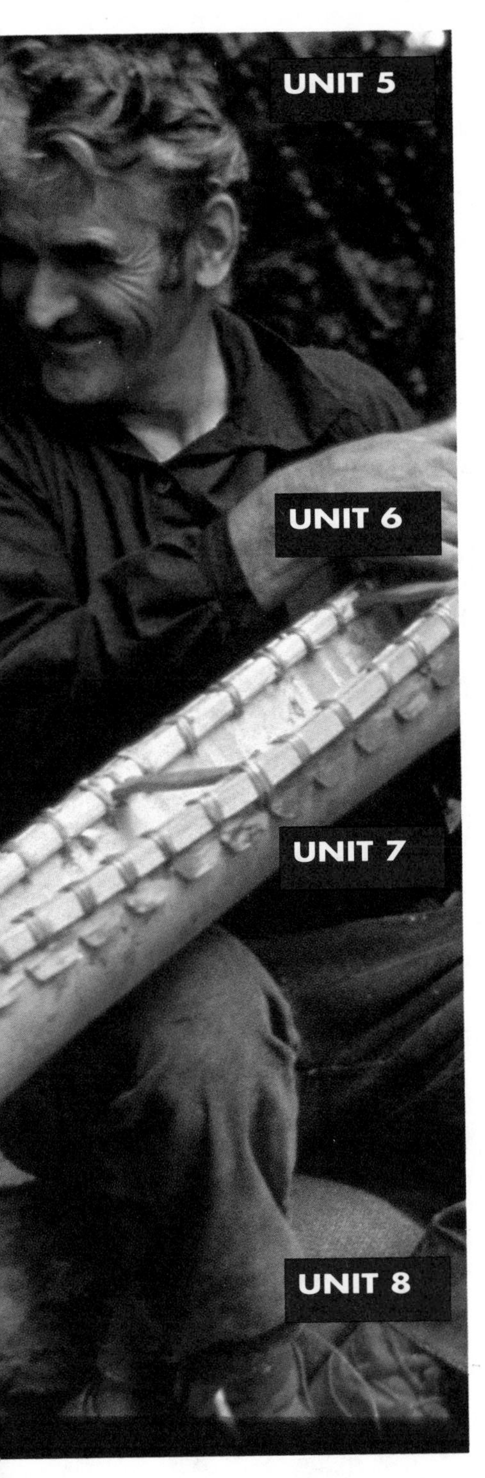

DRIVING DESIGN 87

THE JOB DECISION 111

THE OUTER SHELL 131

TV CHANNELS 149

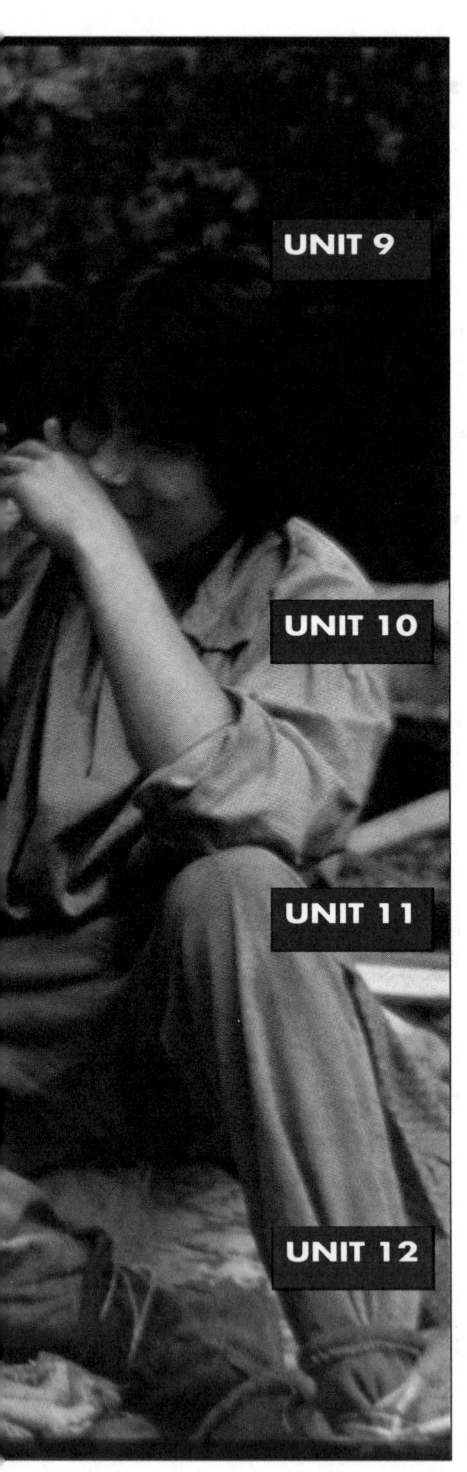

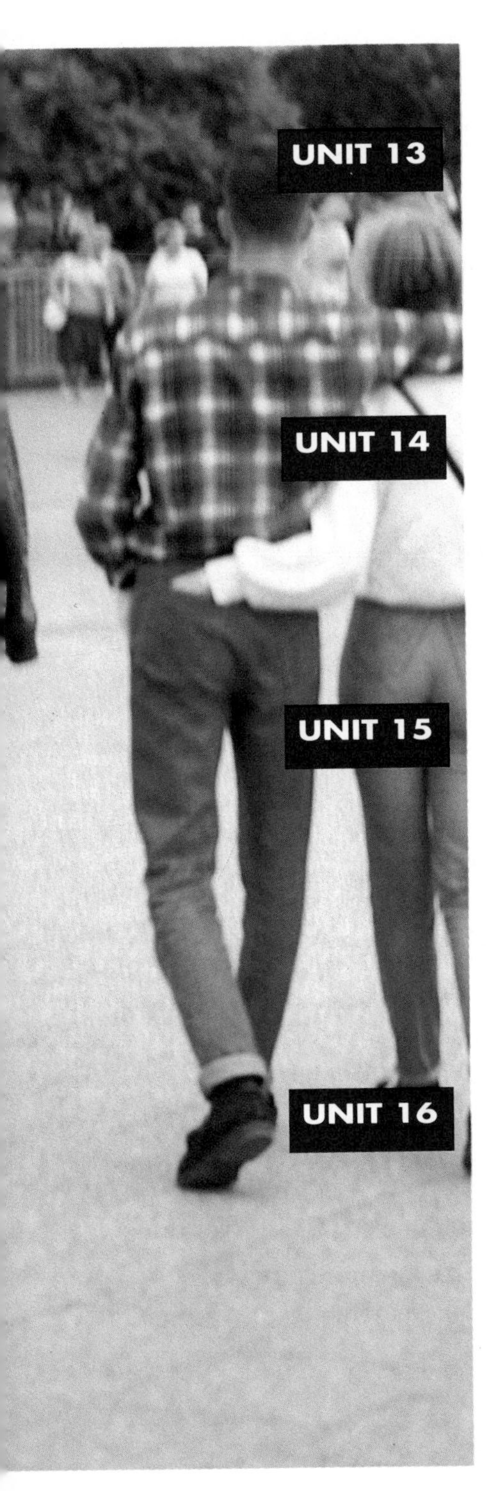

RESOURCE UNITS

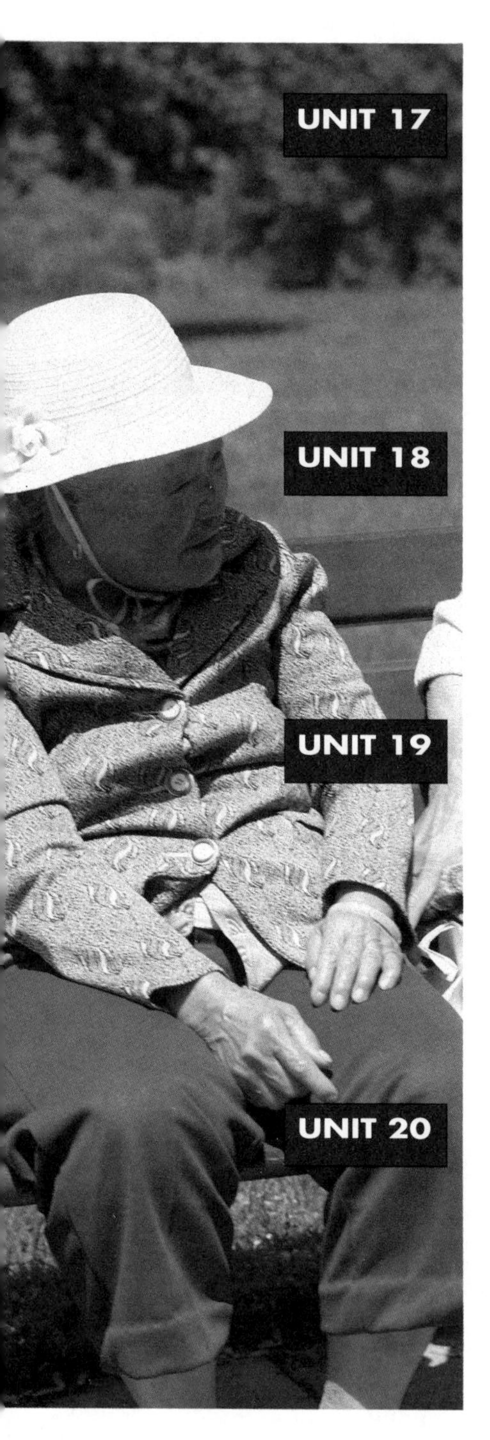
UNIT 17
UNIT 18
UNIT 19
UNIT 20

UNIT 21 LEARNING SKILLS 343

LITERATURE CONTENTS

ACKNOWLEDGEMENTS

As series editor, I extend to the editorial staff at Prentice-Hall appreciation for the care they have given this textbook. I acknowledge the good humour and good sense of Acquiring Editor David Steele, whose work inspired this series, and the editorial judgement of Project Editors Lavinia Inbar and Mary Beth Leatherdale. I am grateful, too, for the work of the editorial and production staff at Prentice-Hall: Production Editor Elise Levine, Manufacturing Buyers Lois Enns and Crystale Sheehan, and Designer Derek Chung Tiam Fook.

I especially appreciate the work of the contributing authors to this textbook, all classroom teachers who did their work on weekends and holidays. I have come to value their creativity and their practical wisdom. Their concern to reach students in general-level classrooms has made this project possible. To the unknown teachers who reviewed the manuscript and provided sound and helpful criticism, I also extend our appreciation. And to Jane and Karen Robinson, who sat long hours at the keyboard going through the many revisions of this textbook, thanks for the help when I needed it most.

Sam Robinson,

Series Editor

HOW TO USE THIS BOOK

ORGANIZATION

- This book is comprised of Core units and Resource units. Each Core unit focuses on an interesting topic or issue. Resource units focus on a particular process such as writing, reading, listening, speaking, viewing, working in groups, and studying.
- This book is flexible and has been designed to be used in any order or sequence depending upon your own interests and needs.
- Each unit is divided into sections containing reading selections, visuals, and activities. The section titles appear in blue ink. Sections within units are linked together by topic and theme, but they can also stand alone and can be used independently, if you desire. The names of all the units and sections are listed in the Table of Contents.

LITERATURE

- All reading selections in this book are highlighted with a coloured screen. These selections offer a variety of short stories, poems, essays, articles, and autobiographies that explore a particular theme.
- All the reading selections are listed in the Literature Contents at the beginning of the book.

VISUALS

- This book also includes a wide variety of photographs, paintings, illustrations, advertisements, and cartoons. They are numbered according to the unit in which they appear and the order in which they appear within the unit. For example, Figure 7-2 refers to the second figure in Unit 7.
- Each visual has a caption that asks you to think about the image and its relationship to the unit.

ACTIVITIES

- This book contains a variety of activities. These activities are highlighted with a magenta box in the margin and are designed to allow you to explore a theme through reading, writing, listening, speaking, and viewing. Sometimes you may be asked to complete the activities independently. In other cases you will work with a partner, a small group, or the whole class.
- The last activity in each Core unit includes a list of possible Extension Ideas for the unit. These activities suggest larger projects that will help you continue your exploration of the theme through independent study or group work.

INFO-BOXES

- Throughout the book you will notice Info-boxes highlighted with a broken magenta border. These boxes offer information about literature, language, and media that relate to the topic of the unit and help you complete the activities in the units. A list of these boxes is provided in an Index at the back of the book.

UNIT 1

★ ★ ★ ★ ★ ★ ★

PEOPLE BUILDING

★ ALL ABOUT ME
★ NAMES AND NUMBERS
★ MORE ABOUT ME
★ THE BETTER TO SEE YOU WITH
★ REPORT CARDS

INTRODUCTION

Prejudice destroys understanding, yet understanding destroys prejudice. When you pre-judge, you don't see people as they are, and you don't understand them. Sometimes new people and new places can make you feel a little unsure about them. But the more you learn about new people and new places, the less you feel uncertain.

When you complete the activities in this unit you will understand your classmates a little better – and perhaps you will become more comfortable in your classroom. And while you are getting to know others, you will probably start to understand yourself a little better, too.

ALL ABOUT ME

If understanding is to destroy prejudice, you need to take risks. One form of risk-taking involves something called self-disclosure. Self-disclosure does not mean confessing all your weaknesses publicly, but it does mean telling others something about yourself. When you tell others about yourself, you help them to understand you. One easy way to begin is by answering a few questions. And who knows, you may get to understand yourself more in the process.

This first activity asks these questions: What do you like? What don't you like? And what interests you? The second activity will ask you to think about your English course and how you can get the most out of your work in English.

LEARNING ABOUT ME

1. Create a data sheet about yourself. Use this list of possible items to organize your data:

- birthday
- birthplace
- ambitions
- favourite things
- pet peeves
- role models
- a brief description of a good person
- what you like to read
- a description of your idea of a perfect day

You might also attach a favourite picture to your data sheet. The picture could be a photograph of yourself (at any age), a friend, or a scene; or it could be a magazine illustration or a drawing.

2. Select two or three different or unusual items from your data sheet to mention in class.
3. In your notebook, list the names of all your classmates and your teacher. Listen as your classmates read their items. As individuals mention something that you feel is important, make a note about this information beside their names. For example, "Chan – spent summer as bee keeper's helper." Be sure to keep this list to use with Activity 2 and to leave an extra space between lines to add more information.
4. In your notebook, state what you learned about yourself in this activity.

DATA SHEET

NAME:
BIRTHDAY:
BIRTHPLACE:
AMBITIONS:

FAVOURITE THINGS:

PET PEEVES:

ROLE MODELS:

A GOOD PERSON:

FAVOURITE READING (including magazines):

A PERFECT DAY:

FAVOURITE PICTURE:

Figure 1-1 The data sheet is just a quick sketch of you. You might want to attach to your data sheet a picture of yourself as a child.

ACTIVITY 2

WHAT I EXPECT FROM THIS COURSE

1. Write a brief statement explaining what you hope this year's English course will be like. For example, "In past years all we ever did was read stories and answer questions. I hope that's not all we're going to be doing this year. Instead it would be nice if ...."
2. Share answers as a class. As you listen to the responses from each person, note one thing she or he wants from the course. For example, "Sarah – lots of group work." Use the same class list that you used for Activity 1.
3. As you complete this list of responses, look for the similarities among students' statements. Look also for the differences. What does this information tell you about the kind of English program your class would like?
4. What does this discussion tell you about yourself and your expectations for your English class? What can you do to achieve your expectations?

NAMES AND NUMBERS

For centuries, people have been interested in discovering the secrets of the unknown – of their own and others' futures, and even of their own personality and that of others. And people have used some extraordinary ways to try to uncover these secrets. They have used means such as tea-leaf reading, phrenology (feeling the bumps on a person's head), Ouija boards, crystal-ball reading, seances, hand-writing analysis, and numerology. The next activity will focus on one of these practices: numerology.

You may not believe in numerology – many people don't. In fact many people don't know that numerology is the study of numbers and the way numbers seem to affect their lives. And even if they do know this definition, they still may not believe in numerology. They don't believe that the numerical value of your name, for example, will influence the kind of person you are and the kind of life you will lead. This next activity is about numerology – something for you to do... just for fun!

ACTIVITY 3

NUMEROLOGY

1. Read the first two paragraphs of "The Magic in Your Name," below.
2. Use these paragraphs to determine the number of your name and, as a class, group yourselves according to your numbers (all ones form a group, all twos form a group).
3. Read the rest of the article and continue this activity as a small-group assignment.
4. Choose someone in your group to outline the description in the article of the characteristics of your group members. Report this outline to the class.
5. Have each member of your group comment on how accurately the article describes himself or herself (for example, "I'm not conceited; I'm just good-looking").
6. Refer to your class list from Activity 1. As you listen to your group members comment on the accuracy of their number, note one quality that you observed about each person (for example, "Sylvie – hard-working").

"In the modern world, numerology may seem to be just an amusing game, but in ancient civilizations it was a very serious concern."

THE MAGIC IN YOUR NAME

Conrad King

Does your name have anything to do with your fortune? Numerologists believe that it does. A numerologist is a person who believes that he can foretell events or discover hidden knowledge by the use of numbers. Your name is one of the ways you are set apart from other people, but to a numerologist, your name is the key to all the qualities that make you what you are. Since there are millions of different names, the job of finding what each one means appears to be impossible. The numerologist solves this problem with a system in which each letter of the alphabet is given a number from one to nine.

1	2	3	4	5	6	7	8	9
A	B	C	D	E	F	G	H	I
J	K	L	M	N	O	P	Q	R
S	T	U	V	W	X	Y	Z	

To find the number of your name, write out your name as you normally use it. If you're called Bob Jones instead of Robert Jones, use Bob Jones. Underneath each letter of your name write the number that letter has on the chart, and then add together all the numbers. You will probably get a two-digit number. If so, add those two digits together. If you get a number from one to nine, that is the number of your name. If you get another two-digit number, add *these* digits together and you will have the number of your name. For example:

R I C H A R D   M A R T I N

9+ 9+ 3+ 8+ 1+ 9+ 4 + 4+ 1+ 9+ 2+ 9+ 5 = 73

Then 7 + 3 = 10 and 1 + 0 = 1

The number of Richard Martin is one.

Numerologists say that people whose number is one are powerful, stubborn, and self-reliant. They have *one*-track minds. They concentrate on what they are doing and have good memories. They are pioneers and leaders and do not take orders well or cooperate with others. Don't try to give ones any advice because they will usually ignore it. Ones don't have much interest in love or friendship, and when they are friendly it is probably because they think they can gain some advantage. They try to dominate everyone and are basically people who "look out for number one."

"One of the ways numerologists try to prove their powers is by the analysis of the names of historical figures."

In the modern world, numerology may seem to be just an amusing game, but in ancient civilizations it was a very serious concern. Names and numbers became connected in ancient times because two important languages, Hebrew and Greek, used the letters of the alphabet to stand for numbers. The Hebrew *aleph*, the first letter in the alphabet, stood for the number one, for example. It was quite natural for a Hebrew or Greek to think of a name as being a group of numbers.

→

> "If you work out the fortunes of yourself and your friends, you may be surprised by their apparent accuracy."

Among primitive peoples people have two names, one for everyday use and a "real" one that is kept secret. If the "real" name is discovered, it is believed that an enemy can use it to destroy the person. In ancient Greece, those who wished to murder someone simply wrote that person's name on a piece of clay and buried it with an appropriate curse. When the name was buried, it was believed that it wouldn't be long before the person joined it.

Some of this superstition survives in the tradition, common among some people, of never naming a child after a living relative. If this is done, the belief is that the relative will die immediately because there is no room in the family for two people with the same name. On the other hand, some fear that the child will die instead of the relative, since the angel of death might become confused by the identical names and take the younger one.

Modern numerology attempts to make a science out of these superstitions. One of the ways numerologists try to prove their powers is by the analysis of the names of historical figures. Napoleon Bonaparte, for example, originally spelled his name Napoleon Buonaparte, which (by a slightly different system than we have been using) adds up to the number one. One is the number of strength, leadership, and domination and it fits Napoleon's early career. He later changed his name, dropping the "u" from Buonaparte, which made four the number of his name. Since four is the number of defeat and failure, to a numerologist Napoleon's downfall was inevitable.

Numerologists, as you may suspect, choose their historical examples very carefully, avoiding the names of people whose fortunes don't seem to fit their actual lives. However, many of the numerologists' explanations of the past and predictions of the future seem to be too close for chance. If you work out the fortunes of yourself and your friends, you may be surprised by their apparent accuracy.

Suppose your number is two. Then you have a soft, sweet nature and are quiet and tactful. You love peace and harmony and tend to play second fiddle. Twos are followers not leaders, and they don't like to assert themselves. They are shy and tend to change their minds and put things off.

People whose names add to three are imaginative, brilliant, and energetic. Threes are witty, charming, and likely to be very successful in life. They are easy-going and lucky – their success seems to come without any effort. Proud and ambitious people, threes are used to having their commands obeyed. They often have artistic talent, but they try to do too many things at once and sometimes suffer because they refuse to take anything seriously. Threes are also a little too eager for popularity and approval.

"People whose names add to three are imaginative, brilliant, and energetic."

Fours are solid, practical, and dull. They are efficient organizers and like to think of themselves as respectable members of society. They like steady, hard work and are not sympathetic to people who don't. Fours are likely to be grim and suspicious and any success they have in life will not come easily.

Fives are nervous, clever, and impatient. They love the new and unusual – travel, new people, different surroundings. Fives also enjoy gambling and risks. They are attractive and make excellent salespeople even though they are sometimes conceited and sarcastic. They hate responsibility and are often inconsiderate. Fives have interesting but unstable love lives.

Sixes are kindly and reliable. Their loyal and affectionate nature makes them well-suited for family life. Wholesome and conventional, they may be more successful in the long run than threes and fives, especially as artists or teachers. They don't usually do well in business and are happiest in a quiet group of family and friends. They sometimes tend to be conceited and gossipy.

Seven stands for the scholar and the philosopher. Sevens like to withdraw from the world and meditate. They are dignified, serious, and self-controlled, and they have no patience with foolishness. Sevens have no interest in money or physical comfort. They have powerful minds, but there is a strange, dreamy side to their character. They are bad at explaining themselves and dislike being questioned.

Eight is the number of power and money, material success or failure. People with this number are tough and practical, successful businessmen and politicians, but their way in life is not easy. Their careers are full of hard and difficult work. They can be selfish and unscrupulous and these qualities often make them unpopular. Beneath their efficient surface eights are often rebels. They are constantly balanced between overwhelming success and crushing failure.

According to numerologists, if your number is nine you are a person of high mental and spiritual achievement. Nines are romantic, impulsive, and charming. They have a great desire to help people and to serve humanity at large. They make brilliant scientists, teachers, and artists, but they are often condemned by others as wild and impractical. They are easily imposed upon and readily fall in and out of love. Nines hate ugliness, poverty, old age, and unhappiness for themselves and everyone else. Their desire to do good may be expressed in a conceited and self-centered way. Sometimes they seem too busy loving people in general to bother with individuals.

"Numerology shows us that, even though we may think we are modern and logical, there is still a great deal of superstition left in human nature."

There are several reasons why the predictions of numerology often seem to be true. First, the characteristics given to a number are broad enough to fit just about anyone. Suppose, for example, the number of your name is eight. Eights are supposed to be selfish, and, since everyone probably feels they're a little selfish, the fortune is "true." Second, since we read a fortune hoping it is true, we tend to ignore the parts that don't apply. Eights are supposed to be tough and practical, but, if you are not, you will probably pass over that part of the fortune without blinking an eye and look for the next thing that fits you.

Numerology shows us that, even though we may think we are modern and logical, there is still a great deal of superstition left in human nature. When your friends are surprised by the accurate fortunes you can make from their names, remember that what you are doing is not far removed from the actions of the Greeks who believed they could dispose of their enemies by burying their names. And you don't believe that, do you? ◆

MORE ABOUT ME

Despite what you might have heard, read, or seen poetry can be very simple. Poetry is ...

- ***talk:*** someone (the poet) is saying something (the poem) to someone else (you)
- ***indirect:*** poetry respects your intelligence by using interesting figurative language to say a great deal using few words
- ***musical:*** like songs, all poems have a rhythm and, sometimes, a rhyme scheme

You can use the following pattern to write a descriptive "I Am..." poem about yourself. Writing this poem will get you to think more about yourself – and will provide others with information about you.

Line 1: Begin with the words "I am."

Line 2: Write three nouns about which you have strong feelings. Begin each with a capital letter.

Line 3: Write a complete sentence about two things that you like.

Line 4: Begin with three nouns that describe qualities you like to see in other people. End the sentence with these words: "...are important to me." Capitalize each noun.

Line 5: Write a sentence containing a positive thought or feeling. It can express what you like about yourself.

Lines 6 and 7: Write a sentence in which you show something negative in yourself or in others; however, the sentence must finish by showing that out of something bad can come good. Use the conjunction "but" to link the bad and the good.

Lines 8, 9, and 10: For each line write a short sentence describing something that you have strong feelings about – either likes or dislikes. These likes or dislikes do not have to relate to each other or to the previous lines you have written.

Line 11: End your poem with the words "This is me. I am!"

Here is an example of a poem that was written using the "I Am..." pattern:

I Am...

I am
Videos, Cory Hart, Blue jeans
I like long weekends and rowdy parties.
Honesty, Humour, and Adventure are important to me.
I like listening to my friends' problems.
I hate to follow directions,
But I don't like to hurt other people's feelings.
I like sleeping in.
I hate alarm clocks.
Friday afternoons are like money in the bank,
This is me. I am!

You may not like to follow a pattern for your "I Am..." poem. You may wish to write a free verse "I Am..." poem. Here is an example:

I Am...

So there it was Friday afternoon again
And I saw this girl standing by her locker.
So what you doing this weekend? I asked.
Not much, she said. Got a car?
Yep. Got a VCR? So I went to the
Video shop 'cause I like
Cars and Videos and Friday nights.
But the tape might as well have been
Herbie Goes Into Outer Space –
When I got home that night
Sister Jessie had the family wheels
On the road.
I think I'm crossing girls off my
Top ten list.

WRITING AN "I AM..." POEM

1. Use the "I Am..." pattern to write a descriptive "I Am..." poem about yourself. Or, if you don't like to follow the pattern, write a free verse poem about yourself.
2. Your "I Am..." poem reflects the things that make you a unique person, different from others. Listen while others in your class read their poems. This activity should give you more personal information about each other than you found in the previous activities.
3. Select magazine illustrations or pictures that portray those things that you mentioned in your poem. Find pictures, for example, of your favourite rock star, car, or actress.
4. On a piece of Bristol board or other art paper, surround your "I Am..." poem with the illustrations you have selected. You could use your own art work instead of the magazine cuttings.

THE BETTER TO SEE YOU WITH...

So far in this unit you have thought about yourself and your classmates in order to come to a better understanding of yourself and of people in general. It seems that the better you understand other people, the more you come to know yourself and to accept who and what you are. The story in this section is about someone who was able to understand and recognize the uniqueness of another individual. By doing so, he was able to destroy the prejudice that he previously had toward this person. As he comes to understand this other person, he comes to know something more about himself as well. And in the process he comes to recognize that while prejudice destroys understanding, understanding destroys prejudice.

"His little bunch of flowers was the most incongruous thing you could imagine. It was a corsage. A corsage of simple flowers, such as a young boy sends his girl for her first formal dance."

LONG, LONG AFTER SCHOOL

Ernest Buckler

I ran into Wes Holman the very day I was collecting for Miss Tretheway's flowers. But it never came into my head to ask him for a contribution.

Miss Tretheway had taught Grade Three in our town for exactly fifty years. She had died the night before in her sleep. As chairman of the school board I had thought it would be fitting if all the Grade Three alumni who were still around made up enough money to get a really handsome "piece." She had no relatives. If I'd given it an instant's consideration I'd have known that Wes himself must have been in Grade Three some time or other; but I didn't.

Wes was just coming through the cemetery gate as I was going in. He "looks after" the cemetery, and I sometimes take a short cut through it on my way to work. I should say that Wes is our local "character." His tiny house up behind the ball park is furnished with almost nothing but books, and he can quote anyone from Seneca to Henry James. But that's his job: caretaker-about-town.

When I spoke to him about Miss Tretheway, a curious change came into his face. You couldn't say that he turned pale, but his stillness was quite different from the conventional one on such occasions. I had expected him to come out with some quote or other, but he didn't say a word.

He didn't go to her funeral. But he sent her flowers of his own. Or brought them, rather. The following day, when I took the short cut again, I surprised him on his knees placing them.

His little bunch of flowers was the most incongruous thing you could imagine. It was a corsage. A corsage of simple flowers, such as a young boy sends his girl for her first formal dance. And more incongruous than its presence in the circumstances of death was its connection with Miss Tretheway herself. I'm quite sure that Miss Tretheway never once had a beau send her flowers, that she'd never been to a dance in her whole life.

I suppose it would never have occurred to me to question anyone but Wes about his motive for doing a thing like that. But I asked Wes about it with no thought of rudeness whatever. Wes's privacy seemed to be everyone's property. There was probably a little self-conscious democracy in the gesture when we talked to him at all.

"She was so beautiful," he answered me, as if no other explanation was needed.

"Wes's privacy seemed to be everyone's property. There was probably a little self-conscious democracy in the gesture when we talked to him at all."

That was plainly ridiculous. That Miss Tretheway was a fine person for having spent a lifetime in small, unheralded services could not be disputed – but obviously she hadn't *ever* been beautiful. Her sturdy plainness was never transfigured, not even for an instant, by the echo of anything winsomer which had faded. Her eyes had never been very blue, her skin very pink, or her hair very brown. She wasn't very anything. Her heart might have been headlong (I think now that it was), but there was always that curious precision and economy in her face which lacks altogether the grain of helter-skelter necessary to any kind of charm. In short, even when she'd been a girl, she'd been the sort of girl whose slightest eagerness, more than if she were ugly or old, a young man automatically shies away from.

"But, Wes," I said, half joking, "she wasn't beautiful. What made you say that?"

His story went something like this. He told it with a kind of dogged, confessional earnestness. I guess he'd come to figure that whenever we asked him a personal question he might as well satisfy our curiosity completely, first as last.

"Perhaps you remember how the kids used to tease me at school," he said. (I didn't. I guess those things stick in your mind according to which end of the teasing you happen to be on.) "If the boys would be telling some joke with words in it to giggle over, they'd look at me and say, 'Shhh... Wes is blushing.' Or if we were all climbing up the ladder to the big beam in Hogan's stable, they'd say 'Look at Wes. He's so scared he's turning pale.' Do you remember the night you steered your sled into mine, going down Parker hill?"

"No," I said. "Did I do it on purpose?"

"I don't know," Wes said. "Maybe you didn't. I thought you did."

Maybe I did. I don't remember.

"I was taking Mrs. Banks's wash home on my sled, and you were coasting down the hill. The basket upset and all the things fell out on the snow. Don't you remember...Miss Tretheway came along and you all ran. She helped me pick up the stuff and shake the snow off it. She went with me right to Mrs. Banks's door and told her what had happened. I could never have made Mrs. Banks believe I didn't upset the stuff myself."

"I'm sorry," I said. I probably *had* done it on purpose.

"That's all right," he said. "I didn't mind the boys so much. It was the girls. You can't hit a girl. There just wasn't anything I could do about the girls. One day Miss Tretheway was showing us a new game in the school yard. I don't remember exactly how it went, but that one where we all made a big circle and someone stood in the centre. I put my hand out to close up the ring with the biggest Banks girl, but she wouldn't take it. She said, 'Your hands are dirty.' Miss Tretheway made us both hold out our hands. She said, 'Why, Marilyn, Wes's hands are much cleaner than yours. Maybe Wes doesn't like to get *his* hands dirty, did you ever think about that?' She took Marilyn's place herself. Her hand felt safe and warm, I remember...and I guess that's the first day I thought she was beautiful."

"The only Wes I could seem to remember was the Wes of adolescence: the tough guy with the chip on his shoulder."

"I see," I said.

I did, and yet I didn't. The Wes I remembered would hate anything with the suggestion of teacher's pet about it. The only Wes I could seem to remember was the Wes of adolescence: the tough guy with the chip on his shoulder.

He was coming to that. But he stuck in an odd parenthesis first.

"Did you ever notice Miss Tretheway," he said, "when...well, when the other teachers would be talking in the hall about the dances they'd been to over the weekend? Or when she'd be telling some kid a story after school and the kid would run off right in the middle of a sentence when she saw her mother coming to pick her up?"

"No," I said. "Why? What about it."

"Oh, nothing, I guess." He drew a deep breath. "Anyway, I decided I'd be stronger and I'd study harder than anyone. And I was, wasn't I? I did. Do you remember the year they voted me the best all-round student in High School?" (I didn't. It must have been after I'd graduated.) "I guess I just can't remember how happy I was about that. I guess I was so happy I could believe anything. That must have been why I let the boys coax me into going to the closing dance." He smiled. "I thought since they'd voted for me... but you can't legislate against a girl's glance."

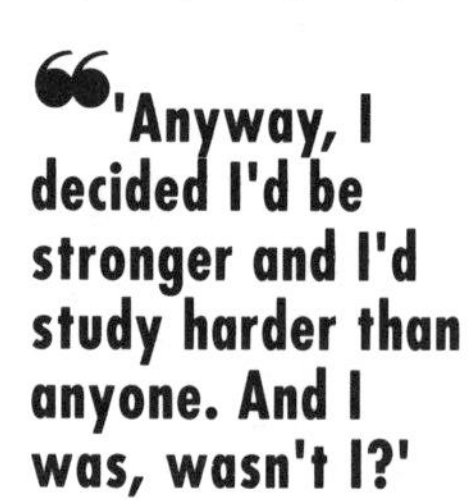

Those were his exact words. Maybe he'd read them somewhere. Maybe they were his own. I don't know. But it was the kind of remark which had built up his quaint reputation as the town philosopher.

"I didn't want to go out on the dance floor," he said. "I'd never danced a foxtrot or anything. The girls all had on their evening dresses, and somehow they looked different altogether. They looked as if they wouldn't recognize *themselves* in their day clothes. Anyway, the boys grabbed hold of me and made me get into a Paul Jones. I was next to Toby Wenford in the big ring. Jane Evans was right opposite me when the music stopped, but she danced with Toby instead – and the girl next *to* Jane just glanced at me and then went and sat down. I guess it was a pretty foolish thing to do, but I went down in the basement and drove my fist through a window."

"Is that the scar?" I said. I couldn't think of anything else to say.

"Oh, it was a lot worse than that," he said. He pulled up his sleeve and traced the faint sickle of the scar way up his arm. "You can hardly see it now. But I almost bled to death right there. I guess I might have, if it hadn't been for Miss Tretheway."

"Oh?" I said. "How's that?"

"You see, they didn't have any plasma around in bottles then," he said, "and in those days no one felt too comfortable about having his blood siphoned off. I guess no one felt like taking any chances for me, anyway. Mother said I could have hers, but hers wasn't right. Mine's that odd type – three, isn't it? Miss Tretheway's was three, too... and that's funny, because only seven percent of people have it. She gave me a whole quart, just as soon as she found out that hers would match."

"I see," I said. So that was it. And yet I had a feeling that that *wasn't* it – not quite.

"She used to come see me every day," he said. "She used to bring me books. Did you know that books... well, that for anyone like me that's the only way you can...?" He hesitated, and I knew that that wasn't quite it either.

"Not until he spoke again, when he spoke so differently, was I sure that only now was he coming to the real thing."

Not until he spoke again, when he spoke so differently, was I sure that only now was he coming to the real thing.

"Do you know what Miss Tretheway said when I thanked her for the transfusion?" he said. "She made a joke of it. She said: 'I didn't know whether an old maid's blood would be any good to a fine young specimen like you, Wes, or not.' The thing I always remember, I knew that was the first time she'd ever called herself an old maid to anyone, and really felt like laughing. And I remember what I said. I said: 'Miss Tretheway, you're making me blush.' And do you know, that was the very first time I'd ever been able to say *that*, and laugh, myself."

There was quite a long silence.

"She was beautiful," he added softly. "She was a real lady."

The cemetery is right next to the river. I looked down the river where the cold December water lapped at the jagged ice thrown up on the banks, and I thought about a boy the colour of whose skin was such that he could never blush, and I thought about a girl who had never been asked to a dance. I thought about the corsage. My curiosity was quite satisfied. But somehow I myself had never felt less beautiful, or less of a gentleman. ◆

The Saturday Evening

POST

March 17, 1956 – 15¢

JAN PEERCE, of the Metropolitan Opera, Advises Would-Be Singers, "DON'T BE A SUCKER, JUNIOR!"

Figure 1-2 How do you feel about each of your teachers? Has your perception of teachers in general changed over the years?

ACTIVITY 5

DEALING WITH PREJUDICE

1. Read "Long, Long After School."
2. In your notebook, mention one characteristic of Miss Tretheway that you liked. Briefly explain why you like that quality in a person.
3. In the story, the narrator misjudges Miss Tretheway because he doesn't know and understand her. By the end of the story his understanding of her destroys his prejudice. He comes to realize that she is an exceptional person. In your notebook, relate an incident in which you first prejudged someone but then came to understand that person better, and your prejudice was destroyed.

Figure 1-3 What is there about you that makes you a unique person?

REPORT CARDS

By now you know that teachers are more than information-givers. Similarly, your teacher knows that students are more than information-receivers. As the following poem "Report Card Writing" shows, teachers and students have a great deal in common – they're all human beings. Before reading this poem, think about a favourite teacher from elementary school. What was that teacher like... as a teacher?... as a person?

REPORT CARD

RELATIONSHIPS (e.g., friendliness, caring)

P	S	E	
poor	satisfactory	excellent	/5

Comments:

PERSONALITY (e.g., sense of humour, pleasantness)

P	S	E	
poor	satisfactory	excellent	/5

Comments:

BEHAVIOUR (e.g., patience, listening, consideration, student awareness, teaching style, helpfulness)

P	S	E	
poor	satisfactory	excellent	/5

Comments:

GENERAL OPINION:

/15

Figure 1-4 Do you think that such a report card gives enough information with which to judge a person's character?

REPORT CARD WRITING
(Some Things You're Not Supposed To Do)

Pat Sadowy

When writing report cards
for the final term
you're not supposed to use any colour but green,
you're not supposed to use the word "promoted,"

You're not supposed to be too vague
you're not supposed to be too negative.

When writing report cards
for the final term
you're not supposed to apologize
for all the mistakes you made
for all the things you intended to do
but never quite got done
for all the times you ignored a child
or hurt a child with thoughtless words
or failed to say "Thank you" though you were thankful
for all the encouragement,
attention,
advice
that you failed to give.

And most of all
when writing reports
for the final term
you're not supposed to say
I loved you.

and you're not supposed to be sitting up after midnight
crying
just because the kids you loved
are leaving.

DESCRIBING FEELINGS

1. Have someone read aloud "Report Card Writing" (p. 21).
2. As the poem is being read, think about the human qualities that the poem reveals about the teacher. List three or four of them in your notebook. For example, "The teacher in the poem worried about having said something that hurt a student."
3. When has someone older than you unknowingly said something to you that hurt your feelings? Write a brief description of the incident in your journal in which you consider:

    a) how you reacted in the situation
    b) how you should handle such a situation

ACTIVITY 7

WRITING A REPORT CARD

1. Refer to Activity 5 and the story "Long, Long After School."
   Using the information in the story about Miss Tretheway, write a report card for her commenting on qualities such as personality (for example, sense of humour), behaviour (for example, patience), and relationships with others (for example, friendliness).

Figure 1-5 What is this comic strip saying about criticizing others?

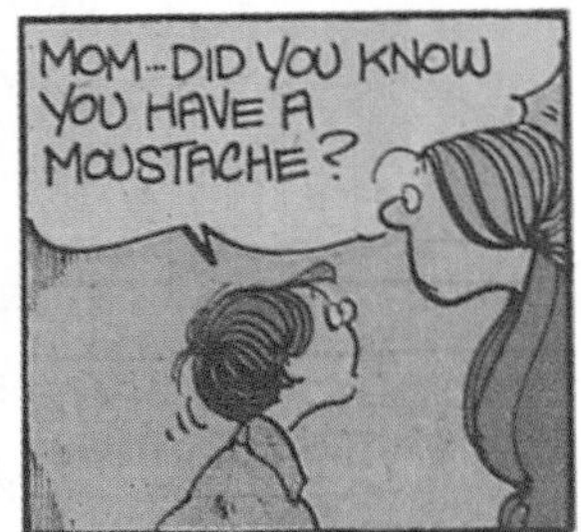

END THOUGHTS

By now you should all know each other fairly well. And knowing each other is a step toward building better people. When communication is open and honest, classrooms become places where both teachers and students want to be, not have to be. This is because open communication leads to people who understand each other, and when people understand each other, they are better people. So when you build better people, you build a better classroom. Each person in your classroom has the ability to work toward the best experience you can create for yourselves.

ACTIVITY 8

EXTENSION IDEAS

1. Write a letter to your local school board in which you ask about their expectations for today's students. Report your answer to your class.
2. Invite a member of your school board to your classroom to find out how they go about building a better school system.
3. Read *Why Shoot the Teacher* by Max Braithwaite (McClelland and Stewart, 1965). This is the story of a young man who goes to teach in an isolated prairie school during the great depression. What does he learn about himself from this experience?
4. Think about and answer these questions:
   - How can we build a better community?
   - How can we build a better nation?
   - How can we build a better world?
5. Write in your notebook about the ideal student-teacher relationship. How can you make such a relationship happen?
6. Collect several cartoons on the theme of communication and human relations. Make a collage and give it a title. The title should describe the specific aspect of the theme that your particular collection of cartoons reflects.
7. You used the cartoon in Figure 1-3 to think about this problem: what is there about you that makes you a unique person? Now expand your thinking to consider how you can make certain that you develop your unique characteristics in spite of what others say about you – or do to you. Discuss this topic with a classmate. Use this conversation as a source of ideas for an article about your unique characteristics.

UNIT 2

★ ★ ★ ★ ★ ★ ★

EYEWITNESS

☆ RIGHT ON TARGET
☆ CRIME STOPPERS PROGRAM
☆ MISTAKEN IDENTITY

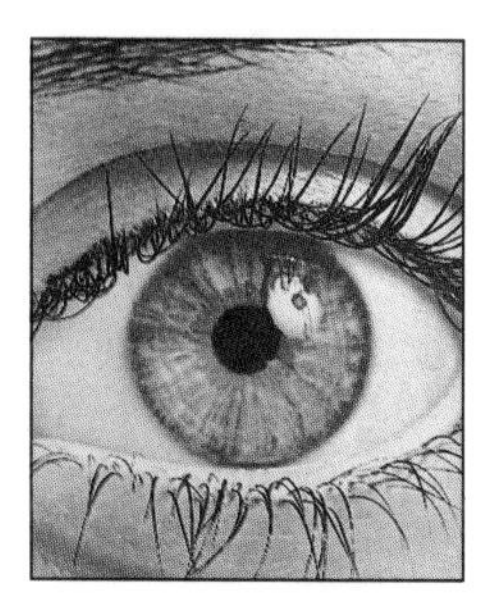

Figure 2-1 Bring your world into sharp focus. View, don't just watch.

INTRODUCTION

Viewing demands that you look as carefully as a situation requires, and that you closely analyze what you've seen. Looking, on the other hand, is simply the act of gathering visual detail. Accurate viewing skills are essential in all aspects of your daily life.

One area where viewing skills are critical is in the prevention of crime, where a good viewer can make the difference between a safe or an unsafe neighbourhood and, occasionally, between life and death. In order for the information viewed to be useful, you must be able to accurately describe what you have seen. This unit will show you how to become better crime stoppers by becoming better viewers and describers.

RIGHT ON TARGET

WITNESSES

Pat Gray and Audrey Elchuk

Marcel Lavoie looked down at his feet. On the other side of the large oak desk, George Greyeyes, crown prosecutor, soothed the uncomfortable young man.

"Just tell me the details as carefully as you can, Marcel," Greyeyes urged....

"'I gotta get out of here,' clanged in his head, and instantly he tried to rise to his feet."

He had stared absent-mindedly out the bus window paying little attention as the bus thumped and bumped its way toward his apartment. The trip required little or no concentration on his part. He'd been doing it for five years, ever since he'd taken on the job as evening host at L'Habitant. He did, however, notice one thing – the icy chill that showed on the gaudy streetlights glaring in the dark night.

Unexpectedly the brakes on the bus tugged and hissed.

"Another passenger," Marcel had reflected.

With the exception of himself, the bus had been empty. Marcel continued to stare out the window and had been only mildly surprised when the new passenger, a young man, sat down beside him.

His reverie disturbed, Marcel quickly glanced at his new seatmate who seemed to be occupying more of the seat than courtesy allowed. His eyes scanned a rough-looking, unshaven youth.

"About nineteen," he thought.

The man's shiny hair, too long to be neat, too short to be messy, peaked over the collar of his grey denim jacket.

His attire, Marcel considered, was totally inappropriate for the weather. Almost as a response, Marcel fastened the top button of his green woollen coat. He began to feel uncomfortable.

He felt the man push against him and reluctantly Marcel slid against the cold window.

"I gotta get out of here," clanged in his head, and instantly he tried to rise to his feet.

"Sit down," the man grunted roughly. "Don't move a muscle."

Marcel felt a pointed edge against his arm.

The bus ride became a nightmare. Each hiss of the brakes became a scream. Familiar buildings assumed grotesque shapes. He felt himself to be in a videotape run by some madman as time distorted beyond recognition. Moments and movements would fast forward breathlessly and then crawl painfully.

"The bus ride became a nightmare. Each hiss of the brakes became a scream. Familiar buildings assumed grotesque shapes. He felt himself to be in a videotape run by some madman as time distorted beyond recognition."

"Out," the assailant muttered, and suddenly Marcel was being shoved out the back door of the bus and heading towards another bus.

"Where are we?" Marcel whispered.

"Shut up. Get on the bus. Don't make a sound or you're finished."

Unmercifully, the new bus was also empty, and Marcel mutely upbraided himself for not having the courage to speak to the driver. A signal. Something. Anything.

The new route was unfamiliar to him. Residential mostly, the lights of the airport at the edge of town were clearly visible. At one of the last blocks before the airport, Marcel's abductor signalled to the driver that they wanted to get off.

The icy pebbles covered with a thin layer of snow stung Marcel's face as he was shoved roughly onto the ground in a back alley.

Marcel watched in sudden astonishment as his assailant's head whipped around and his frame was frozen in the glare of headlights from an approaching car.

The man cursed, and bounded over a nearby fence.

Almost unbelievably, the approaching vehicle was a police cruiser involved in a routine residential patrol.

"A man," Marcel began. And so relayed his story to the police officer....

It was the same story that George Greyeyes had read two days later on the police transcript. Greyeyes, long experienced with such cases, sighed as he reviewed the file and reflected on his interview with Marcel.

"Only an eyewitness," he noted to himself. A conviction was, at best, remote.

Marcel had identified an ex-con from a series of photographs he had been shown. He had been absolutely positive that the photograph was of his assailant. But Greyeyes still regarded the case as a long shot.

The alleged attacker appeared to have an airtight alibi and was overly anxious to offer blood samples, hair samples, clothing samples, anything that would clear him. It was at moments like this that Greyeyes wished he were prosecuting in traffic court.

Greyeyes reviewed the Lavoie file, all the while recalling his knowledge of the reliability of eyewitness testimony. The bottom line was that it was bad testimony. First of all, people were not videotape machines. They were people. And because they were people, they made mistakes. He remembered reading about a case in which a person had been wrongfully convicted even though he had been identified by twenty-three eyewitnesses.

"People are not machines," he mused. People have this horrible flaw which has become known in prosecutor circles as the 'please me' effect. Believing that they are doing the right thing, and confronted by the supportive assistance of people in authority,

"The icy pebbles covered with a thin layer of snow stung Marcel's face as he was shoved roughly onto the ground in a back alley."

> “...people were not videotape machines. They were people. And because they were people, they made mistakes.”

eyewitnesses fill in gaps for which they have no knowledge to please the encouraging authority figure. In such circumstances, mustaches could appear and disappear, eye colour could change, and hair length could vary. On top of that, there were the physical conditions under which Marcel had observed his attacker. Night time on a dimly lighted bus. Then, of course, there was his highly emotional state when the police had picked him up. It was also, Marcel remembered, at the end of a busy day of work at the restaurant and he was probably tired.

"A long shot," Greyeyes thought again....

The day of the trial, April 23, did not begin well.

"Cold and drizzly," Greyeyes thought. "Figures."

Taking off his overcoat, Greyeyes surveyed the courtroom. Scattered in the audience section were a few tired faces.

"Regulars," Greyeyes mused. "Beats game shows and soap operas."

a)

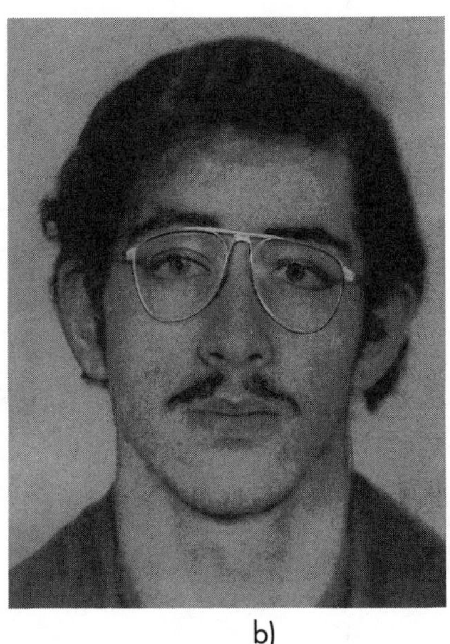

b)

c)

Figure 2-2 Although the man in b) was guilty, the men in a) and c) were picked out of police lineups by witnesses.

The jury had already taken their places.

To his right, sat Lisa Mah, lawyer for the defendant. Vic Shofel, who sat beside her, looked soberly toward the judge's vacant bench. Hair combed neatly, cleanly shaved, and dressed in a blue sports jacket, white shirt with matching tie and grey slacks – a casual onlooker would have difficulty discerning who the lawyer was, Mah or the accused.

Greyeyes was shuffling his papers as Steve Henderson, court officer, announced the arrival of Judge LaFreniere.

When her turn came, Mah called witness after witness for the defence, each swearing earnestly and, Greyeyes noted, believably, that Shofel had been with them the night of the crime. A few drinks and a hockey game on the tube, each one reiterated. Even Shofel's wife, Debbie, with a smile like a July morning, swore that the men had been at their place. She knows, she said. She was there too. None of the witnesses was shaken under cross-examination. In fact, Greyeyes had to admit, their testimony served only to strengthen the defence's case.

"Believing that they are doing the right thing, and confronted by the supportive assistance of people in authority, eyewitnesses fill in gaps for which they have no knowledge to please the encouraging authority figure."

The trial went as George Greyeyes had predicted it would. He called Sam McClellan, the officer who had found Marcel on that evening. The Officer's testimony was limited, to say the least. He and his partner, on a routine patrol, had seen two people go down an alley and, on a hunch, had followed. There was no doubt that Marcel had been assaulted. But McClellan couldn't say who had done it since the assailant had vanished before he got out of his patrol car. The best McClellan could say was that Marcel had been dazed when they found him.

Greyeyes's star witness, Marcel Lavoie, fared only slightly better. He thought he remembered Shofel from that night, but the clothes, hair, and clean, clean shaven appearance shook Marcel's confidence.

As she rose to address the jury in her final summation, Mah began quietly. "Your Honour, ladies and gentlemen of the jury. You have been entrusted with two tasks. The first is to answer the question. On the night of February 16, on or about the time of 7:10 p.m., was Marcel Lavoie assaulted? Secondly, was his assailant, the defendant, Vic Shofel? I think you will agree with me, ladies and gentlemen, the answer to the first question is a definite yes. Mr. Lavoie is a credible young man. And if he says he was attacked, then we have no reason to doubt him. In fact, his attack was confirmed by officer McClellan. As to whether or not Mr. Lavoie was attacked by Mr. Shofel, the answer must, and can only be, a resounding no. This morning you have heard witness after witness confirm the fact that Mr. Shofel was where he said he was on the night of February 16th, at home with his wife and a few friends watching a hockey game. The crown has based its entire case on the testimony of one man. Mr. Greyeyes has asked you to believe that Mr. Lavoie is a machine who is able to accurately record the features of a person observed under the most adverse conditions a number of months ago and to make a positive identification of that person.

"Even Shofel's wife, Debbie, with a smile like a July morning, swore that the men had been at their place."

"Ladies and gentlemen, as you all well know, people are not machines, and even if they were, machines do break down. Numerous psychological studies have documented the frailties of human perception and memory, revealing that such evidence cannot be trusted. In the most notorious instance of mistaken identification, an accused was mistakenly identified by twenty-three witnesses. It is clear that a person's original perception of a face or an event can be influenced, not only by physiological factors that affect the fallibility of all perceptual judgments, but also by such subjective factors as stress, personal prejudices, expectations, biases, group pressures, ego involvement, psychological needs, emotional states, social attitudes, and stereotypes. Both visual memory and verbal description of images retained in memory are similarly affected by many things. The number of witnesses able to make an accurate identification is always low – in some cases, no greater than chance."

The jury listened eagerly. In his chair, Greyeyes slumped.

"In conclusion, ladies and gentlemen of the jury," Mah went on, "eyewitness testimony, then, is a dangerous form of evidence because it is unreliable. There is no doubt, ladies and gentlemen, that on the night of February 16th on or about the time of 7:10 p.m.,

> **In the most notorious instance of mistaken identification, an accused was mistakenly identified by twenty-three witnesses.**

Marcel Lavoie was abducted and assaulted. But it was not, I can assure you, by Vic Shofel. To think otherwise would be to wrongfully condemn an innocent man."

The jury deliberated for no more than ten minutes, and came back with, as Greyeyes had earlier anticipated, a verdict of not guilty.

The courtroom cleared quickly, leaving alone the two lawyers, Mah and Greyeyes.

"Good case, Lisa," Greyeyes smiled.

"Piece of cake," Mah replied. "Eyewitness testimony. You know the story."

"Yeah," Greyeyes shrugged.

"You know what?" Greyeyes brightened. "Let's phone a babysitter for the kids and treat each other to supper."

Arms around each other's waist, they walked out of the courtroom into the April drizzle. ◆

Figure 2-3 State the truth, and only the truth, please.

BECOMING A BETTER VIEWER

1. From the story "Witnesses," find and list in your notebook at least five reasons why eyewitness testimony is unreliable.
2. Decide on four ways that you can become a better viewer. Write these viewing tips in your notebook. For example, "Try to remain as calm as possible."

Figure 2-4
Eyewitness description chart

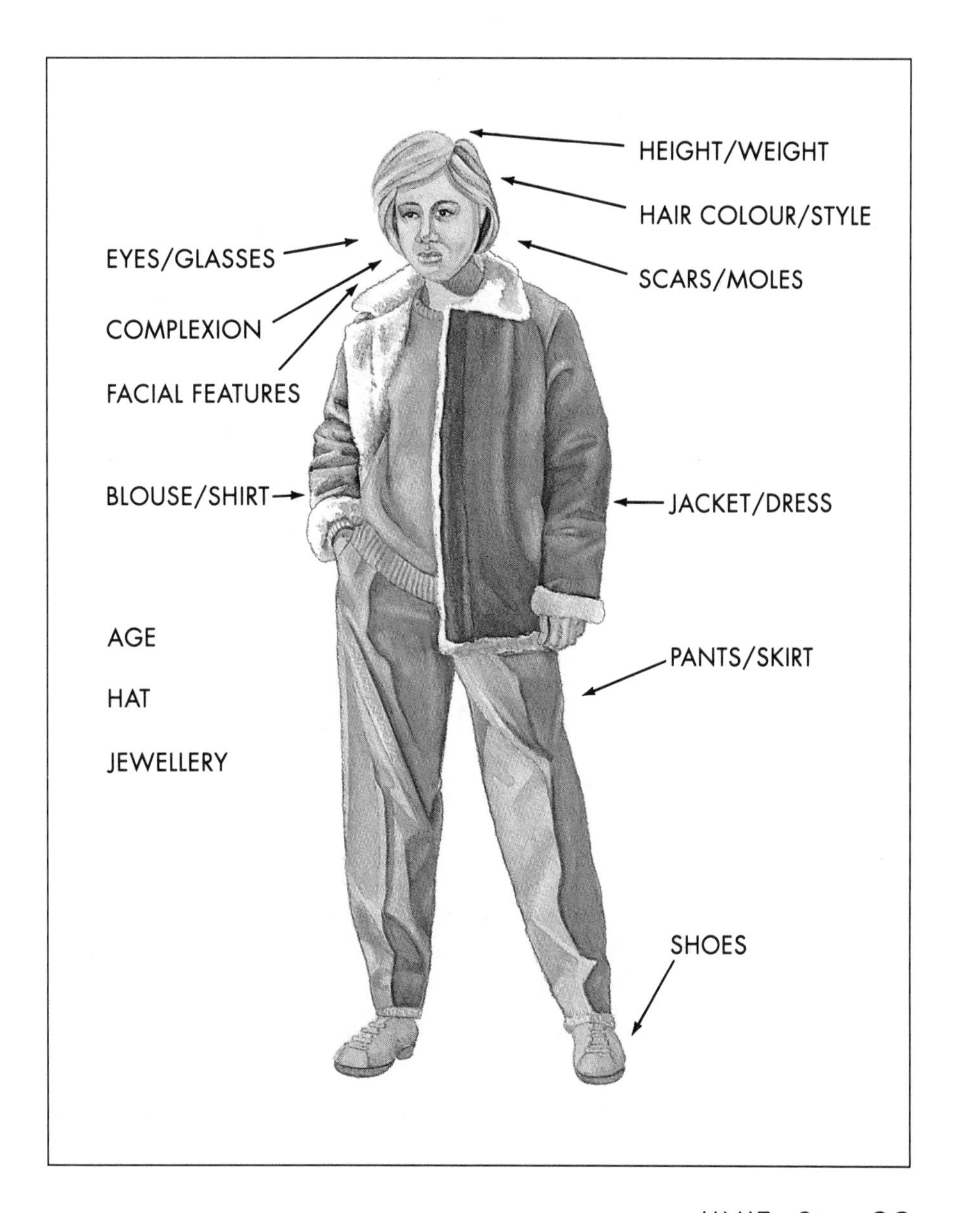

ACTIVITY 2

EYEWITNESS DESCRIPTION

To complete this activity, you will need to copy the eyewitness description chart (Fig. 2-4) into your notebook.

1. Ask someone who is not a member of your class to make a five-second appearance in your class and then leave.
2. As soon as this person has left, complete the chart to describe this person. Take three minutes to fill it out as accurately as you can.
3. After three minutes, have your guest return. Check how accurate your viewing was by comparing what you wrote on your chart with what your guest actually looks like.

WRITING A THREE-MINUTE COMPOSITE

Imagine that you and your classmates have all witnessed a crime. As a class, decide on the nature of the crime (for example, an armed bank robbery). Even though you've had only a brief glimpse of the suspect, the police still want to know as much as you can tell them. If they collect enough descriptions, they'll be able to put together a composite picture to help them catch a criminal.

1. In three minutes, write a two- or three-sentence description of the person you have seen (for example, "He had brown hair to his shoulders"). Be sure to use only specific physical descriptions. For example, don't say that the suspect was ugly, because "ugly" is an opinion and isn't helpful in putting together a description.
2. After three minutes, pass your description sheet to the person behind you.
3. When you have received a new description sheet from a person in your row, take three minutes to read it and to add two or three specific details to the list.
4. After three minutes, pass your paper to the person behind you and repeat step 3 until every student's paper in your row has been read and added to by every student in your row.
5. Write *different* details each time you read a new composite description.
6. End the activity when you receive your own paper back.

7. Silently read over the entire composite description, editing those details that cannot be seen. For example, delete "He had bad breath."

8. Have some students read their composite descriptions aloud to the rest of the class.

9. Alone or with a partner, use clippings from magazines to transform your written composite into a visual composite. Be as accurate as you can. For example, if your written composite does not mention a nose, your visual composite cannot have a nose.

10. Write your composite description in paragraph form on a piece of Bristol board and attach your visual to it.

Figure 2-5 Bank tellers are frequent victims of crime.

CRIME STOPPERS PROGRAM

The Crime Stoppers program in which unsolved crimes are visually depicted or reenacted on television is a huge success. Each telecast usually brings hundreds of phone calls from people who think that they may have information that could lead to the arrest of the suspect. The article "Public can fight back with Crime Stoppers" will provide you with some information on the Crime Stoppers program.

PUBLIC CAN FIGHT BACK WITH CRIME STOPPERS

Gary Taljit

A new weapon in the war against crime was introduced in Saskatoon today.

Crime Stoppers, a program under which anonymous tips can be phoned to the police and rewards for information can be offered, began today.

A joint venture of city police, the public and the media, it has two main features that will lead to its success, says co-ordinator Staff Sgt. Ron Ross: It overcomes public apathy by offering cash rewards and fear of retaliation by offering anonymity.

"It overcomes public apathy by offering cash rewards and fear of retaliation by offering anonymity."

Funded by public donations, rewards are paid when arrests are made.

The program has operated in other major Canadian cities in the West and in Ontario for several years and has proven effective in solving previously unsolvable crimes and in recovering stolen property, said Ross.

In 1982, Calgary became the first Canadian city to get the program and Regina has had one for nearly three years. Saskatoon, which is the sixth city in the province to adopt it, lagged behind until last spring when the program began to germinate.

After seeing successes elsewhere and being pressured by service clubs and the media, the city police department assigned Ross to co-ordinate the program.

With the exception of his salary, Crime Stoppers doesn't cost the public anything, said Ross, who is in his 27th year as a policeman.

Everything from promotional brochures to reward money is being provided by businesses, service clubs and individuals.

A volunteer 17-member board of directors made up of businessmen and professionals will establish policy, raise funds and oversee reward payments.

Rewards, which can range up to $2,000, are based on the value of information provided and the type of crime solved.

Tipsters in Saskatoon can call 931-8477 (or 931-TIPS). Calls

> "...many people feel helping the police is more important than money."

are not traced or recorded but the callers are issued code numbers to ensure anonymity. If their information leads to an arrest, they become eligible for a reward.

Ross will set up a mutually agreeable time and place for tipsters to receive their reward.

However, statistics show only about half actually collect, said Ross, adding that's an indication many people feel helping the police is more important than money.

Media outlets, including the Star-Phoenix, have agreed to publicize a weekly segment known as the Crime Of The Week.

CFQC-TV will film re-enactments of crimes using police department staff.

Tipsters can call in about any crime, not just the ones featured in the media, Ross stressed.

All donations to Crime Stoppers are tax-deductible.

The program has several thousand dollars in its coffers already and $25,000 is the goal for its initial stages of operation. ◆

ACTIVITY 4

BECOMING A CRIME STOPPER

1. In small groups, look through a magazine or a newspaper to get as much information about an unsolved crime as you can.
2. List the information you have gained from your research and answer the following questions:
   a) Who was involved? (Include real or imagined descriptions.)
   b) What happened?
   c) Where and when did the crime take place?
3. Prepare and present a silent enactment of the crime you have researched. Be accurate. Use appropriate props such as a clock on the wall to indicate time, a calendar, and costumes. Present your skit either live or on video tape.
4. While each group's 'crime' is being enacted, make notes about the following:
   a) Who was involved? (Include detailed descriptions of the suspects.)
   b) What happened?
   c) Where and when did the crime take place?

5. Based on the information you have just noted, write a description for the Crime Stoppers program. The following is an example:

   "On Tuesday, the 29th of November, 1999, at 3:00 a.m., two men walked into the Circle Square Confectionery store at 927 Ash Street and at gun point demanded that the cashier hand over all the money in the till. Both men wore ski masks. One is described as being 180 cm tall and of slender build. He had a noticeable limp. The second suspect is described as a heavy-set man of approximately 115 kg ...."

MISTAKEN IDENTITY

When you began this unit, you were reminded that the failure to view accurately could make the difference between life and death. In the following poem, "The Execution," the truth of this comment is brought to light in a very tragic way.

Figure 2-6 Across Canada the Crime Stoppers program has achieved major success.

THE EXECUTION

Alden Nowlan

On the night of the execution
a man at the door
mistook me for the coroner.
"Press," I said.

But he didn't understand. He led me
into the wrong room
where the sheriff greeted me:
"You're late, Padre."

"You're wrong," I told him. "I'm Press."
"Yes, of course, Reverend Press."
We went down the stairway.

"Ah, Mr. Ellis," said the Deputy.
"Press!" I shouted. But he shoved me
through a black curtain.
The lights were so bright
I couldn't see the faces
of the men sitting
opposite. But, thank god, I thought
they can see me!

"Look!" I cried. "Look at my face!
Doesn't anybody know me?"

Then a hood covered my head.
"Don't make it harder for us," the hangman whispered.

WRITING AN ARTICLE

1. Imagine that you are a reporter for your local newspaper and you have discovered the grisly mistake that has occurred at the prison – they've hanged the wrong person! As a reporter, you feel it is your duty to expose this terrible tragedy. Write an article that describes the case of mistaken identity that has occurred in the prison.

END THOUGHTS

Looking is an act done primarily with the eyes, whereas viewing is an activity of the mind. When you look you simply gather visual information. When you view you not only gather, but you also analyze and interpret that information.

ACTIVITY 6

EXTENSION IDEAS

1. On Bristol board make up a *Crime and Punishment* poster including biographies of famous criminals and newspaper clippings of publicized crimes. You might wish to contact a judge to obtain information on sentences given out for particular crimes. Include these in list form on your poster (for example, "Break and Enter – 6 months in jail").
2. After reading the book *Court Jesters* by Canadian lawyer Peter MacDonald, Q.C., arrange for a meeting with a local law enforcement official to discuss humorous crimes. Give a report on this incident to your class.
3. Using your own or a school camera, prepare mug shots and descriptions of friends and anyone else you can convince to pose for you. Of what crimes are they accused? Using your picture and description, make up a humorous *Wanted* poster.
4. Use magazine illustrations of famous people to make up humorous *Wanted* posters. Your *Wanted* posters could be displayed as a mobile.
5. The argument about capital punishment has been going on for years. What is your opinion about capital punishment? Are you for or against it? Briefly state your opinion and provide arguments to support it. Arrange for a panel discussion on the issue of capital punishment.
6. If possible, contact the Investigation Section of your local police department to interview a police officer about the nature of his or her work. Rewrite a report on how they collect evidence to solve a crime.
7. Arrange to have an ex-convict speak to your class about life in prison. An excellent contact to find such a guest is the John Howard Society.
8. As a class, discuss the Crime Stoppers program. Is it right to give money to inform on people? Could this program be misused? Do you think there are other ways to deal with crime in your community?

UNIT 3

★ ★ ★ ★ ★ ★ ★

ALL THAT I HAVE MET

"It's Vince, all right. It's his nose, his mouth, his fur ... but his eyes — there's something not quite right about his eyes."

- ★ ANIMAL RIGHTS
- ★ ALL TOGETHER NOW
- ★ THE FACTS
- ★ CHILDHOOD AND POVERTY
- ★ CAPITAL AND CORPORAL PUNISHMENT
- ★ WORLD PROBLEMS

INTRODUCTION

The poet Tennyson once wrote this line in a poem called "Ulysses": "I am a part of all that I have met." Tennyson was thinking about experiences in life. Any experience that you have in your past will influence you. Praise for doing something well, for example, will make you work harder and achieve more.

No doubt you are like Tennyson – even though he lived over a hundred years ago – and you are part of all that you have met. Think of all the people and happenings that have influenced you: your friends, TV, a scare or sorrow that you once had. All of these experiences join together to influence you and shape your way of thinking.

Try reversing Tennyson's idea and thinking this way: "I have influenced everything that I have met." Your sister, your friends, your parents – all have been influenced by you, and you have helped to shape what they are and the way they think. In fact, try thinking of yourself as a person who can influence the world and make it a better place for all to live in.

"Me," you ask, "influence the world?" You can start by being aware of what is going on in the world. In other words, you can try to understand some of the social issues around you. A social issue is a concern or problem that touches society as a whole. People take different sides on these issues – some are in favour; others, opposed. Such matters might require a lot of discussion before you can make up your mind about where you stand. This unit will help you think and talk about some current social issues.

ANIMAL RIGHTS

Animal rights is one of the social issues in our society. People form groups, such as the Society for the Prevention of Cruelty to Animals, to protect animals. The trapping of wild animals has become a complex issue for Canadians. Some people are strongly opposed to setting traps to catch animals. For others, trapping is their way of life. The following newspaper article shows just how complex this issue really is.

INDIANS AND ANIMAL ACTIVISTS DUEL AT EUROPE'S PARLIAMENT

Edward Greenspon

Canadian differences over fur trapping went on full display before European parliamentarians yesterday as an aboriginal delegation and a Toronto animal-rights activist engaged in a bitter and often emotional verbal duel.

The natives had come to the modernistic, smoked-glass home of the European Parliament to put their case for the preservation of an ancient way of life.

Measures being considered in the European Community to require the labelling of imported fur products caught in leg-hold traps would harm 250,000 natives. It would destroy markets for one of their traditional industries, David Monture, secretary of Indigenous Survival International, warned.

"'While a trap has no choice of what animal it catches, a person does have a choice of what they wear...'"

The ultimate aim is a total ban, he added. "Even if a device was designed that delivered a fatal injection – that would not be enough for most animal-rights activists."

But Mr. Monture and two Indian chiefs faced an aggressive counter-attack from Michael O'Sullivan, Canadian field representative of the World Society for the Protection of Animals.

"While a trap has no choice of what animal it catches, a person does have a choice of what they wear," he said in pushing for warning labels on furs.

If that doesn't work, he supports a total ban on fur products from countries that refuse to outlaw leg-hold traps.

The approximately 30 Euro-MPs who attended the session tend to find the leg-hold traps a cruel method of capturing animals.

The Parliament has already passed a labelling motion that is being considered by the European Commission, the executive arm of the 12-nation European Community.

But the MPs are also concerned about the possible harmful effects of such a measure on native Canadians.

However, Mr. O'Sullivan said the fur trade has only impoverished Indians and their defence of trapping is based on designs to become major capitalists.

He portrayed natives as possessing constitutional privileges not accorded other Canadians and of sitting on a gold mine they will cash in when land claims are settled.

To pursue their claims, natives must demonstrate that they require the land for such natural uses as fur trapping, he said. "So the issue is being used to support a legal land claim – a larger agenda."

"'We may be primitive to some people, but we are people who have some idea of preservation. We know that if our inheritance disappears, we disappear, too.'"

As well, aboriginal groups are taking advantage of land settlements to get into all sorts of businesses from mining to construction and shopping centres, he said.

A recent land claim deal in the Northwest Territories has made 13,000 natives there "the largest private landowners in the world," he noted.

Aurelian Gill, chief of the Montagnais band in northern Quebec, delivered an impassioned reply to "our friend from Toronto." He noted that Indians have higher unemployment, suicide and infant mortality rates than other Canadians.

"If we were in such a good position, we wouldn't have such appalling statistics," he said.

"We may be primitive to some people, but we are people who have some idea of preservation. We know that if our inheritance disappears, we disappear, too.

"These are some things that perhaps are not known in Toronto."

Afterwards, Mr. Gill button-holed Mr. O'Sullivan outside the hall and accused him of wanting to colonize natives.

Mr. Monture said his adversary has "a European mentality. He seems to know what's best for animals and best for people."

The politicians seemed no more satisfied with the answers to their questions. Above all, they wanted their aboriginal guests to address the question of cruelty.

However, the native delegation kept returning to the theme of conservation.

Rosie Mosquito, chief of the Bearskin Lake nation in Northern Ontario, recounted that band elders had advised her the greatest cruelty is to allow animal populations to grow "in a manner that they will die and eat up each other."

“Michael Kilby, an MP from Britain, said European politicians are responding to the concerns of the electorate in pursuing the issue.”

A European elder, Dutch member Hemmo Muntingh, advised her outside that she will have to be more political and less diplomatic in tackling the cruelty issue. The natives appear before another committee in Brussels next week.

The arguments put forth by Mr. O'Sullivan were strong and impressive, Mr. Muntingh said, but they didn't wash with him. It didn't make sense that natives are both rich and poor.

Although a supporter of labelling, he said native groups could stop it in its tracks with a sincere offer to examine alternatives to leg-hold traps.

Michael Kilby, an MP from Britain, said European politicians are responding to the concerns of the electorate in pursuing the issue. He warned that natives are squandering their natural goodwill with Europeans.

He has received 100 to 150 letters over the past four years, he said, from people outraged after watching television programs on "the unspeakable cruelty" of leg-hold traps.

"If you see a television program about the way of life in northern Canada, what comes across is a beautiful country, a people with a long history and culture and a fascinating way of life. That has great appeal and people are on the side of the native people.

"Then they see another television program, same area, perhaps the same people. And then they are shocked at the animals trapped and dying a lingering death." ◆

ANIMAL TALK

1. Form groups of three to five students. Talk about the two cartoons.
   a) What does the cartoon in Figure 3-1 make you think of? Is this cartoon for or against hunting?
   b) Next, talk about the cartoon in Figure 3-2. Is it all right for scientists to experiment with live animals? Why?

Figure 3-1 This cartoonist is making a statement about animal rights.

Figure 3-2 This cartoonist is commenting on the use of animals in experiments.

2. Plan a chart to display the different arguments presented by your group on the topics in question 1.
   a) Decide what ideas suggested in your discussion you should show on the chart.
   b) Decide what kind of chart you might use to display these ideas.
   c) Divide the work of constructing this chart.
   d) Complete the chart and display it in your classroom.

Figure 3-3 Is it right or wrong to use animals for the purpose of high fashion?

LONG OVERDUE By John Long

ALL TOGETHER NOW

To complete Activity 1, you had to work in a small group. This section will help you think about the skills you need to work with others in small groups. You will be able to use your small-group interaction skills in other chapters in this book, and you will likely use these skills later in life. For example, when an organization needs to do something or to make a decision, it will often have small groups work on the problem and then report to the whole group.

ACTIVITY 2

GROUP-INTERACTION CHECKLIST

1. Take a few minutes to think honestly about how your group operated while making the chart for Activity 1. In your notebook, note which of the following statements are true of how your group worked.

a) Everyone participated in our group discussion.
Some people didn't contribute to our group discussion.
b) Our group encouraged everyone to share ideas.
Our group didn't encourage all the members to share ideas.
c) Our group generally agreed on which of the ideas suggested in our discussion we would show on our chart.
Our group didn't agree on the ideas that we came up with.
d) Our group stuck to the task of generating ideas and displaying them on our chart.
Our group wandered off the task and never really discussed what we were supposed to do.
e) Our group seemed to enjoy working together.
Our group didn't get along well at all.

2. What else can you say about how your group managed its task of discussing animal rights and creating a display of the main ideas in the discussion?

3. Using the same group that you had for Activity 1, review your achievement in working together.

a) Use the statements in question 1 to start your thinking.
b) Add the ideas you had in thinking about question 2.
c) Decide how effective your group was in completing the group task.

Working Well – Together: You worked at a group discussion in the last activity – and thought about what happened while you were involved in the discussion. Now, what can you do, or not do, to improve the way a small group works? When you answer this question, you will come up with suggestions on how to be a better group member.

MAKING SMALL GROUPS WORK

1. As a class, look at the results from your thinking about the checklist in Activity 2.

   a) What were the positive things that happened as you were talking in small groups about this checklist?
   b) What were the negative things that happened?

2. Think about your experience in your discussion of animal rights and develop a list of do's and don'ts for group interaction.

3. In your notebook write an answer to this question: Why is it important for people living in your community to know how to work in small groups?

Listening: Groups operate best when all involved listen to each other. Group members need to listen to each other. Group leaders need to listen to the group members. This might sound easy, but it's hard to do. You need to concentrate on what others are saying and to ask yourself questions to make certain that you understand their opinions or ideas. Even if you don't agree with their ideas, try to understand them. To do this, ask yourself, "What is the position that he or she is taking?" Often this kind of listening means that you have to wait to put your own opinion forward in order to understand the ideas of others first. Then you can express your own ideas, not to overpower the other group members but to share your thoughts.

The play on page 50 is about listening, or more exactly, it's about not listening. This dialogue is an interview with Bobby Clobber, 'star' hockey player. Bobby's way of listening is definitely his own.

BOBBY CLOBBER: RADIO HELMET

The Royal Canadian Air Farce

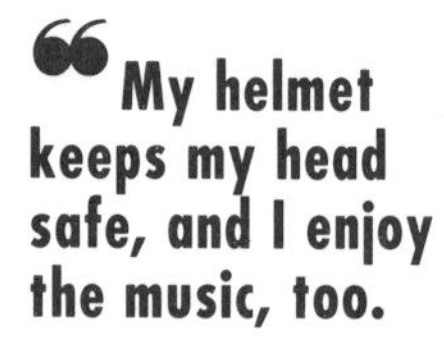

My helmet keeps my head safe, and I enjoy the music, too.

MUSIC	CLOBBER THEME. ESTABLISH AND HOLD UNDER
BIG JIM	Well, thanks, Fergie, and hi, sports fans Well, I've got some bad news and some good news about hockey star Big Bobby Clobber. Just minutes ago, Bobby was coming up to our broadcast booth here, and the bad news is: as Bobby was walking up the stairs, his skates slipped and Bobby went flying and smashed his head right through our desk. The good news is: the desk can be repaired. Here he is now... Big Bobby Clobber.
MUSIC	*OUT*
BIG JIM	Hi, Big Bobby.
BOBBY	I sure am, Big Jim. I'm sorry about the top of your desk. They don't make marble as strong like they used to.
BIG JIM	It's a good thing you were wearing your helmet.
BOBBY	I'm glad you mentioned that, Big Jim. My helmet keeps my head safe, and I enjoy the music, too.
BIG JIM	Bobby, I can't hear any music. Are you sure you didn't hurt yourself when you banged your head on the desk?
BOBBY	(LOUD) How's that, Big Jim?
BIG JIM	I said I can't hear any music.
BOBBY	(LOUD) Neither can I.

→

BIG JIM	That's a relief.
BOBBY	The news is on now. I know this looks like an ordinary helmet, Big Jim, but it's really the official "Bobby Clobber AM-FM Stereo Head Protector and Personal Entertainment Centre Hockey Helmet".
BIG JIM	Do you wear that during games?
BOBBY	Yeah, you can tune in the play-by-play and find out who's got the puck.
BIG JIM	This "Official Bobby Clobber Radio Helmet"... Is this another of your many business ventures?
BOBBY	No way, Big Jim. I'm makin' money with it.
BIG JIM	How many helmets have you sold so far, Big Bobby?
BOBBY	Let me think about that for a minute, Big Jim. I gotta remember the sales figures. Let's see... There was uh... Halifax... (COUNTS ON FINGERS) Moncton... Drummondville... Pembroke... Sudbury...Thunder Bay... Winnipeg... Saskatoon... Red Deer...Revelstoke... Penticton...New Westminster Nanaimo... Port Alberni... And there was Gloria...and her friend, Evelyn... What was the question?
BIG JIM	How many helmets did you sell?
BOBBY	One.
BIG JIM	The one you're wearing?
BOBBY	No. This is a freebie. My mom bought the one we sold.

“I know this looks like an ordinary helmet, Big Jim, but it's really the official 'Bobby Clobber AM-FM Stereo Head Protector and Personal Entertainment Centre Hockey Helmet.'”

BIG JIM	Well, Big Bobby, I think after seeing the way your official Bobby Clobber Radio Helmet protected your head when you crashed into the marble desk, I'm sure a lot of youngsters will want to rush out and buy one.
BOBBY	What would a kid want with a marble desk?
BIG JIM	No, I mean wouldn't it be great if all the kids went out and bought your official Bobby Clobber Radio Hockey Helmet. You'd be richer than you already are.
BOBBY	No question, Big Jim. As on the other hand... All seriousness besides... to me, Big Jim, life has to be more than just a hockey helmet. Like I want to say to all the youngsters who might be watching in to us at this radio interview... whether you are sports-like or not, you don't have to. And even more, it's not whether you lose.
BIG JIM	Big Bobby, that doesn't make any sense!
BOBBY	I know, Big Jim, but when you're makin' the kind of money I am, who cares!
BIG JIM	Thank you, Big Bobby Clobber!
MUSIC	*PLAYOFF* ◆

“... to me, Big Jim, life has to be more than just a hockey helmet.”

ACTIVITY 4

LISTENING WARM-UP

1. Read the play "Bobby Clobber: Radio Helmet" to yourself.
2. With a partner read the dialogue out loud twice; switch parts the second time.
3. Discuss with your partner any similarities or differences between your interpretations of the same parts.
4. In your notebook, write an entry on how an oral interpretation may influence a listener's response to a text.

LISTENING EXERCISE

1. Read the newspaper article "Canadian fishery agents fire warning shots at U.S. trawler" to learn about an international problem.
2. Form groups of three and count yourselves off – "1, 2, 3."
3. Have person #1 speak for exactly one minute, giving his or her opinion of the topic in the newspaper article.
4. As soon as person #1 stops talking, have person #2 tell in his or her own words what they understood person #1 to have said. Stop at the end of one minute.
5. Now have person #3 explain person #1's remarks. Again, stop at the end of one minute.
6. Discuss this experience with your group, using these questions to guide your discussion:
   a) Did you feel the restatements were accurate? If not, what do you think caused the errors?
   b) Was it hard to concentrate? Why or why not?
   c) What are the implications of this experience for other discussions you might have?
7. Repeat this activity using your own topics as the focus for discussion.

CANADIAN FISHERY AGENTS FIRE WARNING SHOTS AT U.S. TRAWLER

Associated Press

NEW BEDFORD, Mass. – The captain of the scalloper Donna Lynn, which was chased after it ignored warning shots by Canadian fishery agents, says the boat never left U.S. waters and the Canadian officials needlessly endangered his crew.

"I thought I was in the Persian Gulf," Douglas Makie said after returning from his fishing trip Tuesday.

Makie claimed that Canadian fisheries officials trumped up charges against him because "they want the boat for past violations of past skippers."

"'I thought I was in the Persian Gulf,' Douglas Makie said after returning from his fishing trip Tuesday."

The incident took place Oct. 1, when a Canadian fisheries patrol boat fired warning shots from a machine-gun and chased the 28-metre scalloper within 160 kilometres of Nantucket when Makie refused to let fisheries officials board his boat.

Canadian officials have asked the U.S. government to press charges against the Donna Lynn, owned by Richard Flood of Mattapoisett. The trawler could face a number of charges in the United Sates, including entering U.S. waters with an illegally obtained cargo.

The Chebucto, the Canadian fisheries enforcement boat, radioed Makie asking him to clear two crew members from the bow because warning shots were coming. Makie said the crew members refused to move.

"You could see the bullets dancing across the water just three or four feet from the boat," Makie said in an interview. "If the Chebucto had rolled – they would have hit the Donna Lynn. My nerves were so shot. I was heaving I was so scared."

Makie said he gave a statement to U.S. National Marine Fisheries officials who are investigating the Canadian claims for the U.S. State Department.

Makie claimed he and his crew were set up by the Canadians because they want to seize the $1-million U.S. boat for alleged past offences.

"I was hitting the line (between the two countries) and then turning back. I already made my turn and was coming back when the six (men) in a black rubber raft pulled up next to me and said they wanted to board me and talk to me."

Makie refused to let the fisheries officials board, he said, because he believed he was not violating the boundary line that splits Georges Banks between the United States and Canada.

"I told the guy by radio, I'm in my own waters," Makie said. "He says to me, 'It looks like you're on the line.' And I said, 'What is the line?' He says, '32.' I looked at my Lorans (navigational devices which pinpoint location) and they say 33.8. That put me a quarter mile into my own waters. I told him this was harassment."

The 50-year-old skipper said this was his first trip as the new skipper of the Donna Lynn.

The rich fishing ground of Georges Bank used to be fished by both countries until the World Court divided it up. The United States was awarded 90 per cent of the territory, but Canada's 10 per cent contains most of the fish. ◆

"'I already made my turn and was coming back when the six (men) in a black rubber raft pulled up next to me and said they wanted to board me and talk to me.'"

For Me and For Others: The next activity is a method of self-training that you can practise anywhere, any time, for the rest of your life. This exercise is particularly useful when disagreements arise in a small group – since the purpose of the activity is to help you think yourself into the mind of another.

ACTIVITY 6

UNDERSTANDING GROUP TALK

1. Form groups of three. Have two people speak with each other while the third person observes.
2. Use one of these topics for your talk, or agree on one of your own:
   - Women should be allowed to play in the NHL.
   - Hockey players are paid too much money.
   - Our community should spend more money on sports facilities.
   - All secondary students should be required to spend two hours a day in physical training.
   - TV wrestling is bad (or good) entertainment.

3. When the first two students talk they must follow this rule: Person #2 must first restate person #1's remarks. Only then can person #2 add to the dialogue.

4. The observer's job is to enforce this rule, making sure that the speakers paraphrase each other's remarks before adding their own. Stop the discussion if necessary and ask them to repeat the ideas in the previous statement.

5. Have the observer keep track of the following items to report to the speakers at the end of this discussion:

   - Did they have difficulty getting a conversation started?
   - Who took the lead in the discussion and how did he or she get the discussion going?
   - How many times did one speaker forget to restate a partner's remarks?
   - How many times did someone start with "Yes, but..."?

6. After five or six minutes, have the observer tell the two speakers what he or she noticed.

7. In a group of three talk about this activity:

   a) Did you find the experience frustrating? Why?
   b) How much concentration was involved?
   c) How does this paraphrasing experience help you understand the ideas of others?

8. Have the observer report the results of the group discussion to the whole class. Observers should listen closely to what other observers say and not repeat any statements.

9. As a whole class talk about these questions:

   a) What are the problems of listening?
   b) What are the implications of this activity for successful group work?

THE FACTS

Often people want to make a statement about aspects of contemporary society. People comment on issues – from the political to the economic to the social and the personal. To do so, they can write a letter to their local newspaper – and make their opinions known this way. Or they can respond to a radio talk show and have their opinions broadcast on the air waves. This next activity will ask you to explore yet another way to make your opinions known – a visual statement.

COLLAGE

You will need the following materials for this activity:

- 1 large sheet of poster board per group
- 1–2 pairs of scissors per group
- 1–2 glue sticks per group
- 6–8 various old magazines with pictures per group

1. In groups of three or four, decide upon a social issue of interest. Here are some possible topics:

- acid rain
- drugs
- street kids
- racial tolerance

2. Once you agree on a theme, take twenty minutes to construct a collage based on this theme.

3. After twenty minutes, show your collage to the class and explain what it says.

4. Talk to the class about how well your group worked to construct the collage.

- How did you agree on a topic?
- How did you share tasks?
- How did you arrive at decisions?
- What group interaction skills did your group use?

CHILDHOOD AND POVERTY

Many people are not aware of issues concerning the environment or animal rights affecting them directly. However, there are some issues that many people feel affect them directly, such as health care, child care, and poverty. These issues affect the daily lives of many people. Some people cope with such problems; others are defeated by them.

Richard Wright is an American writer. He was among the first of the Black writers in the United States to gain national fame. He often writes about his life of poverty as a young child. His father deserted the family when Richard was five years old. Mrs. Wright had to work as a domestic servant. She received very low wages and had to leave Richard and his brother alone during the day to look after themselves. Mrs. Wright, who was ill during this time, gradually became completely paralyzed and had to send her sons to live with relatives. Richard did not fit in very well and his relatives found him hard to manage.

The following excerpt from his autobiography *Black Boy* is a personal account of poverty. It is also the story of a young boy – and his mother.

HUNGER

Richard Wright

Hunger stole upon me so slowly that at first I was not aware of what hunger really meant. Hunger had always been more or less at my elbow when I played, but now I began to wake up at night to find hunger standing at my bedside, staring at me gauntly. The hunger I had known before this had been no grim, hostile stranger; it had been a normal hunger that had made me beg constantly for bread, and when I ate a crust or two I was satisfied. But this new hunger baffled me, scared me, made me angry and insistent. Whenever I begged for food now my mother would pour me a cup of tea which would still the clamour in my stomach for a moment or two; but a little later I

“Hunger had always been more or less at my elbow when I played, but now I began to wake up at night to find hunger standing at my bedside, staring at me gauntly.”

would feel hunger nudging my ribs, twisting my empty guts until they ached. I would grow dizzy and my vision would dim. I became less active in my play, and for the first time in my life I had to pause and think of what was happening to me.

"Mama, I'm hungry," I complained one afternoon.

"Jump up and catch a kungry," she said, trying to make me laugh and forget.

"What's a kungry"?

"It's what little boys eat when they get hungry," she said.

"What does it taste like?"

"I don't know."

"Then why do you tell me to catch one?"

"Because you said that you were hungry," she said, smiling.

I sensed that she was teasing me and it made me angry.

"But I'm hungry. I want to eat."

"You'll have to wait."

"But I want to eat now."

"But there's nothing to eat," she told me.

"Why?"

"Just because there's none," she explained.

"But I want to eat," I said, beginning to cry.

"You'll just have to wait," she said again.

"But why?"

"For God to send some food."

"When is He going to send it?"

"I don't know."

"But I'm hungry!"

She was ironing and she paused and looked at me with tears in her eyes.

"Where's your father?" she asked me.

I stared in bewilderment. Yes, it was true that my father had not come home to sleep for many days now and I could make as much noise as I wanted. Though I had not known why he was absent, I had been glad that he was not there to shout his restrictions at me. But it had never occurred to me that his absence would mean that there would be no food.

"Whenever I begged for food now my mother would pour me a cup of tea which would still the clamour in my stomach for a moment or two; but a little later I would feel hunger nudging my ribs, twisting my empty guts until they ached."

"I don't know," I said.

"Who brings food into the house?" my mother asked me.

"Papa," I said. "He always brought food."

"Well, your father isn't here now," she said.

"Where is he?"

"I don't know," she said.

"But I'm hungry," I whimpered, stomping my feet.

"You'll have to wait until I get a job and buy food," she said.

As the days slid past the image of my father became associated with my pangs of hunger, and whenever I felt hunger I thought of him with a deep biological bitterness.

"As the days slid past the image of my father became associated with my pangs of hunger, and whenever I felt hunger I thought of him with a deep biological bitterness."

My mother finally went to work as a cook and left me and my brother alone in the flat each day with a loaf of bread and a pot of tea. When she returned at evening she would be tired and dispirited and would cry a lot. Sometimes, when she was in despair, she would call us to her and talk to us for hours, telling us that we now had no father, that our lives would be different from those of other children, that we must learn as soon as possible to take care of ourselves, to dress ourselves, to prepare our own food; that we must take upon ourselves the responsibility of the flat while she worked. Half frightened, we would promise solemnly. We did not understand what had happened between our father and mother and the most that these long talks did to us was to make us feel a vague dread.

Whenever we asked why father had left, she would tell us that we were too young to know.

One evening my mother told me that thereafter I would have to do the shopping for food. She took me to the corner store to show me the way. I was proud; I felt like a grownup. The next afternoon I looped the basket over my arm and went down the pavement toward the store. When I reached the corner, a gang of boys grabbed me, knocked me down, snatched the basket, took the money, and sent me running home in panic. That evening I told my mother what had happened, but she made no comment; she sat down at once, wrote another note, gave me more money, and sent me out to the grocery again. I crept down the steps and

> 'You just stay right where you are,' she said in a deadly tone. 'I'm going to teach you this night to stand up and fight for yourself.'

saw the same gang of boys playing down the street. I ran back into the house.

"What's the matter?" my mother asked.

"It's those same boys," I said. "They'll beat me."

"You've got to get over that," she said. "Now, go on."

"I'm scared," I said.

"Go on and don't pay any attention to them," she said.

I went out of the door and walked briskly down the sidewalk, praying that the gang would not molest me. But when I came abreast of them someone shouted, "There he is."

They came toward me and I broke into a wild run toward home. They overtook me and flung me to the pavement. I yelled, pleaded, kicked, but they wrenched the money out of my hand. They yanked me to my feet, gave me a few slaps, and sent me home sobbing. My mother met me at the door.

"They b-beat m-me," I gasped. "They t-t-took the m-money."

I started up the steps, seeking the shelter of the house.

"Don't you come in here," my mother warned me.

I froze in my tracks and stared at her.

"But they're coming after me," I said.

"You just stay right where you are," she said in a deadly tone. "I'm going to teach you this night to stand up and fight for yourself."

She went into the house and I waited, terrified, wondering what she was about. Presently she returned with more money and another note; she also had a long heavy stick.

"Take this money, this note, and this stick," she said. "Go to the store and buy those groceries. If those boys bother you, then fight."

I was baffled. My mother was telling me to fight, a thing that she had never done before.

"But I'm scared," I said.

"Don't you come into this house until you've gotten those groceries," she said.

"They'll beat me; they'll beat me," I said.

"Then stay in the streets; don't come back here!"

I ran up the steps and tried to force my way past her into the house. A stinging slap came on my jaw. I stood on the sidewalk, crying.

"Please, let me wait until tomorrow," I begged.

"No," she said. "Go now! If you come back into this house without those groceries, I'll whip you!"

She slammed the door and I heard the key turn in the lock. I shook with fright. I was alone upon the dark, hostile streets and gangs were after me. I had the choice of being beaten at home or away from home. I clutched the stick, crying, trying to reason. If I were beaten at home, there was absolutely nothing that I could do about it; but if I were beaten in the streets, I had a chance to fight and defend myself. I walked slowly down the sidewalk, coming closer to the gang of boys, holding the stick tightly. I was so full of fear that I could scarcely breathe. I was almost upon them now.

"I clutched the stick, crying, trying to reason."

"There he is again!" the cry went up.

They surrounded me quickly and began to grab for my hand.

"I'll kill you!" I threatened.

They closed in. In blind fear I let the stick fly, feeling it crack against a boy's skull. I swung again, lamming another skull, then another. Realizing that they would retaliate if I let up for but a second, I fought to lay them low, to knock them cold, to kill them so that they could not strike back at me. I flayed with tears in my eyes, teeth clenched, stark fear making me throw every ounce of my strength behind each blow. I hit again and again, dropping the money and the grocery list. The boys scattered, yelling, nursing their heads, staring at me in utter disbelief. They had never seen such frenzy. I stood panting, egging them on, taunting them to come on and fight. When they refused, I ran after them and they tore out for their homes, screaming. The parents of the boys rushed into the streets and threatened me, and for the first time in my life I shouted at grownups, telling them that I would give them the same if they bothered me. I finally found my grocery list and the money and went to the store. On my way back I kept my stick poised for instant use, but there was not a single boy in sight. That night I won the right to the streets of Memphis. ◆

Figure 3-4 Hunger is a problem throughout the world.

Stephen Spender, the poet who wrote "Rough," grew up in England. Although his story is similar to that of Richard Wright's, Spender's problem was not personal poverty. Rather, he felt the results of the poverty of others.

ROUGH

Stephen Spender

My parents kept me from children who were rough
Who threw words like stones and who wore torn clothes.
Their thighs showed through rags. They ran in the street
And climbed cliffs and stripped by the country streams.

I feared more than tigers their muscles like iron
Their jerking hands and their knees tight on my arms.
I feared the salt coarse pointing of those boys
Who copied my lisp behind me on the road.

They were lithe, they sprang out behind hedges
Like dogs to bark at my world. They threw mud
While I looked the other way, pretending to smile.
I longed to forgive them, but they never smiled.

WRITING ABOUT YOURSELF

1. Read both Richard Wright's autobiographical account and Stephen Spender's poem.
2. Hold a class discussion on "Hunger," following these rules:
   a) Select ten students to comment on "Hunger."
   b) Do not stop to discuss these comments. Rather, have the ten students speak one after the other.
   c) Then allow anyone to comment on this literary selection.
   d) Have one or two students summarize the class discussion on "Hunger."

3. Hold a class discussion on "Rough." Follow the guidelines for discussion that are outlined for question 2.
4. Use these questions to begin a class discussion on "Hunger" and "Rough":
   a) Compare these two literary selections. In what ways do they talk about the same idea? How are they different?
   b) These selections talk about the problem of poverty. Look at Figure 3-4 and consider how serious this problem is throughout the world. What is a solution to the problem of poverty in your community? In Canada? In the world?

CAPITAL AND CORPORAL PUNISHMENT

A social issue that prompts much controversy is punishment for people who have done wrong. Politicians have to deal with the issue of capital punishment for criminal offenses. In homes and schools, corporal punishment – strapping or spanking children – can be an issue. Some people believe that schools must retain the right to strap students because strapping is a last-resort measure that is needed for some students. Other people believe that parents should not be allowed to spank their children. In Sweden, for example, spanking is a criminal offence. This next activity will help you explore your ideas on the social issues of corporal and capital punishment.

The following activity uses a technique called a "fishbowl." This technique actually has many names: cluster design, goldfish bowl, micro lab. The purpose of the technique is always the same – to show a group in operation so that you can observe what is going on. This will allow you to provide helpful suggestions to a group and, in turn, other groups will help improve the way you operate in a small-group situation.

ACTIVITY 9

FISHBOWL

1. Pair off in two groups of four or five students each. Have one group sit in a closed circle in the centre, and have the second group sit in an outer ring. The inner group interacts and the outer group observes.

2. Have the inner group talk about capital punishment. Set a time limit, say ten minutes, to talk about this topic. Ask someone to act as timekeeper.

3. After the discussion, invite the outer group to offer its observations on what happened during the inner group's discussion. The outer group can base their observations on the following questions:

- What incident showed someone in the inner group as an active listener?
- When did someone in the inner group use paraphrasing to help the discussion?
- What individuals in the inner group complimented someone for adding a good idea to the discussion?
- Who summarized the discussion as a means of helping the group think about what was discussed and of finding a new direction for the discussion?
- How did the discussion get started? How did it come to a close?
- How did members of the inner group decide to change topics during their discussion?

4. Repeat this activity, with the groups changing roles. Ask the new inner group to talk about corporal punishment.

WORLD PROBLEMS

Social issues are not limited to your community or to Canada as a nation. Social issues can be world wide. The newspaper article about Brazilian rainforests on page 67, for example, shows just how serious such problems can be. Many issues have an impact on the well-being of the entire world, such as the depletion of the ozone layer and the warming of the average temperature on earth, the pollution of the air, the quality of water, and the garbage disposal crisis. And there are the many human rights issues – the oppression caused by military rule, the jailing of people because of their beliefs, the existence of hunger and famine, and the problem of illiteracy.

"If world governments can't make things better, what can I possibly do?" You may be tempted to give up because these issues seem so huge and difficult to solve. But by ignoring world concerns, you can't possibly work toward a better world. What, then, is a starting point that makes sense? One answer is understanding. You need to know the questions before you can find the answers. As you read the article "To save the rainforests of Brazil," note what kinds of questions are being considered in the article. Does this article leave some important questions unanswered?

TO SAVE THE RAINFORESTS OF BRAZIL

The Globe and Mail

Brazilian president Jose Sarney has grudgingly agreed to douse some of the thousands of man-made fires which threaten to reduce the world's greatest rainforest to ashes and dust. International lenders, concerned about the global impact of deforestation, have forced President Sarney to call a truce in Brazil's furious war on the tropical forest of the Amazon. If Brazil can be prevailed upon to keep its promises, the entire world will benefit.

"The Amazon rainforest, more than five million sq km in size, represents one-third of the world's tropical forests and is being destroyed at an unprecedented rate."

Photographs taken from orbiting satellites have revealed that about 6,000 man-made fires are burning in the Amazon every day. Airports in the capitals of five Brazilian provinces were forced to close temporarily this year because the smoke in the atmosphere was so dense pilots could not see to set down their aircraft. Most of the fires have been kindled by land-starved peasants clearing wilderness plots so they can plant crops to feed their families. But the giant blazes have been set by cattle ranchers – who want grassy plains, not rainforest – miners and Brazilian government workers commissioned to lay down highways.

The destruction has been so rapid because the fragile Amazon soil has proved poor for farming or grazing land. Crop-producing nutrients leach away within only two or three years, and peasant farmers must move on and once again set the land ablaze.

The scale of destruction is staggering. Brazil's Atlantic rainforest, estimated to have covered more than 350,000 square kilometres in colonial times, has shrunk to just over 10,000 sq km. The Amazon rainforest, more than five million sq km in size, represents one-third of the world's tropical forests and is being destroyed at an unprecedented rate.

"The stakes for all citizens of this endangered earth could not be higher....Officials at the Canadian branch of the World Wildlife Fund calculate that, at the present rate of destruction, one species is lost every day."

Until now, Mr. Sarney has argued that Brazilians should be as free as North Americans were to raze their forests. He believes the Amazon must be exploited to help ease the crushing social and economic burdens which weigh upon Brazil's 135 million people. But environmentalists, and latterly international lending agencies, have begun to worry that both the elimination of the Amazonian plant life and the terrible conflagration itself are contributing to a potentially catastrophic global warming effect.

In the past Brazil has made, and broken, pledges to safeguard the forests and the forest dwellers. In the early 1980s, the World Bank agreed on only the most restrictive terms to lend Brazil money to construct a highway deep into the interior near the border with Bolivia. But after the road went in, more than one million immigrants were permitted to flood the region and to slash and burn an area the size of the Netherlands.

As well, despite dire warnings from scientists, the Brazilian government is permitting the development of what will be the world's largest iron ore mine with 20 iron smelters, all of which will use wood – not coking coal or oil – as the chief form of energy.

The stakes for all citizens of this endangered earth could not be higher. Tropical forest makes up 7 per cent of the world's surface and contains half of all plant species. Every year between 10 and 15 million hectares of tropical forest are lost. Officials at the Canadian branch of the World Wildlife Fund calculate that, at the present rate of destruction, one species is lost every day.

The WWF has launched a campaign to raise money for the preservation of tropical forests. Canadians have been asked to "buy" a parcel of tropical forest to save it from destruction. Already $500,000 has been raised to hire and train wardens for rainforest preserves in Central America.

Perhaps the developed nations could adopt a similar model in providing inducements – in addition to the threats already issued by lenders – to encourage Brazil to spare the Amazon, and the whole world, a bleak future. ◆

GROUP REPORT

Prepare to form small groups. Each group will report on an important issue of which the impact is not limited just to your community or just to Canada.

1. Using the group-interaction skills that you practised throughout this unit, decide on the following matters:

a) How will the groups be formed?
b) Where will the groups meet?
c) How long will the groups have to complete their reports?
d) How will the groups present their reports to the rest of the class?
e) How will the different groups be scheduled?
f) How will the class provide feedback on these reports?
g) Should the reports be marked? If yes, how should they be marked and who should do it?

2. Form small groups and prepare your report. Decide how you will operate as a group. Keep in mind the communication and cooperation skills practised in this unit.

3. When you are finished working on your report, look once again at the Group Interaction Checklist in Activity 2.

a) Complete this chart one more time, based on your experience with the group report in this activity.
b) Compare the results of the two checklists. Did you improve as a result of the exercises in this unit?

info-box

WRITING A GROUP REPORT

A group report can take many shapes.

1. Decide upon a topic or theme.
2. Then do some initial exploration of this topic, both as a group and independently.
3. Next, as a group, decide how to organize the report and how to present it to your class. You can use a number of different techniques. You can lecture to the class. You can use audio-visual material. You can present your ideas through mime or through drawings.... You are limited only by your imagination.

END THOUGHTS

In this unit, you have thought about social issues. Some of these issues are personal – concerns that you or your family have. Other issues are concerns of your community. And still other issues are global concerns, issues that touch nations. You may be tempted to say, "These issues are so complex, so huge and so far away from me that I can't do anything about them. Why bother?" You might find an answer to this question in the cartoon in Figure 3-5 on page 71.

EXTENSION IDEAS

1. In a small group, plan and carry out an event to support a local charity or one that your school is involved with. You might, for example, plan a party for some young children in your community. Or you might volunteer to do door-to-door canvassing for a group such as the United Way or Community Chest.
2. Set up a class project. Divide the class into small groups so that each group has a specific task. When you put all the group efforts together, you have completed the project.

Figure 3-5 What does this cartoon say about the ideas presented in this unit ?

3. Invite a speaker to your classroom to talk about a social issue that has caught your interest. Make sure that you have prepared some questions to ask this speaker ahead of time.

4. Use your knowledge of a social issue to write a letter to the editor of your community newspaper, giving your point of view on this issue.

5. Follow your local newspaper for two weeks. Cut out articles dealing with social issues. Make your own bulletin-board display of these issues.

6. Develop a survey in which you list several social issues. Conduct your survey in your school to determine the response of students in your school to each of these issues. Publish the results in your school newspaper.

7. Find a pen pal in another part of Canada. Write to him or her about social issues in your community and ask about social issues in your pen pal's community. Are they the same?

UNIT 4

FRIENDSHIP AND RESPONSIBILTY

- ★ A CASE STUDY OF FRIENDSHIP
- ★ HAIKU

INTRODUCTION

We all need friends. Friends are different from family members because friends choose us. We choose friends because we like them, and this is what makes friendship so valuable.

We can't treat our friends in just any way. We may have a lot of freedom of action when it comes to our friends, but there are limits to our behaviour toward them. This unit is about friendship and the responsibilities that go along with it.

Figure 4-1 "A Time to Dream"

ACTIVITY 1

THINKING ABOUT FRIENDSHIP

1. Look at Figure 4-1 and use this picture to think about the nature of friendship.

a) Look at the picture and think about a time when you and some friends shared some time together.

b) Do some free writing about your thoughts. Start to write – and put down anything that comes to mind. Write without stopping for five minutes. If you can't think of anything to say, keep rewriting the word 'friendship' until other thoughts come to mind.

2. Form groups of about four members to consider your answers to question 1.

a) Share your experiences of friendship with others in your group and discuss the nature of friendship.
b) Make a group list of characteristics of a good friend.

3. Draw some conclusions about the responsibilities that you have to a friend.

a) Discuss how you would complete these statements:

- "A friend should ...."
- "A friend shouldn't ...."

b) As a group, make a list of responsibilities that you have to your friends.
c) Present your ideas to the class, and listen to the other students' ideas about friendship.

ACTIVITY 2

A PUZZLE FOR DISCUSSION AND WRITING

1. Read this anecdote, and then discuss this question with a partner: How did he know her name?

John Thomas stepped off the train in Calgary and met a friend he had not seen in years. Beside his friend was a little girl.

"John," shouted his friend. "How delightful to see you! Did you know that I am married. This is my daughter."

"No, I didn't," said Thomas to his friend. "What is your name?" he asked the girl.

"The same as my mother's," replied the girl.

"Then you must be Anne," said Thomas.

2. After solving the puzzle, consider the following questions with a partner:

a) Talk about your first response to this puzzle. Why did you think this way?
b) What does this anecdote say about friendship and responsibility?

3. Create your own puzzle. Write it in anecdote form using conversation. Make a neat copy on a card. Pass the cards around, solve the puzzles, and discuss the causes of any misunderstandings.

A CASE STUDY OF FRIENDSHIP

This cartoon shows how superficial some people can be about friendship. Which would you rather be: liked by other people or popular? The following story examines this question. It is about friendship and responsibility and it demonstrates the danger of seeking popularity for its own sake.

Figure 4-2 Two ways of looking at friendship.

THE TRADE OFF

Paula Mitchell

I just wanted to have friends. That's the only reason I did it. I didn't mean to hurt anyone. But I guess that sometimes when you want something desperately enough, you can be blinded by your own selfishness. You're so busy reaching for that tiny glimmer of hope, that one-in-a-million chance you think is just within your grasp, that before you know it, the damage has been done.

There I go rationalizing again. Actually, point-blank lying to myself. The truth is, I was perfectly aware of what I was doing, and the possibility that I might hurt someone was not foremost in my mind. And when I say "friends" I guess I'm lying to myself there, too. I didn't want friends, I wanted... a clique; I wanted to belong – to the group of popular, cute, energetic girls whose names are known in every high school across the country. You know, the girls who wear oversized varsity sport jackets, and mill excitedly around their lockers, giggling and flirting and earnestly whispering as if what they have to say is so earth-shattering it can't wait another second. And it didn't matter about their dangerous escapades, that beneath the facade they did more back-stabbing than Arabian knights, or that with my aspirations (good grades = good college = good job) I had virtually nothing in common with them. Worst of all was my mother's old line, "Once high school is over their lives are headed nowhere." None of these things made a difference to me – I would have jumped at the chance to trade in my one-best-friend life for their secure cluster.

I'll admit that's the reason I tried out for cheerleading last September. I'd had an incredible brainstorm one dull Saturday afternoon while blow-drying my hair. I was sitting cross-legged on the bathroom counter top in my own little world of monotonous, electronic whirring, when the idea suddenly took shape. It seemed painfully obvious. Why hadn't I thought of it before? I could be a cheerleader! I'd never exactly had a burning desire to win that title, but the girls I wanted to be friendly with were the cheerleaders – I mean, they practically invented the word. Football season will be here soon, I thought, and then I'll try out and make the squad and be at all their practices and then they'll have to notice me because we'll be spending so much time together and, anyway, we'll get to be friends because all the cheerleaders are friends – everyone knows that – and ... my mind surged off on a delirious fantasy. I imagined myself at one of their wild parties, at the homecoming dance.... Yes, it could finally happen. And becoming a cheerleader was the key. From there, it looked so easy.

"I imagined myself at one of their wild parties, at the homecoming dance.... Yes, it could finally happen. And becoming a cheerleader was the key."

I was prepared for tryouts by the one and only Janice Whitaker, established cheerleader, and tenth-grade Homecoming Queen – after I consented to let her cheat off me on a chemistry test. I figured my assimilation into the top echelon of Cedar Grove High would begin with a close friendship with Janice, formed during those few days she coached me. I don't know where I got the idea that one thing would lead to another – I mean, I fantasized about her coming over to my house and our chumminess building to such a point that on her way out the door, she'd casually invite me to all the best parties, and introduce me to the most gorgeous guys in the world.

Meanwhile, real life intruded on my plans. My best friend, Melina, suspiciously asked me why I'd been walking with Janice Whitaker the other day after school. (I couldn't suppress a gleam of triumph, at least someone had noticed me in such impressive company, even if it was only Melina.) "I didn't know you were friends," she remarked coldly, kicking her locker shut and looking up at me. It was times like these that she really grated on my nerves.

"We're not – I mean...." I'd avoided mentioning the tryouts to Melina for fear of jinxing the outcome, but at that moment, the lie wouldn't come fast enough, so I told her the truth.

Melina's eyes bulged in astonishment, "You're going to be a cheerleader? That's great!" she gushed.

"Shhh," I hissed, glancing wildly toward the people within earshot. A few of the more popular set were clustered about five

feet away; I didn't want them to know my plan until I'd succeeded – until I was absolutely, positively a cheerleader. "Be quiet, Mel. I don't want anyone to hear –."

"Why not?" she asked. "It's fantastic!" despite her usual anti-jock sentiments. She refused to step within a five-mile radius of any football games, because she didn't like any of "those people."

Melina's ecstatic reaction didn't surprise me. She tended to worship nearly everything I did. I wished I felt the same way about her. She had no doubt in her mind that I would make it. I noticed that every time I started to talk about the squad, or anything to do with that group, her eyes would glaze over, and I would pretend not to hear the tears in her voice.

"I noticed that every time I started to talk about the squad, or anything to do with that group, her eyes would glaze over, and I would pretend not to hear the tears in her voice."

Two weeks later, on the night I was officially made a Cedar Grove Varsity Football Cheerleader, I found Melina at my house with a cake, waiting to celebrate. There had been a party that night for cheerleaders. Everyone went except me. Nobody asked me along.

As we got into the season, there were more parties, and I wasn't invited to these either. I have to stop kidding myself, they're never going to ask me along.

What is wrong with me? I constantly demanded of myself, choking on tears of self-pity in the privacy of my bedroom.

My mother heard my sobs and came to see what was wrong. I told her, but her response was not what I expected.

"You're being foolish," she snapped. "Those girls aren't looking for friends – they don't need you. And what ever happened to Melina? And your friends from last year, Kirsten and – ."

"Oh, spare me," I said. I wanted sympathy, not a lecture. She shrugged indicating it was my loss, and informed me that dinner was almost ready.

To complicate matters more, I called Melina and found out from her mother that she was confined to bed all weekend with a stomach virus, so I couldn't even turn to her.

By Wednesday, she still hadn't shown up in school, so I phoned her again. Talk about the unexpected this time. Her mother informed me that Melina had been taken to the hospital to be tested for what they thought was mono. It was two days later that Melina called. And what Melina told me was so bizarre, so like a sick nightmare, that I still get a chill every time I recall it.

The mono story had been to save face. It turned out that she had been so depressed these past few months that her parents decided it would be better if she went away for a while. She was now at a place most kids refer to as 'Loony Tunes School' – an alternative facility for people who are undergoing too much emotional stress to function adequately in public high school. (I'd seen the brochure.) The place where all the crazies go.

"The entire squad looked in my direction. I could feel the beads of sweat beginning to spill down my forehead. I was excited, that I was finally being recognized. Enveloped by this heady sensation I began to talk so fast that the words tripped over themselves."

The last thing I remember her saying before she hung up was, "Just promise me you won't tell anyone where I am, okay?"

Out of the blue, at my next cheerleading practice, somebody asked where Melina Paterson had gone. The entire squad looked in my direction. I could feel the beads of sweat beginning to spill down my forehead. I was excited, that I was finally being recognized. Enveloped by this heady sensation I began to talk so fast that the words tripped over themselves.

"You see," I began, savouring my stardom, "she was feeling really depressed...."

When I got started, I couldn't stop. The whole story spilled.

"Omigosh," Chrissy whispered. "That's horrible." In hushed, awed tones, we all reflected on just how horrible it was, until Kelly pointed out that it was getting late, and since we'd done nothing but talk all week, we really had to practise for tomorrow's game.

I was waiting for my mom to pick me up when it finally hit me – the full impact of what I'd just done. The exhilaration I had felt while telling the story had died as soon as I was finished, and there's no adjective to describe the cheap hollowness I felt then, especially when half those girls walked out the door without even saying good-bye to me. No, there's no adjective to describe that, just as there was absolutely nothing I could say to Melina when she returned to school two weeks later, to a senior class that treated her like a leper.

I tried everything – even my good old rational thinking to

convince myself that what I'd done wasn't all that terrible. But when I approached Melina in the hall, ready with a lame apology I'd run through my head a billion times the night before, all it took was the pained expression on her face to inflame mine with shame, and force my gaze elsewhere. Without a word, she told me that she never wanted to speak to me again. And even though I miss her, I guess I can't blame her. Her silence is more than I deserve. ◆

ACTIVITY 3

THINKING ABOUT "THE TRADE OFF"

1. Answer the following questions about this short story:

a) What one word that is found in the pages of this story best captures its meaning? Why?
b) What other word do you believe best captures the meaning of this story?
c) Why is this story called "The Trade Off"?

2. Judge the narrator of this story, using your list made for Activity 1 on page 74.

a) Is the narrator a good friend in some ways?
b) According to your list, what does she do that makes her a poor friend to Melina?

3. Write the ending of this story as Melina might have told it.

4. Not everyone has expressed a positive attitude toward friendship, as this well-known saying reminds us: "With friends like these, who needs enemies?" Here are four other rather cynical views on friendship:

- Defend me from my friends; I can defend myself from my enemies.

  – *Marechel de Villars*

- I can be on guard against my enemies, but God deliver me from my friends!

  – *Charlotte Bronte*

- I am not worried about my enemies. It is my friends that keep me awake nights.

  – *Warren Harding*

- Most friendship is feigning, most loving mere folly.

  – *William Shakespeare*

Which of these sayings best describes the friend that the narrator proves herself to be in "The Trade Off"? Explain your choice.

HAIKU

Haiku is an ancient Japanese form of poetry that has been adapted for use by English writers. Haiku look easy to write because they are very short, but they do, nevertheless, follow very strict rules. Here are some haiku written by the Japanese poet Issa on the theme of human relations.

TWO HAIKU

Issa

Under the cherry-blossoms,
None are
Utter strangers.

We human beings,
Squirming about among
The flowers that bloom.

info-box

CHARACTERISTICS OF HAIKU

the white cloud drifts west
on a wide blue sheet – punctured
by a sharp jack pine!

– *Clare Henderson*

1. In haiku a sensory image is presented but is not explained. The reader must experience it. In the above example the picture is of a white cloud drifting across a blue sky.
2. Traditionally only imagery of nature and the seasons could be used. Usually the images were gentle, such as drops of rain on lotus blossoms. Writers of modern English haiku use any kind of image to achieve the effect they desire.
3. Haiku has three lines. There are five syllables in the first and third lines and seven syllables in the second line. There is no rhyme.
4. The verbs are always in the present tense. For example, the cloud *drifts* instead of *drifted*. This enhances the reader's sense of the experience by making it seem more immediate.
5. There is a twist in the third line. The image is established in the first line, is developed in the second line, but is altered in the third line. This surprising twist may be ironic, humorous, or just a new point of view on the topic. For example, the white cloud drifts across the peaceful sky – until it is punctured by a sharp tree.
6. You may add a title. Many haiku have no title. What would you call the haiku in the example above?

ACTIVITY 4

FRIENDSHIP AND HAIKU

Write a number of haiku about friendship and make a collection of the best ones. Illustrate your collection.

1. Much poetry writing involves playing with words. Start by getting words down on a page. As you do this, concentrate on creating images and don't worry about line length.
2. After you have developed your idea, start the revision process. Keep revising your words until they take the shape you need. Count the syllables in the lines. Try strengthening the feeling your images create by playing with your words to get the right line length. And don't forget the twist!
3. Write a number of haiku in this manner. When you are satisfied with what you have written, begin a selection process. Check your poems against the Characteristics of Haiku on page 83. Let other people read and comment on them.
4. Select your three best haiku. Type them centred on one page and single space them as in the example on page 82. Leave a space between each haiku. Type your name after the last one. If you are using a word processor, centre all of the lines. In any case, make the haiku look attractive because the appearance of poetry on a page is very important to your visual appreciation of it. Try putting your work together with that of others to create a book of haiku.

FRIENDSHIP

1. To summarize your thoughts on this unit, write a personal statement on friendship by responding to each of the following topics (each topic should form a paragraph):

   a) Your personal definition of a friend. For example, you could start out, "To me the word 'friend' means ...."
   b) Your thoughts on responsibility. You might begin, "I think that responsibility to a friend is shown in these ways:...."
   c) Your personal thoughts about friendship with people of the opposite sex. Start with "I think that ...."
   d) Your personal experiences with friends. "I have had ...."
   e) Conclude with a statement about your own behaviour. "From now on I...."

2. Put these five paragraphs together to form a personal statement about friendship.

   a) Write an introductory paragraph for your statement. Make each of your responses to question 1 a paragraph.
   b) If necessary, write a concluding paragraph.
   c) Give your personal statement a title.

END THOUGHTS

This unit has dealt with the importance of having friends. It has also drawn your attention to the other side of the coin – the responsibilities you have to your friends. And you have explored the idea of friendship in the form of the short story and in haiku.

EXTENSION IDEAS

1. Write a number of poems on friendship. Select three or four of the best ones to include in a small anthology. Create a cover page. Type the poems one to a page and neatly centred. If you do this as a group, include a table of contents and type the author's name on each page.
2. Read *Of Mice and Men* by John Steinbeck. Steinbeck's book is a short novel about friendship and the responsibilities that go with it. Create a collage or a mobile to describe George's friendship with Lennie.
3. Decide what you should do in this situation: Your best friend has just told you about a very serious problem.You know that you can't help your friend because you don't know exactly what to do. But you know that he or she really needs help. Your friend, however, refuses to seek help by talking with anyone – a parent, a school counsellor, a teacher. What should you do?

   Use these guidelines to arrive at your decision.

   a) Form a discussion group of three or four people.
   b) Choose a fairly serious problem that someone might have.
   c) As a group, brainstorm to create a list of choices that you

could make in response to this imaginary person's situation. Remember: in brainstorming, you do not criticize or reject any idea. All ideas must be written down and considered later.

d) Talk about your list of ideas after the brainstorming session is over. Look for the advantages and the disadvantages of each idea.
e) Rank the possible choices from most valuable to least valuable.
f) As a group, prepare a report on your discussion. Use the following headings as an outline for this report:

   - The Situation
   - The Choices
   - The Best Action
   - The Reason for Our Choice

g) Decide upon an interesting way to present your report to your class.

4. Look at "A Time to Dream" on page 74. What overall impression does this photograph make on you? Examine each of the following elements as you look at this photograph:

- the content
- the colour
- the composition

Collect several pictures about friendship from magazines. Examine the elements of these pictures. Prepare a short talk to deliver to your class to show what elements make the photographs effective.

5. Complete the following statements in your notebook or journal.

- "A friend is..."
- "A friend isn't..."
- "A friend will..."
- "A friend won't..."
- "A friend should..."
- "A friend shouldn't..."
- "A friend can..."
- "A friend can't..."

UNIT 5

★ ★ ★ ★ ★ ★ ★

DRIVING DESIGN

- ★ THE MAGIC OF A CAR
- ★ THE MARKETPLACE
- ★ VISUAL APPEAL
- ★ CHANGES TO THE MOTOR CAR
- ★ POWER IN SYMBOLS
- ★ "WON'T YOU BUY ME A MERCEDES BENZ"
- ★ THOSE WHO DARE TO BE DIFFERENT
- ★ JUNK YARD
- ★ CARS AND PEOPLE

INTRODUCTION

Cars are more than just transportation. They also send out messages about the kind of person who owns them. In other words, your car can be seen as an extension of your values, hopes, and dreams. In this unit you will have the opportunity to look briefly at cars and to see how they can reflect the values and attitudes of the people who use and own them.

THE MAGIC OF A CAR

Cars have fascinated people of all ages for a hundred years. Car enthusiasts everywhere devote time, energy, and money to their cars: they build models, collect antiques, work on cars, and participate in car races and rallies. In one way or another cars are, for these people, a source of entertainment and enjoyment.

DEKE'S FIRST CAR

Gary Hyland

Now I'm supposed to terrorize
cuttin doughnuts every corner
duals burpin, radio blastin
buzzin chicks on the street
and I will, I know, I'll haveta.

But I'd rather spin around alone
when the houses are goin dark,
slow through rain-wet streets,
engine hummin thick with power,
wet lickin sounds of tires,
paint and chrome rain-beaded
like jewelry in the lights,
the snugness and warm car smell,
and next to me a half-lit place
waitin for a girl who can feel
the special magic of a car.

DREAMING ABOUT CARS

1. What is Deke's dilemma in the poem "Deke's First Car"? That is, what does Deke have to do and what does Deke want to do? Does Deke make the right choice? Why? Is this the choice that you would make?
2. Find two or three examples of visually descriptive language in "Deke's First Car." What do these words tell you about Deke?
3. Write an account in your notebook in which you describe the special features that your dream car must have.
    a) Compare your list with that of a partner's. What items are only on your list?
    b) Do these items reflect your particular values and attitudes?
4. Write a short poem that describes you driving your special car.

THE MARKETPLACE

For many people, the most important consideration about a car is what it looks like. Car manufacturers are well aware of this. They put a great deal of effort into designing cars that will be visually appealing to buyers.

As you look at the cars in this unit, remember that you will interpret what you see based on your particular background and previous experience. Your answers to the questions in the next activity will not necessarily be the right answers for someone else.

ACTIVITY 2

VISUALLY SPEAKING

Figure 5-1 Why might antique cars appeal to a collector?

1. Look at the car in Figure 5-1. Do you like the look of it? Why or why not?
2. Who do you think was the original owner of this car? What would he or she have been like? What visual clues in the picture lead you to these conclusions?
3. Did your class react to the visual clues in the picture in the same way? What caused the similarities or differences in opinion?
4. How do the backgrounds and personal experiences of the people in your class prompt them to see and interpret this picture in different ways?

There are a great many models of cars, and the marketplace is competitive. Looking for a car can be time consuming and sometimes frustrating. Most people, however, have certain things that they want when they go looking for a car, depending on their needs, tastes, and preferences. Here are some of the characteristics that various people may value in a car: speed, power, appearance, luxury, economy, performance, safety, comfort, durability, convenience, and uniqueness.

Figure 5-2 Here are three potential car buyers.

Figure 5-3 As you look at these clippings from automotive brochures, try to identify some of the characteristics that people may be expected to value in an automotive vehicle.

EXPECTATIONS AND VISUAL ASSOCIATIONS

1. Select the car from Figure 5-3 that you believe each of the buyers in Figure 5-2 would purchase (p. 91). Give the reasons for your choices.
2. If you were choosing a car for yourself, which of those in Figure 5-3 would you choose? Why? Which car would you not choose because it would project the wrong image of you?
3. Many people choose their possessions in order to project a particular image or picture of themselves and to live up to social expectations – through their possessions they are 'keeping up with the Joneses.' Describe some examples of people choosing cars to project a specific image of themselves.

VISUAL APPEAL

People who sell cars say that there are two kinds of buyers: those who look for good performance and those who are interested in appearance. Those who look for performance consider aspects such as the gas mileage, the horsepower, and the repair record of the car. Those who look for appearance think about aspects such as shape, colour, and size. Sales statistics show that more people buy cars for their visual appeal than for any other reason.

Those who look for appearance respond to the visual appeal of a car. They might consider, for example, the interior upholstery and the chrome trim. They might look, too, at extras such as stereos and hub caps. In addition, they might respond to the colour of the car. Some people want a car that is exciting – sporty and speedy. Often such people will choose a red car. Others who want their cars to suggest something more serious will likely choose a darker colour such as grey or black. Closely connected with the colour of a car is its shape. Some shapes suggest speed and excitement and other shapes have a more classy and sedate look – something an owner would drive only to deposit money in a bank!

THE PEOPLE'S CHOICE

1. What colour of car do you think each of the people in the following list would choose – and why?

a) a person selling computers
b) a manager of a large department store
c) an NHL hockey player
d) the prime minister of Canada
e) a male hero of an afternoon soap opera
f) an announcer who reads the CBC-TV nightly news

2. What feeling do you have for the shape of each of the cars in Figure 5-4? Why?

3. What message does each car in Figure 5-4 give you about the kind of person who would drive it? What kind of society does this person live in? For example, the shape of one car might suggest a society that is interested in space and aerodynamics.

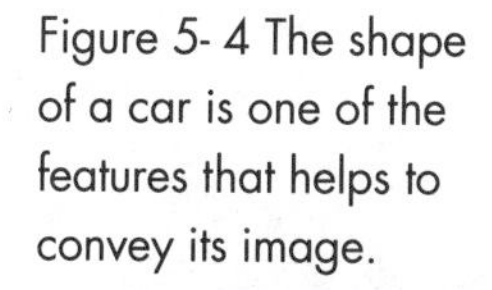

Figure 5- 4 The shape of a car is one of the features that helps to convey its image.

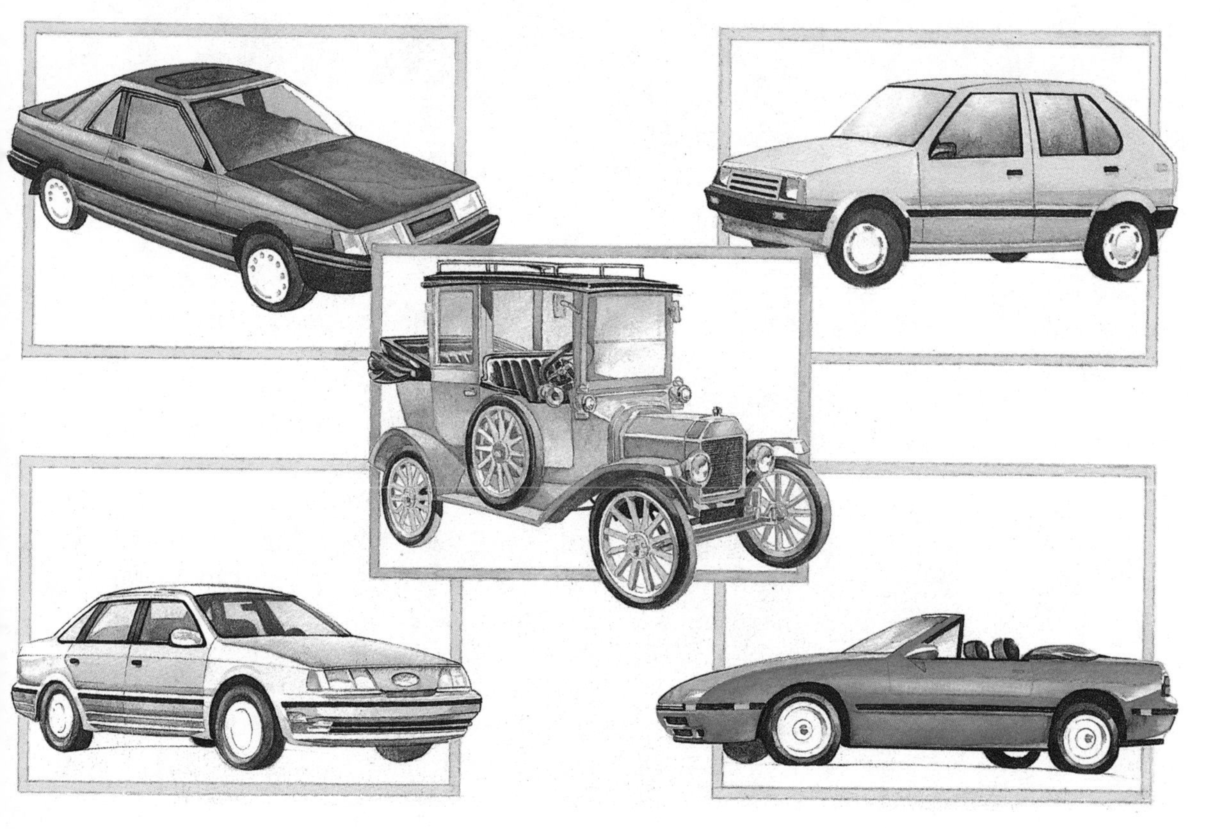

CHANGES TO THE MOTOR CAR

When the first car was invented, the designer took ideas about shape and design from the horse-drawn buggy. It took a long time for the average person to accept the 'horseless carriage' as a reliable means of transportation. The car did not become popular until the early 1930s. Over the years it has taken the work of both engineers and car stylists to change the original box-like design of the car to a design of rounded corners and graceful sweeping lines. It has changed into a machine of motion.

Figure 5-5 What reaction do you have to the shape and colour of the car from the 1920s in a) and the car from the 1930s in b) ?

Car designers constantly try to capture the mood of the time in which they live. The designers of the cars of the 1950s showed their desire for a change from the common design. They were looking for a radical, new look for cars. People of the 1950s were beginning to think about space travel. These thoughts influenced the design of cars as designers looked to jet planes and space rockets for ideas. They developed big, ostentatious cars, with powerful V-8 engines, that drew attention to themselves.

With the world energy crisis in the 1970s, North American manufacturers began to produce cars that were smaller and more fuel efficient – with streamlined designs emphasizing aerodynamics. At this time, too, imported cars from Europe and Japan gained in popularity, forcing the major North American manufacturers to redesign their cars from the big sedan to the smaller, sportier car. Stick shifts on the floor became popular; clutches returned to replace automatic gear shifts.

ACTIVITY 5

A VIEW OF THE FLAMBOYANT '50S

Figure 5-6 Look for these features on the cars of the 1950s: fins and space-rocket tail lights; chrome-plated grilles and air scoops; wraparound windshields; long and bulky hood lines; dual exhaust outlets; excessive chrome trim; vibrant colour combinations with, for example, pinks and mauves; and flashy hub caps.

1. Look at the pictures of the car in Figure 5-6, then draw a line down the middle of a page and on one side list the design features you notice about this car. On the other side, list the design features you have noticed about today's cars. Compare the two lists and write a brief statement in your notebook about the major differences in design features between the two eras.

2. Interview people in your community who remember the 1950s. Ask them about their memories of the cars of that time. Also ask them how they feel about how cars look now as opposed to what they looked like then. Be prepared to report your findings to your class.

3. Conduct an interview with people who remember cars from another era such as the 1940s or the 1930s. Again tell your class what you find out about the feelings that these people have for the cars of 'their' era.

ACTIVITY 6

THE FAST LANE

Figure 5-7 What do you associate with sports cars?

1. What is there about the Corvette in Figure 5-7 that gives it a racy appearance of speed and power?
2. Bright colours such as intense reds and yellows are more common in sports cars than in other cars. Why?
3. What features, besides shape and colour, give this car spirit?
4. What kind of person would likely buy this car?

POWER IN SYMBOLS

People as far back as the stone age have relied on symbols to express feelings and meaning. Today school teams, for example, sometimes adopt names such as Tigers and Hawks to suggest animal-like strength and ability. Car manufacturers choose names for their cars very carefully because these names help sell the cars. This is because the name projects an image – and many people buy cars for the image they project.

ACTIVITY 7

WHAT'S IN A NAME

"Do you have something suitable for a person who tends to be chicken?" November 12, 1964

Figure 5-8 Image is an important factor in the marketing of cars.

1. What point is the cartoonist in Figure 5-8 making about cars and car names?
2. Car names are important. Like colour and shape, the name tells you something about a car. Car manufacturers frequently use names symbolically to give their cars an image. For example, cars are frequently called by animal names such as *Mustang, Colt, Cougar, Jaguar*, and *Rabbit*. Sometimes people give cars a name such as the *Beetle*. Look again at Figure 5-4 on page 93 and suggest a name for each car that will increase its buying appeal.
3. Make a list of names of cars. You might find it helpful to browse through magazines and car brochures.
4. Categorize your list of cars, using this chart as a model.

CAR NAMES

	Animals	Astronomy	Exotic Places	Nobility	Others
Name	Mustang	Mercury	New Yorker	Monarch	
Symbol	wild west	space rockets	style	classic, high brow	

Figure 5-9 What other names and symbols can you think of ?

5. Use your chart to write a short report on the names of cars. Include a discussion of how the visual images brought to mind by a particular name might attract a particular type of car buyer. Do you think they really do? Begin your report with a strong statement in a topic sentence like this one: "Car manufacturers choose a wide variety of names to give their cars a definite image."

"WON'T YOU BUY ME A MERCEDES BENZ"

This title comes from a song made popular by pop singer Janis Joplin. This song is about people's desire to impress others with their material possessions. Many people use cars more than any other possession as a symbol of their status and prestige. Some celebrities customize their cars to make a statement about themselves: their cars tell about their pride and wealth. These celebrities have been known to add specially designed features such as these to their cars: 24K gold-plated grilles, black alligator-hide interiors, mink fur seat covers, and bullet-proof wind shields.

While some people use their cars to make a statement about power and wealth, other people may use their cars to satisfy different emotional needs, as Harry Harrison's short story shows.

"Out of the garage the great machine charged, down the drive and into the street with the grace and majesty of an unleashed 747."

SPEED OF THE CHEETAH, ROAR OF THE LION

Harry Harrison

"Here he comes, Dad," Billy shouted, waving the field glasses. "He just turned the corner from Lilac."

Henry Brogan grunted a bit as he squeezed behind the wheel of his twenty-two-foot-long, eight-foot wide, three hundred and sixty-horsepower, four-door, power-everything and air-conditioning, definitely not compact, luxury car. There was plenty of room between the large steering wheel and the back of the leather-covered seat, but there was plenty of Henry as well, particularly around the middle. He grunted again as he leaned over to turn the ignition switch. The thunderous roar of unleashed horse-power filled the garage, and he smiled with pleasure as he plucked out the glowing lighter and pressed it to the end of his long cigar.

Billy squatted behind the hedge, peering through it, and when he called out again, his voice squeaked with excitement.

"A block away and slowing down!"

"Here we go!" his father called out gaily, pressing down on the accelerator. The roar of the exhaust was like thunder, and the open garage doors vibrated with the sound while every empty can bounced upon the shelves. Out of the garage the great machine charged, down the drive and into the street with the grace and majesty of an unleashed 747. Roaring with the voice of freedom, it surged majestically past the one-cylinder, plastic and plywood, one hundred and thirty-two miles to the gallon, single-seater Austerity Beetle that Simon Pismire was driving. Simon was just turning into his own driveway when the behemoth of the highways hurtled by and set his tiny conveyance rocking in the slipstream. Simon, face red with fury, popped up through the open top like a gopher from his hole and shook his fist after the car with impotent rage, his words lost in the roar of the eight gigantic cylinders. Henry Brogan admired this in his mirror, laughed with glee and shook a bit of cigar ash into his wake.

“Roaring with the voice of freedom, it surged majestically past the one-cylinder, plastic and plywood, one hundred and thirty-two miles to the gallon, single-seater Austerity Beetle that Simon Pismire was driving.”

It was indeed a majestic sight, a whale among the shoals of minnows. The tiny vehicles that cluttered the street parted before him, their drivers watching his passage with bulging eyes. The pedestrians and bicyclists, on the newly poured sidewalks and bicycle paths, were no less attentive or impressed. The passage of a king in his chariot, or an All-American on the shoulders of his teammates, would have aroused no less interest. Henry was indeed King of the Road and he gloated with pleasure.

Yet he did not go far; that would be rubbing their noses in it. His machine waited, rumbling with restrained impatience at the light, then turned into Hollywood Boulevard, where he stopped

> "Simon's face was flushed with rage and he danced little angry steps upon the sidewalk."

before the Thrifty drugstore. He left the engine running, muttering happily to itself, when he got out, and pretended not to notice the stares of everyone who passed.

"Never looked better," Doc Kline said. The druggist met him at the door and handed him his four-page copy of the weekly Los Angeles Times. "Sure in fine shape."

"Thanks, Doc. A good car should have good care taken of it." They talked a minute about the usual things: the blackouts on the East Coast, schools closed by the power shortage, the latest emergency message from the President; then Henry strolled back and threw the paper in onto the seat. He was just opening the door when Simon Pismire came popping slowly up in his Austerity Beetle.

"Get good mileage on that thing, Simon?" Henry asked innocently.

"Listen to me, dammit! You come charging out in that tank, almost run me down, I'll have the law on you –"

"Now, Simon, I did nothing of the sort. Never came near you. And I looked around careful like because that little thing of yours is hard to see at times."

Simon's face was flushed with rage and he danced little angry steps upon the sidewalk. "Don't talk to me like that! I'll have the law on you with that truck, burning our priceless oil preserves –"

"Watch the temper, Simon. The old ticker can go poof if you let yourself get excited. You're in the coronary belt now, you know. And you also know the law's been around my place often. The price and rationing people, IRS, police, everyone. They did admire my car, and all of them shook hands like gentlemen when they left. The law likes my car, Simon. Isn't that right, Officer?"

O'Reilly, the beat cop, was leaning his bike against the wall, and he waved and hurried on, not wanting to get involved. "Fine by me, Mr. Brogan," he called back over his shoulder as he entered the store.

"There, Simon, you see?" Henry slipped behind the wheel and tapped the gas pedal; the exhaust roared and people stepped quickly back onto the curb. Simon pushed his head in the window and shouted.

"You're just driving this car to bug me, that's all you're doing!"

His face was, possibly, redder now and sweat beaded his forehead. Henry smiled sweetly and dragged deeply on the cigar before answering.

"Now that's not a nice thing to say. We've been neighbours for years, you know. Remember when I bought a Chevvy how the very next week you had a two-door Buick? I got a nice buy on a secondhand four-door Buick, but you had a new Toronado the same day. Just by coincidence, I guess.

Like when I built a twenty-foot swimming pool, you, just by chance, I'm sure, had a thirty-foot one dug that was even a foot deeper than mine. These things never bothered me –"

"The hell you say!"

"Well, maybe they did. But they don't bother me any more, Simon, not any more."

He stepped lightly on the accelerator, and the juggernaut of the road surged away and around the corner and was gone. As he drove, Henry could not remember a day when the sun had shone more clearly from a smogless sky, nor when the air had smelled fresher. It was a beautiful day indeed.

Billy was waiting by the garage when he came back, closing and locking the door when the last high, gleaming fender had rolled by. He laughed out loud when his father told him what had happened, and before the story was done, they were both weak with laughter.

"I wish I could have seen his face, Dad, I really do. I tell you what for tomorrow, why don't I turn up the volume on the exhaust a bit. We got almost two hundred watts of output from the amplifier, and that is a twelve-inch speaker down there between the rear wheels. What do you say?"

"Maybe, just a little bit, a little bit more each day maybe. Let's look at the clock." He squinted at the instrument panel, and the smile drained from his face. "I had eleven minutes of driving time. I didn't know it was that long."

"Eleven minutes... that will be about two hours."

"I know it, damn it. But spell me a bit, will you, or I'll be too tired to eat dinner."

"Remember when I bought a Chevvy how the very next week you had a two-door Buick? I got a nice buy on a secondhand four-door Buick, but you had a new Toronado the same day. Just by coincidence, I guess."

Billy took the big crank out of the tool box and opened the cover of the gas cap and fitted the socket end of the crank over the hex stud inside. Henry spat on his hands and seized the two-foot-long handle and began cranking industriously.

"I don't care if it takes two hours to wind up the spring," he panted. "It's damn well worth it." ◆

ACTIVITY 8

LIONS AND BEETLES

1. The author of this short story has presented two very different characters: Henry Brogan and Simon Pismire. Write a paragraph in which you compare their physical characteristics and their personalities.
2. What caused Henry to drive his "definitely not compact luxury car"?
3. Write a paragraph describing situations in which people use a possession other than a car to assert their importance and individuality.

THOSE WHO DARE TO BE DIFFERENT

Not everyone uses classy cars to impress others. There are exceptions. Some people behave in unexpected ways to make a different statement about their values and attitudes. Cars can also be a means of making a statement about one's individuality or even eccentricity.

THE HAPPY COUPLE

1. Look carefully at the photograph in Figure 5-9 on page 103 and list in your notebook everything that you can see. In what way is this scene different from that of a typical wedding?
2. A vehicle is a symbol of people's values and attitudes. What does this truck symbolize about its owners?

Figure 5-9
The wedding day

3. From this wedding scene, what guesses can you make about the life style, hopes, and aspirations of these people?

ACTIVITY 10 ONE-OF-A-KIND DESIGN

Figure 5-10 This car was customized by a high school student.

1. A high-school student customized the car in Figure 5-10. How has she altered the original? Why do you think she altered the original design in this way?

2. An auto body shop has donated a car to your school for a charity raffle. The shop has agreed to customize this car to meet your tastes. The task for your class is to design the changes to make this car appeal to young drivers in order to sell many tickets for the charity.

   a) As a class, brainstorm to generate ideas about how to customize this car.
   b) Then make a final choice of the features that you would like to see this car have.

3. In small groups, design posters that depict this car to help publicize the raffle. Hint: You can make larger sketches by using an opaque projector to project the car image on a screen.

4. As a class, analyze the posters that have been produced. Why are some more successful than others?

info-box

GUIDELINES FOR POSTERS

An effective poster must get attention. It must be direct and easily read. These suggestions will help you with your design.

1. ***Information:*** Determine the most important part of your poster and emphasize it. For example, if the car illustration is the attention-getter, make it as large as possible on your poster.
2. ***Simplicity:*** Make your information brief, direct, and clear. Readers will give only a few seconds of their time, so simplicty is important.
3. ***Lettering:*** Letters should be easy to read and carefully spaced.
4. ***Colour:*** Use colour combinations that will attract attention from a distance. For example, use colours that have a strong contrast in value (between light and dark).
5. ***Unity:*** Unity relates to a sense of oneness in design. Arrange your layout to move the viewer's eyes smoothly from one part of the design to another.

JUNK YARD

Because of the strong competition among car manufacturers and the high standard of living in North America, car designs undergo changes as often as clothing fashions. Slight, superficial changes to, for example, the shape and placement of lights stimulate sales. Promotion agencies focus attention on such features, making last year's models old fashioned or psychologically obsolete before the cars themselves are worn out. Yearly trade-ins provide the car industry with enormous profits – and neighbourhoods with used car lots.

In some countries individuals are not allowed to privately own cars. And in other countries where prospective car buyers must wait for years to buy a new car, old models are in constant demand. In such places, it would be most unlikely to find an old car abandoned along the roadside or piled up in a junk yard.

ACTIVITY 11

JUNK YARD RETIREMENT PLAN

Figure 5-11 At the end of their lives, cars often end up in junk yards.

1. What is your reaction to the photograph in Figure 5-11?
2. What social and environmental concerns does Figure 5-11 suggest to you?
3. Figure 5-11 shows one aspect of the problem of landscape pollution. Is there a better solution to this problem than junk yards? Discuss this as a class.

ACTIVITY 12

IN WORDS, NOT PICTURES

Figure 5-12 The Stegowagenvolkssaurus. Here is a novel way of disposing old car parts. The artist saw a similarity between cars and dinosaurs and used this idea to create this car.

1. Paleontologists, who study fossils, have learned a great deal about dinosaurs by reconstructing their skeletons.
    a) Imagine what one of these scientists might say if, at some time in the future, he or she uncovered the sculpture in Figure 5-12.
    b) Make a list of the sculpture's characteristics that you find most visually striking.
2. Write a short dialogue between two paleontologists in the year 2090. Your dialogue should help to convey a visual description of the sculpture for your audience and could show how these scientists arrive at the name Stegowagenvolkssaurus.
3. What kind of redesign can you think of for a Volkswagen Beetle?

CARS AND PEOPLE

The relationship between cars and people is interesting. Some relationships are warm ones that last for years. In such cases, cars get special care and attention; their owners treat them almost as if they were members of the family or family pets. Such cars share a place in the home, have pet names, are groomed for hours and, of course, are shown off to all the owner's friends.

In other cases, the owner's infatuation with the car quickly fades, and she or he exchanges it for a new one. Sometimes, in such instances, the old family car gets a last face lift and for one final time becomes a star – at a demolition derby.

Demolition derbies are common events in many communities. The main attraction is a competition in which opponents attempt to immobilize each other – as they do in TV wrestling. Unlike in wrestling, however, the losers in demolition derbies don't get up and walk away. Their dismantled bodies are towed away.

SMASH 'EM UP

1. Why do people enjoy demolition derbies?
2. In your notebook, write a journal entry about an experience that you might have at a demolition derby.
3. Look at Figure 5-13 on page 108. As a class, discuss the role that colour and customized accessories play in the competition.

Figure 5-13 Demolition derby: a contact sport for cars.

a)

b)

c)

END THOUGHTS

This unit has been about cars and the appearance of cars. You have thought about what you like in cars and you have considered what others like in cars. Some people like performance; others like the visual appeal of a car. And some like both.

The invention of the car has had a major impact on our way of life. Just think of all the jobs in your community that are related to cars: people sell cars, fix cars, sell gas, sell car accessories – and some people give out speeding tickets. Take away cars, and our whole way of life would change. How would people be able to express themselves? Do you think people in the 'good old days' chose horses to express themselves, just as car owners do today?

EXTENSION IDEAS

1. The Grand Prix and the Indianapolis 500 are two of the most famous races held in different parts of the world. Many people make or have made car racing their profession – people such as Gilles Villeneuve, Janet Guthrie, and Mario Andretti. Other people – for example, actors Paul Newman and Tom Cruise – race cars as a hobby. Find out more information about a car racer and prepare a

Figure 5-14 Janet Guthrie in her stripped-down car at a qualifying race

short report on his or her life. For instance, you might see the film *Heart Like a Wheel,* the story of Shirley Muldowney and her struggle to become a professional race driver, and write about her.

2. Car manufacturers know that people are greatly influenced by advertisements. Surveys and sales figures show that a well-designed advertising campaign can have dramatic effects on the number of cars sold.

   a) Select car advertisements from magazines or newspapers and analyze their promotion schemes. What values and attitudes do car manufacturers promote?
   b) Make a poster of your picture collection. Use print from the advertisements (or write your own 'ad copy') and visuals to communicate your information.

3. Cars are featured in many pop songs. Use visually descriptive language to write a song about a car that you would like to own.

4. Most public libraries have a good selection of car magazines such as *Motor Trends* and *Hot Rod*. Read several articles in these magazines about one topic. Summarize your information and tell it to your class. If you can, illustrate your report with drawings and clippings.

5. Future car designs will reflect new ideas in travel as well as future technological developments and economic conditions. Design a car for the twenty-first century that has accessories such as a computer that will help you find a parking spot on a crowded street. Make an illustration of this car and display it to your class. To get some ideas for this topic, you might want to look in old issues (for example, from the 1950s) of magazines such as *Popular Mechanics* to see what ideas of futuristic cars were like then.

6. Prepare a short talk for your class on buying a second-hand car. How should a high-school student go about this task? What should he or she look for? What should he or she watch out for? How do you finance a car? Books such as *Lemon Aid* or magazine articles may be helpful.

THE JOB DECISION

- ★ PEOPLE IN PART-TIME JOBS
- ★ KIM'S DILEMMA
- ★ DECISIONS, ALTERNATIVES, CONSEQUENCES
- ★ KIM'S DECISION
- ★ TAKING A STAND

INTRODUCTION

What are the advantages of working while going to school? What are the disadvantages? As you try to answer these questions, ask yourself "What is best for me?" This is one of the keys to decision making because each person is unique: what is best for your friends may not be best for you.

ACTIVITY 1 WORK, WORK, WORK

Figure 6-1 Do you sometimes feel this way about school?

Figure 6-2 Police officer Sandy Maxwell at work

1. In one sentence, describe what Figure 6-1 suggests about work.
2. What does Figure 6-2 tell you about jobs today as opposed to jobs twenty years ago? In your notebook, write a paragraph in which you compare jobs now with those in the past.
3. Young children at play often imitate adults at work. Children play at being doctors, nurses, teachers, fire fighters, mail carriers, and many other kinds of workers. Think back to your childhood and recall some of the occupations you played at when you were young.

Figure 6-3 To what extent are we prepared for work as adults by playing at work as children?

PEOPLE IN PART-TIME JOBS

People hold part-time jobs for many reasons. One reason is to earn money. Another is to gain experience in certain areas (for example, in working with people).

Almost everyone has held a part-time job of some sort while growing up. For example, you may have had duties or jobs to do at home: washing the dishes, taking out the garbage, shovelling the walk, mowing the lawn, and baby-sitting your younger brother or sister. If you've done any of these tasks, you've had experience working.

PART-TIME JOBS

Think of all the part-time jobs you have had during the past five years – whether or not you were paid for them.

1. List these jobs in your notebook.
2. Answer these questions about your part-time jobs:

   a) Which one did you enjoy the most? Why?
   b) Which one did you enjoy the least? Why?
   c) What skills have you learned from your part-time jobs? Don't forget to note skills such as learning how to deal with people, handling money, acting responsibly, and working independently.

3. Appoint a recorder to make a list on the chalkboard of all the skills the class as a whole has developed from part-time work.
4. Have someone conduct a survey of the part-time jobs held by members of your class. This survey should include the following information:

   - the kinds of paying jobs held by students
   - any unique part-time jobs students have held
   - the number of part-time jobs that are summer-vacation jobs
   - the number of part-time jobs that are year round
   - the number of people in the class who presently hold part-time jobs
   - the number of people in the class who are presently looking for a part-time job.

ACTIVITY 3

PART-TIME JOBS AND VOLUNTEER WORK

Figure 6-4 What kind of part-time work interests you?

(Figure 6-4 continued)

Each picture in Figure 6-4 shows a person in a part-time job.

1. Look at each picture and in your notebook list the part-time work it represents.
2. After you have completed this list, place an *S* beside those jobs that are seasonal and a *Y* beside those jobs that are year round.
3. Place an *M* (for money!) beside those jobs listed in question 1 that you feel are paid jobs and a *V* beside those you feel represent volunteer or community service jobs.
4. What kinds of volunteer or community service jobs can you do in your community? In your notebook write a short statement to describe how doing volunteer work now could benefit you in the future.
5. After you have completed question 4, assign a class recorder to list on the chalkboard in separate columns the benefits of paid work and of volunteer work.

KIM'S DILEMMA

Kim has a social life and a clunker of a car. But going out with friends and maintaining a car takes money – money she doesn't have! In fact if it weren't for her father – a single parent – she would *really* be broke. But she feels guilty always asking her dad for a handout. He usually is willing to help out but he works hard for his money; and besides Kim there are her younger brother and sister to support.

These problems really bother Kim as she sits in English class trying to concentrate on a group discussion. Kim wants to solve these problems by getting a part-time job, but her dad doesn't want her to because he feels that a job will interfere with her school work. To make things worse, whenever they talk about it, they always seem to have an argument instead of a discussion.

After class Kim complains to her friend Sasha. Kim says she is tired of fighting with her dad.

"Instead of arguing, why don't you show him how getting a job would help both of you," Sasha says. "Let's figure out how much it costs you to live."

The following chart shows Kim's expenses for one week. While Sasha and Kim agree that this isn't necessarily a typical week for expenses, it will still show Kim's dad that they will both benefit by Kim getting a part-time job.

Figure 6-5 How much money do you need each week?

KIM'S WEEKLY EXPENSES

	MONDAY	TUESDAY	WEDNESDAY	THURSDAY	FRIDAY	SATURDAY	SUNDAY
FOOD	CHOCOLATE BAR $.65	FRIES $1.50			PIZZA $2.50	POPCORN $1.50 DRINK $1.50	
CLOTHING	T-SHIRT $17.00						
ENTERTAINMENT						MOVIE $10.00	
CAR EXPENSES *							GAS $10.00
DAILY TOTAL	$17.65	$1.50			$2.50	$13.00	$10.00
TOTAL							$44.65

* And this figure doesn't cover insurance, driver's license, and car repairs.

ACTIVITY 4

DAILY BUDGET

1. Estimate what you spend weekly. Then keep a record in your notebook of your expenses for one week. Be careful to keep track of your expenses every day; otherwise you might forget from day to day.
2. At the end of the week, compare your estimate with that of your actual expenses. If there is a big difference between the two, think about why this happened.
3. Choose a friend with whom you are willing to share your record and compare each other's expenses. What conclusions can you reach about your situation? Do you need a part-time job?

ARGUMENTS

1. In your notebook list all the reasons that you can think of to justify Kim's having a part-time job.
2. Appoint a recorder to make a class list on the chalkboard of reasons for part-time jobs.
3. Read the article, "Odd jobs help youngsters polish their financial skills."
   a) List the arguments presented in this article that support students taking a job.
   b) What is your opinion of these arguments?
4. What reasons can you add to the class list for question 2 to support the argument that Kim should have a part-time job?
5. In your notebook, write a journal entry in which you explore reasons for and against your taking a part-time job while going to school.

ODD JOBS HELP YOUNGSTERS POLISH THEIR FINANCIAL SKILLS

Tony Van Alphen

Your 11-year-old wants to take over the neighbourhood paper route, and your teenager has a chance to tend the cash register at the corner grocery store.

Should you let them?

Most financial experts answer with a resounding "Yes" – with the caveat that the job musn't get in the way of schoolwork or create a "junior workaholic."

Financial counsellor Chris Snyder, author of How to Teach Your Children About Money, says a job doubles the benefits of a regular allowance. It satisfies a child's emotional desire for independence and the practical need for money and, at the same time, teaches management of their earnings, he says.

"Snyder and other experts say a job also gives children habits, skills and experiences that no allowance can provide."

Snyder and other experts say a job also gives children habits, skills and experiences that no allowance can provide.

"It's a fabulous experience where you can learn a lot," says Tom Delaney, a Toronto-based personal financial consultant who watched his two children work part-time while going through high school.

Delaney's daughter, Nicola, says she learned discipline and how to handle people by doing part-time jobs that ranged from ringing up orders at a Dairy Queen to secretarial work.

"It taught me to be diplomatic but, at the same time, hold my own and that helps me now," says Nicola, a 23-year-old assistant to the vice-president of finance at a Canadian film company.

Chartered accountant Jeff Halpern, director of personal financial planning for Royal Trust, says work at a young age can be a big help later.

I hated every minute of the chartered accountant's program," recalls Halpern, who worked as a paper-boy, truck driver and tree planter in his youth. "If I hadn't done those jobs when I was young I wouldn't have been able to build up the resistance to get through the CA's program."

Halpern and Delaney say jobs help children mature and be →

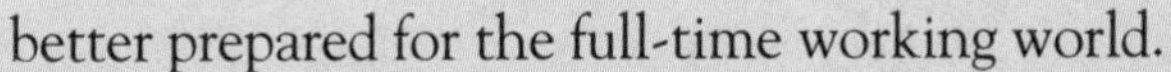

better prepared for the full-time working world.

Children who expect to keep their part-time jobs develop good work habits by necessity. Nicola found her part-time job during the school year meant juggling classes, studying, sleeping, eating and her family and social life while still getting to work on time.

"Children who expect to keep their part-time jobs develop good work habits by necessity."

"When this becomes difficult," says Snyder, "they'll have to decide between, say, more movies and more babysitting. One of the most important habits working children learn is responsibility."

The benefits of early work, like those of handling money at a young age, carry over into adulthood.

"You have a lot more confidence in yourself and you're more willing to try different things," says Halpern. "I also learned the value of a dollar and the art of negotiating for yourself."

He adds that contacts and friendships made in part-time jobs can be helpful when finding a permanent job.

While experts recommend jobs for children, they warn that it should be kept in perspective. Parents should prevent their children working until they're handling schoolwork adequately.

Figure 6-6 Computer skills are becoming increasingly important in today's job market.

"Remember that play is important," says Snyder, president of Toronto-based ECC Financial Planning Group. "You don't want to raise a junior workaholic."

In his book, Snyder cites a study from two social psychologists from the University of California who concluded that 10th-graders can handle up to 14 hours of work a week before their marks suffer and 11th-graders up to 20 hours.

The variety of work ranges among age groups, although they can overlap.

For example, for those under age 11 the job can be washing cars, bottle-collecting or a paper route; under 15, babysitting, mowing lawns or shovelling snow; 15 to 19, construction work, factory jobs, serving fast food or house painting.

There are also opportunities for older teens to get loans to start their own businesses.

Delaney and other experts say parents should try to advise

❝ ...contacts and friendships made in part-time jobs can be helpful when finding a permanent job. ❞

children on how to invest their extra income whether it's in a registered retirement savings plan, Canada Savings Bonds or stocks.

"My experience is that it usually falls on deaf ears in the early stage of their working careers," Delaney says. "One of the reasons they want to work is so they can make money and not have their parents tell them how to spend it."

However, he says, once children earn enough to file an income tax return – at least $4,000 a year – they begin to understand the need for putting money in different investments, like an RRSP.

"But it's not so much a method of saving," he concedes, "as trying to avoid tax." ◆

DECISIONS, ALTERNATIVES, CONSEQUENCES

In the readings and activities in this unit, you will notice that there is no right or wrong answer to the question of whether or not you should work part-time while in school. What it boils down to is this: you need to make your own decision. That decision, however, should be based on a careful consideration of the alternatives and a weighing of the consequences. This means, for example, that if you want to be successful in school but find, as a consequence of working part-time, that your school work suffers, then you might need to change your decision to work. The following poems show that one decision can make a difference.

THE ROAD NOT TAKEN

Robert Frost

Two roads diverged in a yellow wood,
And sorry I could not travel both
And be one traveller, long I stood
And looked down one as far as I could
To where it bent in the undergrowth;

Then took the other, as just as fair,
And having perhaps the better claim,
Because it was grassy and wanted wear;
Though as for that the passing there
Had worn them really about the same,

And both that morning equally lay
In leaves no step had trodden black.
Oh, I kept the first for another day!
Yet knowing how way leads on to way,
I doubted if I should ever come back.

I shall be telling this with a sigh
Somewhere ages and ages hence:
Two roads diverged in a wood, and I –
I took the one less travelled by,
And that has made all the difference.

OPPORTUNITY

Edward Rowland Sill

This I beheld, or dreamed it in a dream:
There spread a cloud of dust along a plain;
And underneath the cloud, or in it, raged
A furious battle, and men yelled, and swords

Shocked upon swords and shields. A prince's banner
Wavered, then staggered backward, hemmed by foes.
A craven hung along the battle's edge
And thought, "Had I a sword of keener steel –
That blue blade that the king's son bears – but this
Blunt thing –!" he snapt and flung it from his hand
And lowering crept away and left the field.

Then came the king's son, wounded, sore bestead,
And weaponless, and saw the broken sword,
Hilt-buried in the dry and trodden sand,
And ran and snatched it, and with battle-shout
Lifted afresh he hewed his enemy down,
And saved a great cause that heroic day.

ACTIVITY 6

POETRY ABOUT DECISIONS

1. Read "The Road Not Taken" (p. 121) and answer these questions in your notebook:

   a) What decision did the speaker have to make?
   b) If the roads appear so similar, why would choosing one now make such a difference many years later?
   c) You have probably made many choices in your life. Select one and describe in your notebook how that decision has made a difference in your life, either positively or negatively.

2. Read "Opportunity" (p. 122) and answer these questions in your notebook:

   a) A *craven* is a coward. What excuses does the craven give for not fighting?
   b) What was the reaction of the king's son?
   c) What is the theme of "Opportunity"? For example, the theme of "The Road Not Taken" could be seen as being that of making choices.

KIM'S DECISION

Kim's dilemma can only be solved by looking at the alternatives and consequences of the decision she is trying to make. Good decision making is based on examining the facts, exploring the alternatives, and then making a decision.

While Kim has what she feels are good reasons for having a job, she knows that her father will have many counter arguments.

COUNTER ARGUMENTS

1. In your notebook, list reasons for not having a part-time job. For example, one reason would be that it would take away from your 'free' time so that you couldn't play on school teams or join in other co-curricular activities. Then form groups of three and talk about the importance of each of the reasons listed.

2. Read the article "An Eye on the Future" and list in your notebook additional reasons to support the argument that people in school shouldn't have part-time jobs.

3. Compare the ideas expressed in "An Eye on the Future" with those expressed in "Odd jobs help youngsters polish their financial skills" (p.118). Which newspaper article do you think gives the best advice?

4. "An Eye on the Future" describes youth in the mid-1980s. Do you think the ideas and attitudes of youth have changed since then? If yes, describe this change.

AN EYE ON THE FUTURE

Jerald G. Bachman

The end of high school is a critical period in the lives of young people. They must make important decisions about education and employment, and they look forward to taking new roles in society, such as those of spouse or parent.

For more than a decade, Lloyd D. Johnston, Patrick M. O'Malley and I have been conducting nationwide surveys of high school seniors, asking about their life-styles and values. The seniors' answers reflect the impact of families, friends, schools and national culture during the years of childhood and adolescence. Our findings suggest that young people today are more tolerant than their counterparts of a decade ago in some respects, but not in others.

The seniors' views about women's rights and family roles have become more flexible. The vast majority of seniors expect to marry and have children, and their tolerance for nontraditional sex roles has increased steadily.

Both young men and women show a growing acceptance of working mothers and wives, although the men consistently express more traditional views than young women do. Most seniors agree that "having a job gives a wife more of a chance to develop herself as a person." Self-interest may play a role in this sentiment: Seniors might believe that both husband and wife will have to work to support their life-style. But there is one contrary note: Looking ahead to their own marriages, most young men and

> “Nearly half of the seniors report that their jobs interfere with their social life, but only one-quarter report much interference with schoolwork or with family life.”

women don't think a mother should work outside the home full-time while her children are young.

Young people's ideas about work are shaped by their own job experiences. Three-quarters of high school seniors hold part-time jobs, working an average of 16 to 20 hours per week and often earning more than $200 a month. Most seniors report that their jobs make little or no use of their skills and abilities, and many characterize their jobs as "the kind of work people do just for money."

Nearly half of the seniors report that their jobs interfere with their social life, but only one-quarter report much interference with schoolwork or with family life. Perhaps social time is the first to be sacrificed for a job, or perhaps its loss is felt most deeply.

Most of the seniors' earnings are not used to help with family expenses, nor are they set aside for college or any other future plans. Instead, young people spend their money on more immediate things: cars, clothing, stereos, TV's, records and other possessions and recreational activities. This "premature affluence" may be poor preparation for adult spending responsibilities. It is also the area in which teenagers see the greatest conflict between their attitudes and those of their parents.

We have also noticed some recent shifts in seniors' long-term job aspirations. Working for a large corporation is now more attractive than working in a small business, and working in a social-service organization has become less attractive than it was 10 years ago. Seniors stress the importance of opportunities for advancement, money and prestige.

Despite this attraction to corporate life, self-employment remains the most attractive option for seniors. They continue to prefer jobs that are interesting and use their skills, and jobs that give them the chance to participate in decision making. Having a job that is worthwhile to society doesn't get many top rankings, but overall it outranks job status or prestige.

One of our most disturbing findings is that long hours of part-time work are linked with weak school performance, low college aspirations and higher drug use. Many other studies have found this connection between long work hours and higher drug use, perhaps because students spend more time with older coworkers who abuse drugs. Although long work hours might contribute to increased drug use, drug problems themselves may create more motivation to work: Youths who use drugs need to earn more money to support their drug life-styles, and have less time for school.

In spite of this, teenagers today see their attitudes toward drugs as closer to their parents' views than teenagers did in the 1970s. Fewer teenagers today approve of the use of marijuana or other drugs. Cocaine is the one troubling exception: Teenagers report that cocaine use rose throughout the 1970s, and it has not declined in the 1980s.

Although they disagree with their parents about certain aspects of their lifestyles, most high school seniors feel their personal values are "very similar" or "mostly similar" to their parents' views. About half say they agree with their parents on political issues; the rest don't disagree – most of them just don't know.... ◆

"Despite this attraction to corporate life, self-employment remains the most attractive option for seniors."

TAKING A STAND

In this unit you have examined the issue of working part-time. To expand your thinking on this issue, divide your class into debating teams of four members each. Use one of the motions presented in Activity 8, or use one of your own motions. Have two members of your debating team support the motion and have the other two argue against it. Follow the rules for debating that are presented in the following Info-box.

DEBATING

1. Choose one of the following resolutions for debate – or develop one of your own.

- Be it resolved that our schools should have work experience as part of the curriculum.
- Be it resolved that students should be paid a salary for attending school.
- Be it resolved that there should be more emphasis on the three "R's" in schools since they are necessary for success in the world of work.
- Be it resolved that all students should take at least one skill-training subject such as industrial arts, typing, computer science, or home economics at each grade level in high school.
- Be it resolved that schools should be run like a business to prepare students for the world of work.
- Be it resolved that any place of employment be allowed to hire students after they have graduated from grade eight.
- Be it resolved that students be allowed to work no more than ten hours per week, including weekends, while attending school.

2. As a class, conduct a series of debates to explore the topic of the place of students in the work force.

info-box

DEBATES

A debate is a formal discussion for which the participants (usually four) have prepared a case for their points of view. It has rules designed so that each side has an equal opportunity to present its case and to answer its opponents.

1. A chairperson presents the subject of the debate in the form of a motion that the debaters want the audience to either accept or reject.
2. The first speaker for the motion introduces the subject and establishes a position on which she or he feels secure. This speaker then proceeds to assert her or his point of view and to prove it.
3. The first speaker against the motion attempts to disprove the arguments made by the first speaker. The first speaker against the motion then proceeds to make points of her or his own.
4. The speaker seconding the motion presents arguments against those made by the first speaker against the motion. The second speaker for the motion then presents her or his own arguments.
5. The second speaker against the motion then does the same thing – he or she disproves the arguments made by the previous speaker and presents his or her own arguments.
6. The motion is then thrown open to questions from the floor, giving the audience a chance to direct questions to any of the speakers.
7. After the open discussion, each side has a final chance for rebuttal. The speaker against the motion and the seconder speak first. The proposer and the seconder, since they opened the debate, have the last word.
8. The chairperson then puts the motion to a vote by the audience and announces that the motion has been carried or defeated by x number of votes.

This is the form of debate used in our national parliament when legislation is discussed.

DECISION-MAKING

Throughout this unit, you have been thinking about whether or not Kim should take a part-time job. Use the discussions from the other activities in this unit to consider what Kim's decision should be.

1. Write two or three paragraphs that summarize your discussions of the pros and cons of students working part-time.
2. Conclude your paragraphs with a statement about what you think Kim's decision should be.

END THOUGHTS

Using the arguments she developed in favour of working, Kim convinced her father that, for her, part-time work was a reasonable choice. Whether part-time work is reasonable for you, however, is a matter of personal choice. The decision is yours.

EXTENSION IDEAS

1. Visit an employer. Conduct an interview to find out what he or she expects from students who are hired on a part-time basis.
2. Talk with students who work. Ask them about the pros and cons of working. Find out what effect working has had on their school progress and on their out-of-school life. Don't talk to just one student – ask several for their opinions and take notes. Write a short report on what you find out.
3. Visit your Canada Employment and Immigration Centre (CEIC) to find out what jobs are available. Or have someone from the CEIC talk to your class. Make a list of jobs that you think might interest you and be prepared to ask the person from CEIC about them.
4. Make an appointment to discuss part-time work with your school counsellor. Or invite your counsellor to visit your class. Make certain that you have prepared some questions to ask him or her.
5. Visit the counselling resource centre in your school. What pamphlets and other materials does the centre have to help you make a decision about working and going to school? How helpful are these materials? Report your findings to your class.

UNIT 7

☆ ☆ ☆ ☆ ☆ ☆ ☆

THE OUTER SHELL

INTRODUCTION

When you first meet people you judge them according to factors such as where you meet, who you meet them with, and what they are doing at the time. But perhaps more than anything else, you base your first impression – either consciously or unconsciously – on the clothing they are wearing. Clothes are an important visual code. They reveal information about people's personalities, values, and attitudes. Clothes even project self-esteem. This unit will focus on clothes as a form of non-verbal communication.

Figure 7-1 Besides for appearance, what is another reason people who ride motorcycles wear leather?

BIRDS OF A FEATHER

Clothing protects people from the weather; but what they wear and when they wear it often has more to do with appearance than with usefulness. In the past, for example, cowhands on the dry western plains wore wide-brimmed hats and neckerchiefs as protection from the heat and dust. Now, many Calgarians – and tourists – dress in pointed-toed boots, neckerchiefs, and wide-brimmed hats to celebrate the spirit of the West during Stampede week. Country musicians, even some who have never been farther west than Nashville, Tennessee, wear western clothes. They do this to gain a sense of identity from the clothing they wear.

ACTIVITY 1

IDENTITIES

1. Use the clues provided by the clothing of the man in the photograph in Figure 7-1 to decide what he is like. Who is he? Where does he live? What interests him? What are his hobbies? What does he eat for breakfast?

2. Use one of the following questions as the basis for a class discussion on clothing and identity:

- Do people make premature assumptions based on their first impressions of others?
- Do items such as uniforms, sunglasses, evening gowns, and black leather jackets give a wearer qualities of personality that he or she might not otherwise have?

- Are there people in your community who wear specific items of clothing to express personal values or group identity?

3. Based on your discussion, write a paragraph on stereotyping and clothing. Use this pattern to guide your writing:

- Title: "The Outer Shell"
- Topic sentence: "Some people may stereotype others after looking at their clothing."
- Example 1: ______________________________
- Example 2: ______________________________
- Example 3: ______________________________
- Concluding sentence: ______________________

DRESSING UP

People have always found visual appearance important. Prehistoric people, for example, used animal skins both for warmth and for their magical powers. They believed that these skins gave them strength in the hunt. People from all cultures dress up in special clothing to celebrate or commemorate special events. There are special clothes for weddings and special clothes for funerals. And each culture has different clothes for these special occasions.

Figure 7-2 Hyacinthe Rigaud. *Louis XIV, King of France.*

Clothes also play an important role in suggesting status and power relationships. Look at the picture of King Louis XIV of France (1643-1715) in Figure 7-2 and note the richness of his clothing. He wore fancy laces, furs, and silks; ladies in King Louis's court wore huge wire crinolines, layers of petticoats, and yards of material. The rich nobility of Europe imitated the elaborate, opulent style of the court of King Louis XIV for several centuries.

King Louis and the nobility of Europe dressed with such opulence to reflect their status. Since the fabrics were delicate, hard to keep clean, and unsuitable for physical work, their clothes showed that they were wealthy and didn't have to work. Their choice of style in clothing clearly set them apart from the people of the working class who had to wear durable clothing.

Today, mass production and cheap transportation have made fashionable clothing accessible to many people in North America. Yet certain clothes continue to project affluence and distinction – especially clothes that are made of rare and exotic fabrics and are created by famous designers.

ACTIVITY 2

STATUS SYMBOLS

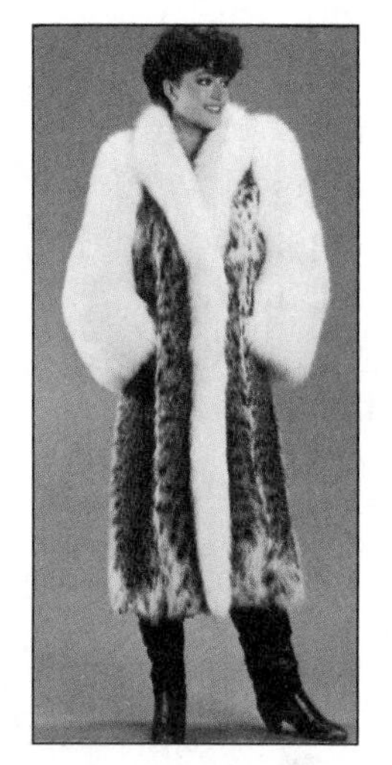

Figure 7-3 This coat is about more than warmth and comfort.

1. The model in Figure 7-3 is wearing a fur coat created by a famous designer. Use one of these questions as the basis for a class discussion on fur coats as status symbols:
   - What image would the owner of such a coat project?
   - What similarities in image are projected in the clothing of the model in Figure 7-3 and King Louis in Figure 7-2?
   - What similarities in image are projected in the clothing of the model in Figure 7-3 and the clothing prehistoric hunters might have worn?
2. Some clothes are prestigious because they are expensive. Others, such as team jackets, are prestigious because they are exclusive. What images are projected by the clothing worn by the students in your school? Are clothes an important factor in the way students treat each other?
3. Divide into small groups and plan an interview with students in an elementary or middle school. Find out how important clothing is for them. You will find sample interview questions in the Info-box on page 135.
4. Compile the results from the interviews conducted by the groups and prepare a class report on the attitude of elementary or middle year students toward clothing. Send a copy of your report to the principal of the school where you did your interviews.

info-box

SAMPLE INTERVIEW QUESTIONS

- Do you like some clothes better than others because of their labels? Give me an example.
- Who are your favourite TV or music personalities? Do you choose your clothes to be like them? Please give me an example.
- Do students in your classroom or school tease other students because of their clothes? What is an example of this teasing?

Figure 7-4 How does this cartoon depend upon the non-verbal messages of clothing?

(May 24, 1969)

INNER SECRETS

There are times when everyone has imagined how life could be different... if we could only change our image with a new hair style or a new body. But often we dream of clothes – how a new jacket, for example, would make us feel and how it would impress our friends. Eric, in the following story, has just this problem. He believes that new clothes will make a new reality.

FASHION

Robley Wilson, Jr.

Eric Worth had never owned a suit that really *fit* him, so one day, when he was stationed with the army in Wiesbaden, he went to a German tailor and had his measurements taken. He picked out a fabric from among several bolts of English wool, then for weeks he lay awake after all the barracks lights were out and imagined how he would look when the suit was finished. He would look exceptional.

"He picked out a fabric from among several bolts of English wool, then for weeks he lay awake after all the barracks lights were out and imagined how he would look when the suit was finished. He would look exceptional."

He pictured himself wearing the suit, feeling it move with him, knowing it would wear all his life because it was *his* – not an article made for some approximation of himself whose name was irrelevant and whose round shoulders were matters of indifference to the cutting machine. He saw himself on furlough, looking impeccable and British, strolling into the Hotel Vierjahreszeiten in Hamburg – a hotel where they did not welcome Americans because it was the Americans who had done the old bombing – smoking perhaps an oval cigarette or, even better, one of those Russian *papyrosi* that smelled like a trash fire, holding the cigarette like Franchot Tone in the early morning movies, between the thumb and the first two fingers with the palm up, the other hand slipped casually and lightly into the pocket of his suitjacket. He saw himself in the hotel dining room, at a small table near a window – one Martini, the lobster with a Riesling he

would let the steward choose, cognac and a leisurely smoke afterward. Not far away, a handsome, blonde, thirtyish woman admiring the well-dressed foreigner....

When the suit was finished and the tailor sent a message to the barracks: "Herr Worth, your suit is ready," he couldn't pay for it, couldn't scrape together the eighty dollars he had committed himself to. He was too embarrassed to face the tailor – the man lived in a tiny apartment above a jeweller's shop – to climb the narrow staircase and say to the German that he had broken his promise, that he could not pay. In the end he sent his buddy David Darby to the tailor. Darby was about the same size; the tailor altered the suit – *his* suit – and it fit David Darby as if he were a man with no name at all, as if the suit were machine-cut but altered as best could be to the shape of David Darby's approximate self. But Eric could never bring himself to imagine David Darby leaving the Vierjahreszeiten with the handsome blond woman on his arm.

"He saw himself on furlough, looking impeccable and British, strolling into the Hotel Vierjahreszeiten in Hamburg..."

As it turned out, the only clothes he brought in Europe were not new at all; they belonged to Corporal Nordstrom. When Nordstrom was killed in a motorcycle accident on the Autobahn, his clothes were auctioned off in the dayroom. Eric bought a gray suit for nine dollars, had it altered by the base tailor, and wore it frequently for many years. His wife never referred to it except as "Eric's dead man's suit." ◆

WISHFUL THINKING

1. Why did Eric want to buy a tailor-made suit?
2. In the end, Eric buys a gray suit. Why does the author make certain that you know that this suit is gray?
3. Here is a rewrite of the middle paragraph in this story:

   "When the suit was finished, the tailor sent a message to the barracks: 'Herr Worth, your suit is ready,' and Eric proudly wrote a cheque for the suit."

   Now rewrite the ending of this short, short story.

PRIM AND PROPER

The Victorian era, during the middle and late nineteenth century, was noted for its rigid standards of social behaviour. Both men and women were expected to adhere to a strict code of conduct. They wore clothing with modest styles to reflect this code. For example, women hid their body shapes with hoops and bustles. It was unthinkable for them to show their ankles from beneath their skirts. Elegantly dressed ladies occasionally fainted – not because they were delicate, but because their tight clothes made breathing difficult.

Many changes have taken place in Canadian lifestyles in recent years. We have relaxed our standards of proper conduct and our criteria for modesty.

ACTIVITY 4 A NEW CODE OF ETIQUETTE

Figure 7-5 Winslow Homer. *Long Branch, New Jersey.*
American, 1836-1910. Oil on Canvas. 16 x 21 3/4 in. Hayden Collection, Courtesy, Museum of Fine Arts, Boston.

1. Look at Figure 7-5. In your notebook, jot down details that describe this scene.
2. Then describe what a similar scene today would look like.
3. Using these notes, write a paragraph to contrast the nineteenth century scene with a similar scene today. You might use this model to write your paragraph:
   - topic sentence to explain what your paragraph is about
   - ideas about the Victorian scene
   - ideas about a modern scene, showing how these items are different from Victorian times
   - closing sentence to sum up your ideas and note the main way these two scenes are different.
4. One change that would shock Victorian society is the freedom in modern social behaviour. Analyze the clothes – their style, colour, and fabric – as well as the posture and facial expressions of the people in Figure 7-6. How has the code of etiquette changed since the Victorian era?

Figure 7-6 Where and when do you feel it would be appropriate to wear these clothes?

A NEW LIFESTYLE

Fashion is an important indicator of social change. We choose clothes to match our way of life and our thoughts about life. For example, schools today tend to be much less formal than they were two generations ago because our attitudes toward life are more relaxed. These attitudes carry over both into how we feel and into how we relate with others.

ACTIVITY 5

DAYS OF WASH AND WEAR

1. Look at Figure 7-7. In a short class discussion, consider how the following changes have affected today's clothing styles:
   - women working outside the home
   - mass production of ready-made clothing
   - the invention of synthetic fabrics
   - mass transportation
   - women's equal rights movement

Figure 7-7 Dress codes are more relaxed now than they were in the Victorian era.

2. Make a list of the ideas expressed in this discussion.Arrange these ideas into a logical sequence.and group them into possible paragraphs. Then, using your notes, write an article on this topic: "How and Why Fashion Changes."

THE PRICE OF BEING FASHIONABLE

Many people have accepted outrageous practices in order to follow fashion. Although history provides examples of both men and women enduring pain for the sake of appearance or fashion, women were often subjected to the most extreme practices.

In the late Victorian era, skin colour was a mark of status. Upper-class women wore large hats, carried parasols, and bathed in mixtures such as buttermilk and oatmeal to ensure that their skin would remain pale. They did not want to be mistaken for a member of the tanned or sunburned working class. In the 1800s, well-to-do women wore corsets made of whalebone and steel. This corset was laced up and tightened to give them the appearance of having a small waist. As a result of this practice, these women often had sore backs and their internal organs became deformed.

Until the beginning of the twentieth century, the daughters of Chinese nobility had their feet bound so that they would not grow. They wanted their feet to look small and dainty. Walking on these deformed feet was difficult or impossible, forcing the women to depend on servants. Their bound feet, then, were visual evidence of their upper-class status.

ACTIVITY 6

FASHION-CONSCIOUS SYNDROME

1. Use these questions to start a class discussion:

a) Why did people in past ages subject themselves to painful and harmful practices in the name of fashion?
b) What are some modern examples of such practices?

2. Divide into small groups to undertake a research study.

a) Select six different magazines from your school library or from a local magazine stand.
b) Count the number of ads or photographs of fashion models in which the central figures are young and healthy, middle aged, and older.
c) Count the number of articles and ads devoted to diets and to fitness exercises.
d) Pool information in your small group and make a graph to dis play your information.

3. Report the results of your study to your class.

TREND SETTERS

Although fashion has changed over the centuries, today mass communication has prompted rapid changes in fashion. Before the 1960s, adult fashion dictated what young people should wear. With the 1960s, folk music and Rock 'n' Roll established a distinctive youth culture. Elvis Presley, the Beatles, the Rolling Stones, and teenaged models such as Twiggy set clothing trends that were quite distinctive. The clothing of the long-haired men and the mini-skirted women was quite different from that of their parents.

In the '70s and '80s a cascade of fashion trends and hair styles have followed in the wake of Punk Rock and Heavy Metal music. Fashion magazines also have an impact upon fashion choice. Much of the content of these magazines is glossy, eye-catching ads sponsored by clothing manufacturers.

ACTIVITY 7

WHAT'S NEW

Figure 7-8 Clothing display in Amsterdam

1. Look through fashion magazines such as *Chatelaine* or *Seventeen* or a men's fashion magazine. Select an advertisement that catches your eye.
   a) Analyze why this ad is effective. Is it because of the striking appearance of the model(s), the new or chic styles of the clothes, or the exotic setting of the ad (for example, a Caribbean beach)?
   b) What is the hidden or indirect message that this ad communicates (for example, business success, good times, adventure, or popularity)?
2. Examine Figure 7-8 and analyze what these clothes would communicate about the person who wears them.
3. Write a journal entry in which you explore the value of fashion in your life.

BLUE JEANS

In the middle of the nineteenth century, Levi Strauss made canvas jeans with seams reinforced with copper rivets. Miners in the California gold fields wore his clothes. For many years, blue jeans were just work clothes. In the 1960s, young people adopted blue jeans as a form of protest against the social conventions of the older generation.

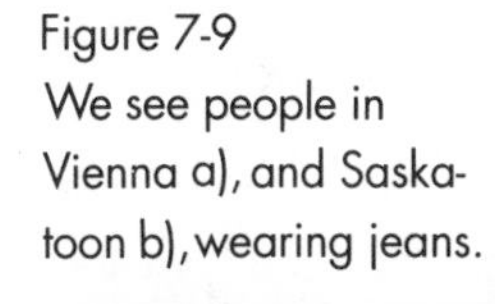

Figure 7-9
We see people in Vienna a), and Saskatoon b), wearing jeans.

Figure 7-9 a)

b)

Blue jeans proved to be comfortable and durable, and people began to wear them for utility, rather than as a protest. Today people of all ages and all social positions wear jeans. They are popular all over the world. Some manufacturers promote them as great social equalizers: you don't have to be rich to be well dressed.

ACTIVITY 8

JEANS ARE JEANS?

1. Do you think that jeans are a great social equalizer?
2. Think of the positive and negative aspects of jeans fashion today. Are all jeans the same in status? Can jeans be worn almost anywhere?
3. As an individual or class project, complete one of these topics:

   a) Design a collage, using blue jeans as the theme or centre of attention.
   b) Do a class project. Plan a 'jeans day' in your classroom or school. Encourage students to be creative in the way they dress up their jeans. Take photographs of your jeans and then if pos-sible arrange a display in one of your local jeans shops.
   c) List the names of the characters from a short story or a novel that you are studying. Decide what kind of jeans each of the main characters would wear. Then, using examples that you cut from old magazines, create a chart to show your choice for each character.

FREE ENTERPRISE IN ACTION

With modern technology, mass communication, and an intensely competitive fashion industry, the pace of change in the fashion industry is greatly increasing. Clothing – especially clothing for young people – has become an important market commodity. For many parents and students, fashion trends in schools have become an economic drain. The pressure to be in 'fashion' or to keep up with the latest fad is part of the everyday reality of our society. Many people, especially in times of economic hardship, must make sacrifices in terms of the clothes they wear.

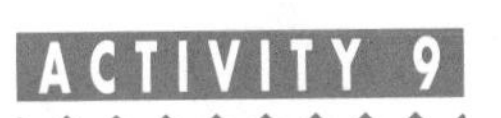

GRADUATION GIFT

1. Read the poem "Deke" on page 146. Compare Deke's graduation gift to those received by Bumper, Zip, and Magoo in terms of both financial and other costs.
2. Why was it so important to Deke's mother that he should have a suit for his graduation ceremony?
3. Deke's graduation suit was unfashionable. Was it appropriate for the occasion?
4. Is the question of clothes for graduation a problem in your school? If it is, what are some solutions to this problem?
5. Write a paragraph in which you explore your thoughts about this poem.

DEKE

Gary Hyland

For graduation
Bumper got a watch
Zip a record player
Magoo a typewriter

Deke living on his own
ousted by his father's fists
got a neighbour's suit
purchased by his mother
for three months worth of tips

The lapel was too fat
the pants too baggy
but he wore it without a word

He sat in the front row
on the wide stage
blushing in the dumpy suit
No record player, no watch
but all she could afford
and he would wear it anywhere

She sat near the side aisle
in her sister's beige dress
shadows and rouge concealing
the other price she paid

FREEDOM OF CHOICE

Dress codes are more flexible now than they have been in the past. Today each person has a greater freedom of choice in what she or he wears. Many people do not blindly follow fads and fashion, but instead attempt to customize their clothing to express their personalities and to suit their lifestyle.

ACTIVITY 10

COATS OF MANY COLOURS

1. Hold a class discussion on teenage clothing trends.

a) How important are fads and fashions to people in your class?
b) Are there opportunities for personal choice in fashion, or is there an unwritten dress code?

2. Look at the students about you and then prepare a short report to be published in your school newspaper or to be circulated in your class. Call your report "Fashion Trends in Our School." If possible take some photographs and interview some students to complement your written report.

Figure 7-10 Clothes express your sense of self.

END THOUGHTS

Some people feel that clothes are all show and no substance, something you should be able to see beyond. They argue that you shouldn't be a slave to fads and fashions because the impact of clothing is soon forgotten. But paying attention to appearance isn't always just a frivolous pastime. It's not so much what you lose by not caring about how you look; it's what you gain by feeling good about your appearance and yourself.

ACTIVITY 11

EXTENSION IDEAS

1. Many musicians and TV personalities choose their clothes to create a certain image. While some performers have special clothes designed for on-stage use only, others carry this 'dressing the role' over into their personal lives. Study the clothing worn by popular TV and music stars. Do the clothes create a specific image? Classify these performers according to the image that they project. There is an old saying: "Clothes maketh the man." (Of course this saying was always meant to apply to women too.) Does the information from your study support this old saying?

2. People often use clothes to symbolize their wealth or rank. Role play different types of people using different kinds of clothing and accessories – for example, hats, belts, shoes – to communicate status and power.

3. Although there are many different standards for modesty and good taste in clothing, people often make assumptions about others whose clothes are different from theirs. These assumptions, however, may be incorrect. Write a short skit to demonstrate how people prejudge others on the basis of their clothes.

4. Look at a film or video and identify the different ways that clothing is used to reinforce the personalities of the actors. Watch for examples of stereotyping.

5. Select two pieces of clothing that you own, one piece that you like and one that you don't like. Analyze why you like one more than the other. Is it because of the colour, the style, or because it projects an image of you that you like?

UNIT 8

★ ★ ★ ★ ★ ★ ★

TV CHANNELS

★ A PROGRAM SCHEDULE

★ NETWORK PROGRAMMING

★ PRIME-TIME PROGRAMMING

★ KEEPING YOUR INTEREST

★ PRIME-TIME CHARACTERS

★ PEOPLE ON TV

★ PLANNING NEXT SEASON

INTRODUCTION

You are a television consumer. You view television at a rate greater than your parents could ever have imagined thirty years ago. In fact, you probably know more about television than you do about any other form of communication – perhaps other than talk. This unit will help you explore your use of television by learning how it communicates ideas and information. Only when you understand what is really happening when you watch television, can you engage in creative viewing.

Figure 8-1 Creative viewing occurs when you understand what TV is all about.

A PROGRAM SCHEDULE

Each region in Canada gets a different mix of channels and programing, based upon location and population. Some regions receive only one or two channels, while others receive additional channels made especially for cable television. People who use a satellite dish can receive as many as a hundred channels. As well, some regions don't receive any American channels, while parts of northern Canada may receive only one Canadian channel.

Each channel usually shows the programs for a different network or television company. Most local stations are affiliated with a major network. Some examples of Canadian networks are the CBC, CTV, and Global TV. Some common American networks are ABC, NBC, CBS, and PBS. There may also be some independent stations in your area who choose not to affiliate with a major network.

To get a clearer idea of the TV schedule in your area, you need to know how to read the listings of programs in your newspaper or in a TV guide. As you read the listings for one evening, try the following self test.

ACTIVITY 1

TV LISTINGS SELF TEST

Choose TV listings for one evening in your viewing area and answer these questions:

1. Which channel(s) is received in your viewing area? Which network(s) is received in your viewing area?
2. Which programs are shown on more than one channel?
3. If you get more than one channel from the same network, do the stations always show the same programs at the same time?
4. How can you tell from the listings when a program ends?
5. Other than sports and movies, what are the longest programs shown in your area?
6. Name one program that is shown on two or more networks.

NETWORK PROGRAMMING

The television industry carefully constructs programs and chooses when they will be seen. Television networks make money by selling advertising. They must get you to watch their programs or they won't be able to attract advertisers who want their commercials to be seen by many people. Some people, in fact, suggest that the function of programs on TV is to collect an audience to look at the commercials.

For this reason, the kinds of programs on TV networks tend to be the same from year to year. In addition, networks tend to copy each other's successes by offering similar programming. This 'success copying' accounts for the fads in TV programming – westerns one season, police stories the next, and dramas about rich and beautiful people the next.

ACTIVITY 2 KINDS OF TV PROGRAMS

Figure 8-2 What type of program does each of these programs represent?

1. As a small group, look at the pictures in Figure 8-2. Brainstorm to produce a list of all the types of shows seen on TV. For example, your categories might include game shows, soap operas, and talk shows.
2. Find examples of each category in the program listings you used in Activity 1.
3. As a class, discuss your lists and agree on a final class list of TV programs.
4. Use your local weekly schedule of programs to create a chart of program types.
   a) As a class, choose a variety of stations (try to choose ones that carry different networks). Then assign a day of the week to each of the groups from question 1.
   b) Working with your group, make a chart of program types for the day of the week assigned to your group. Down the side of the page list the times by half hour from 7:00 a.m. to 11:00 p.m. Across the top of the page list the stations to be used Then complete the chart.

PRIME-TIME PROGRAMMING

TV programmers must attract large audiences in order to sell advertising. Programmers believe that *when* a program is seen is as important as *what* it is about. Prime time on television is the period from 8:00 p.m. to 11:00 p.m. each day – except Sunday when prime time begins at 7:00 p.m. During prime time, more people watch TV than at any other time of the day. Programmers try several techniques to get you to watch their channels and networks, especially in prime time.

Blocking: One technique is blocking. Block programing occurs when a series of similar programs are shown on one evening. The programmer hopes to keep an audience that has tuned in for a particular type of show watching through several programs.

Blunting: Another technique is blunting. To try to keep you from switching networks, the programmer will offer the same program (or a similar one) at the same time as the other networks. After all, to sell commercial time, programmers have to keep people watching their network.

Audience Appeal: A third technique is creating audience appeal. Programmers try to create shows that will appeal to the widest possible audience during prime time. Thus programs that appeal to special audiences such as children's programs, cooking shows, exercise programs, talk shows, or soap operas are not usually shown in prime time. Such programs are shown earlier in the day or later at night. As well, programmers realize that the later in the evening the program is shown, the older and more adult the audience will probably be. For this reason, news programs are shown after 10:00 p.m. or later. Game shows are shown earlier than documentaries and situation comedies are shown earlier than realistic crime stories.

ACTIVITY 3 TELEVISION PROGRAM PLANNING

Working with your group from Activities 1 and 2, examine the chart on prime-time TV that you completed for Activity 2. As you look for examples of programmers' planning, discuss the following questions with your group. Ask one person to act as chairperson to keep your group on topic and to encourage all members to participate. All group members should take notes on the discussion.

1. Discuss the following questions about programming techniques:

a) What type of show is most common on each channel during prime time?
b) How many shows of one type are shown on each of the channels in your chart?
c) Have the programmers tried to block programs on any of the channels?
d) Are the blocks similar on different networks?

2. Look for the same show turning up on different networks. Do these shows occur at the same or different times? Did any of the network programmers try to blunt the other channels during your prime time?

3. If you receive both American and Canadian channels, did the Canadian channels try to blunt the American programs?

4. Think about the audiences the programmers are trying to attract. Use examples as you answer these questions:

a) How do your channels plan for a more mature audience later in the evening?
b) What programs are designed to appeal to mature viewers?
c) What programs for specific groups are offered during prime time?
d) Are any of the shows aimed at people in different social classes or groups?

ACTIVITY 4

REPORTING TV FACTS

As a group, report to the class your findings for Activity 3. Use the following steps to prepare your group report.

1. Meet with your group and divide the questions in Activity 3 so that each member of the group takes part in the presentation.
2. Review your notes so that they include the following points:
   - the idea you are examining
   - a few sentences describing your program schedule
   - several examples that demonstrate the points you are making (be sure to use different channels in your examples)
   - a closing statement that sums up the major programming trends in your community
3. Transfer the ideas in your notes to a new sheet of paper. Use a very short point form. Do *not* use complete sentences. Refer to these notes when you give your presentation.
4. Think about how you can make your presentation effective. The class needs to receive your information in more than one way. Speaking will be one means, but your group must also find a way to present your information visually. A chart, a bar graph, a point form list, or a pie graph could all be used. With your group members discuss the best way to present your information. Read the following Info-box to help you think about this problem. Be sure to refer to your visual display when you present to your class.
5. With your group, practise presenting your information to each other. Group members should look for clear ideas, clear visuals, understandable examples, and logical order. Based on suggestions from the group, make changes to your presentation.
6. Present your information to the class when your teacher asks for your day of the program week.

info-box

VISUAL INFORMATION IN A PRESENTATION

In choosing a visual means of display, first decide what kind of information you want to highlight. Think about which visual form will help you highlight your information.

- Do you want to emphasize the similarities or the differences between shows? Or do you want to highlight the fact that one type of program occurs much more frequently than another type?
- Do you want to present many or few pieces of information?

REFLECTIONS AND ACTION

1. After listening to each group presentation, write a journal entry in which you suggest how you would change the types of TV programs being offered or how you might change the scheduling for the programs on any of the Canadian networks. Also comment on what you like about the programming practices of any network or station.

2. Write a letter to the manager of your local TV station suggesting ways to improve the station's prime-time programming. Make your letter positive and complimentary in tone. Use the following pattern:

   - state a clear position
   - state what is currently happening with programming
   - state why a change should occur
   - provide some examples
   - review your position

KEEPING YOUR INTEREST

Once you decide to watch a television program, the programmer must keep you interested so that you don't become bored and switch to another channel. One common technique is the jolt. A jolt is any sudden movement or change that maintains viewer interest. A jolt can be created through an incident of violence, or through laughter, movement by the actors or the camera, change in sound volume, or change in location. Programmers know that they must deliver enough jolts per minute (JPM) to keep the viewer interested. One jolt every three to four seconds is common.

Different kinds of programs offer different numbers of jolts. Compare an interview show and a prime-time detective show. The interview usually shows one speaker and then the other and so has few jolts. The detective show follows the detective as she or he encounters all kinds of locations, actions, and conversations. As a result, the detective show has many more jolts per minute than an interview.

Television advertising also makes use of the jolts principle. A sixty-second ad may contain as many as twenty different jolts. Some ads will try not to use many jolts while others try to use a great number, depending on the kind of product being offered and the image that the advertiser wants to project for the product.

JOLTS

1. Examine the images from TV programs in Figure 8-3 on page 158. Try to decide how each of the images demonstrates a jolt.
2. Share your answers with your group. Explain why you think each picture provides the type of jolt it does. Then list ways the TV program might create the next jolt *after* each of the images in Figure 8-3.
3. Meet with your class and compare the results of your observations.
   a) Is there a difference in the JPM for the types of programs you have examined? Why might such a difference occur?
   b) Do students find programs more interesting if they have a higher JPM rating?
   c)What kinds of products seem to have a high JPM rating in their TV advertising? What kinds of products have a low JPM rating?

Figure 8-3 Jolts are intended to maintain your interest.

4. In your notebook, write a one-paragraph summary about jolts. (Refer to the following Info-box.) Before you begin, review the material in this section, starting with Keeping Your Interest on page 157.

info-box

A SUMMARY

A summary is a short version of your information. Your summary expresses your main ideas in a logical order.

- Begin with an opening statement that introduces your main idea.
- Then add several important points to support and expand your main idea.
- Close with a concluding statement about your main idea.

PRIME-TIME CHARACTERS

The world you see on TV is very different from your own. Think for a minute about the roles that men and women play in real life and on TV. Do men and women equally play lead roles in action stories on TV? Do they equally play roles that support the main character? Do they play parenting roles to the same degree? Do the roles given to men and women on TV reflect the reality of society today?

Consider the jobs that the main characters of most prime-time programs hold. There are more police officers, lawyers, detectives, nurses, and doctors than, for example, secretaries or factory workers. As well, some programs never indicate what work the major character actually does. Whatever the occupation, the pay is never a problem and the character seems to have a lot of free time to talk or to have adventures.

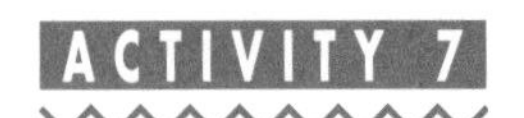

MEN, WOMEN, AND WORK ON TV

Work in your group from the other activities in this unit. Use the prime-time chart that you developed in Activity 2.

1. As a group make a chart showing the name, sex, and job of each of the major characters during prime time for the day of the week you used in Activity 2. Then list this same information for the second most important character on the program. Total your results for the sex and job of the major character and the second most important character.

2. Examine these totals and decide whether they are equally balanced in terms of the types of roles played by men and women. Is a balance important ? Why ?

a) If the types of roles played by women and men are not balanced, what changes would you make to some programs to achieve a more equal balance?
b) What programs would you drop from the schedule to get a better balance?

3. Look at the lists of jobs that the major characters hold.

a) Make another list in which you group similar jobs.
b) Note the number of times similar jobs appear in your schedule.
c) Talk about the impressions you might get about the world and work based on this list.

4. Write a one-paragraph summary of your group's findings. Use the instructions from the Info-box on page 159 to help you write your summary.

5. Using your summary as the basis, present your group's results to the class.

6. Use the class discussion and your notes to write a report in your notebook in which you compare the major roles played by women with those played by men on prime-time TV. Your report should record the important facts that the class discovered, state a position about the facts, and recommend any action that may be necessary by the TV programmers.

PEOPLE ON TV

As you have seen, the jobs and roles according to sex of characters during prime-time TV are often very unlike those of the people you know. The personalities and actions of TV characters may also be very unlike those of people you know. The actors on TV may seem to be people acting out real life, but if you watch them closely they look and behave differently from people in real life. People on TV tend to be much better looking than the majority of people in real life. Find pictures of various actors currently appearing in TV programs and compare these with the people around you! Heroes always seem to be strong, rugged, and handsome; heroines always seem to be beautiful, slim, and unusually well groomed.

Often you see very little of the personality of the major character. Because you see only a few personality traits, not many TV characters are very complex or difficult to understand. These individuals have few flaws in their character. At most, you will see one or two weaknesses that the character usually manages to overcome during the program.

TV characters often do what few people have ever done or will ever get to do. On TV people ride in helicopters, drive fancy cars, meet important people, and travel to exotic locations. Rarely do they spend much time washing dishes, doing laundry, taking a bath, or even watching TV.

Figure 8-4 What does this cartoon say about viewing habits?

TV CHARACTERS

Choose the major character from your favourite detective or suspense program as the basis for this activity.

1. On a separate piece of paper answer the following questions about the program:

a) What key words describe the physical traits of this character?
b) Try to name three people you know who look like this character.
c) Other than physical traits, what positive aspects of the character's personality are you shown?
d) What flaws or weaknesses are you aware of in the character's personality?
e) What unusual skills or abilities does this character have?
f) What three everyday activities does this character not do?
g) Is the financial situation of this character different from that of your family?
h) What situations that you have experienced yourself have you seen this major character in?

2. Write a letter to your teacher explaining how the information you gathered in question 1 supports or disproves the ideas put forward in People on TV on page 161. Be sure to point out several examples that support your position. Use the suggestions in the following Info-box to help you write your letter.

3. When you have written a draft of your letter, give it to a partner to examine. Have your partner use the Info-box on formal letter writing as a checklist for suggesting revisions for your letter.

info-box

LETTER WRITING

Content:

1. Begin with a clear statement of the position you are taking.
2. Give specific examples that prove your position.
3. Complete your letter by reviewing the position you have taken

Style:

1. If you are writing to someone you don't know, you will need to use a formal style. To make it more formal avoid slang and

incomplete sentences. Always try to use the most precise language you can.

2. If you are writing to someone you know, you will want to avoid being too formal. Don't use big words when a small word will do and don't write sentences that are long and complicated. Remember to use precise language: don't say the same thing three different ways.

March 22, 19–

Dear Student,

When your writing partner has finished suggesting revisions you should plan a second draft. Use the suggestions from your writing partner and write your second draft in the same friendly letter format that you see in this note.

The friendly letter uses equal margins on both sides of the page and tries to include roughly equal margins at the top and bottom. It is usually written on unlined paper.

Since it is a friendly letter written between people who know each other, the return address is not included. Just the date is required starting at the middle point of the top of the page.

The closing for the letter also starts at the middle point of the page – but at the bottom.

When you have written your second draft, give it to your partner for final editing and proofreading. Your partner should check carefully for problems in spelling, punctuation, and form. She or he may wish to use the proofreader's trick of starting at the end of the letter and reading backwards one sentence at a time.

You may need to make a final revision of your letter based on the proof reading. When you complete your letter, be sure to attach your notes from question 1 of this Activity to the letter for submission to your teacher.

Sincerely,

The Author

Figure 8-5 A friendly letter

PLANNING NEXT SEASON

Every fall the television networks introduce new shows that they hope will appeal to their viewers. In planning these shows, television programmers need to consider all of the facts that you have examined in this unit.

Before you begin to plan your own programs for the next season, consider what one critic says about the state of TV in the article "Programming for Profit." As you read the article, ask yourself if much has changed since this article was written in 1977 and if the references to American TV programs apply to those in Canada as well.

PROGRAMMING FOR PROFIT

Merrill Panitt

Television's success lies in its strength as an advertising medium. Its programs attract huge numbers of viewers who are sold to advertisers at $6 to $7 a thousand in prime time. The more viewers, the more money. It's that simple – and that complicated, because there is competition for viewers.

"The more viewers, the more money. It's that simple – and that complicated, because there is competition for viewers."

Most of the standard questions the audience has about the medium can be answered with the facts in that paragraph.

- "Why is there so much violence on television?" Because many programs that feature violence attract large audiences.
- "Why must they have so many commercials?" Because commercials mean money, and the networks and stations are in business to make money.
- "Can't they make money with fewer commercials?" Yes, but networks and stations are corporations. Stockholders want dividends to increase. The more money the corporation makes, the happier the stockholders are, and the more likely

the men who run the corporations are to keep their jobs and make more money themselves.

- "Why, if one network schedules a good special, do the other networks schedule good specials at the same time?" Because competition involves keeping the other fellow from getting a big audience, and sometimes it's just as effective to ruin your competitor's blockbuster as it is to schedule a blockbuster of your own.

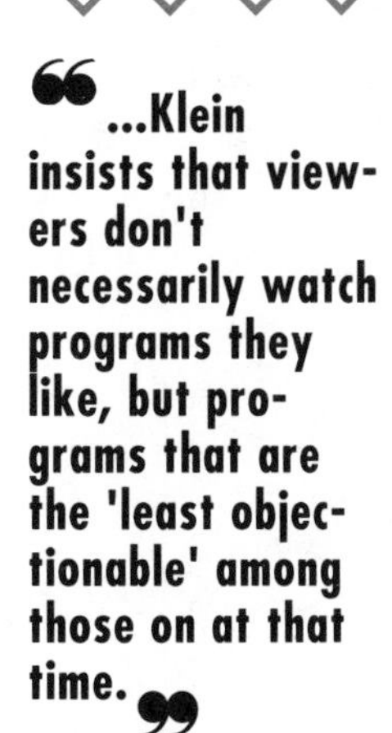

The networks have developed audience-building into a fine art. In the early days it was believed that creative people should have an important voice in setting a network's schedule. That was when men like Pat Weaver, who created *Today* and *Tonight* for NBC, were on that network; and Hubbell Robinson and Mike Dann – who depended upon writers and producers – were at CBS.

As competition increased, along with television's financial rewards, sales experts were brought into programming positions. They were thought to be knowledgeable about what the advertisers wanted, but before long it was not really necessary to suit advertisers.

Researchers came next because they were informed as to what viewers were watching, what performers they liked, the trends that lay ahead. One such researcher, Paul Klein, left NBC for a time, then returned late last year as chief of the network's special programming. His predictions as to which shows will succeed each year have won him a reputation as a television seer – and somewhat of a gadfly, for Klein insists that viewers don't necessarily watch programs they like, but programs that are the "least objectionable" among those on at that time.

Now the networks depend upon men who are experts in several areas, especially at gauging the audience and manipulating it. Today's most successful programmer is ABC's Freddie Silverman, whose uncanny ability to sense public tastes has raised ABC from the third network to the first, in ratings....

Part of his success is in knowing exactly where to schedule his programs (running *Roots* eight consecutive nights was a brilliant gamble), how to zero in on a competitor's weakness, how to bolster his own new or sagging programs by scheduling them between strong ones. Programming is a fine art and Silverman, once its most successful practitioner at CBS, is now repeating his success at ABC.

At the other networks his counterparts have the same motivation and are using the same techniques to try to catch up and pass him.... Still, all of them appear to be more concerned with audience manipulation than the showmanship that begins with outstanding entertainment, more involved with scheduling technique than creativity in programs. It is as if the programs themselves are only incidental to putting together the schedule that will attract most of the $6-$7-a-thousand audience, most of the time.

Complaints about violence or sex or too many commercials can hardly have an effect on men who can judge the popularity of violence and sex by the size of the audiences for *Starsky & Hutch*, *Hawaii Five-O* and *Charlie's Angels*. As for too many commercials, the people watch, don't they? And they must be buying the products or advertisers wouldn't be lining up to buy more time, would they?

One of the networks' most important profit centres is Saturday morning. Children watch television at all hours (a million of them under 11 years old watch after midnight – on week nights!), but on Saturday mornings the audience is concentrated.

[In the U.S.] a campaign by Action for Children's Television and jawboning from the FCC chairman persuaded the networks to reduce the amount of advertising during Saturday morning children's shows and prompted several attempts to try at least a few more substantial programs. But the substantial programs are up against cartoons, and there is no contest. CBS offers short segments of news for youngsters, and there are some movies and sugar-coated educational efforts, but Saturday morning still is nothing television can be proud of.

Daytime television consists of soap operas and game shows, both forms excellent for advertisers with products to sell to women, the shows and the commercials strong evidence that women's lib still has a long way to go.

Some idea of the power of the medium, and proof that others besides the networks are interested in money, is given by the fact that television has succeeded in changing the rules of football and baseball to make those sports more suited to television's commercial needs.

Football carefully measures three timeouts per half for each team. But television commercial timeouts may be called by the referees (promoted by a television technician) whenever the ball changes hands. Baseball play in a televised game does not resume after an inning is ended until the commercials are over.

Football games start at odd times Saturday and Sunday afternoons to make it possible for television to present double-headers. They're playing night games in the World Series now. Last October, because the network had football scheduled on Sunday afternoon, both players and stadium audience shivered in 20-degree cold in Cincinnati so that a World Series game could be played on a Sunday night: the only comfortable man in the stands was Bowie Kuhn, the baseball commissioner, who sat there with his coat off to show it really wasn't a bit chilly.

It is of some interest to note that last year commercial television paid about as much for the rights to televise football games as the [U.S.] government paid the Corporation For Public Broadcasting for the entire public-television system in [that] country.

Although the subject of [this] article is the state of commercial television, it is fair to mention that the audience for public television is growing, although it still is only a small fraction of that enjoyed by commercial television. The networks are rather ambivalent about public television, grateful for the fact that, by presenting serious programming, public TV takes some of the pressure off the networks, but rather displeased because a number of large corporations spend money to underwrite excellent public-television programs. The commercial networks would prefer to have that money flow their way.

It is prime-time commercial television that is most disappointing to those who are aware of the medium's power and who believe the medium could raise America's standards of entertainment. It is possible that innovative programming, perhaps even a regularly scheduled dramatic series in prime-time, might attract enough viewers to warrant the expense. We have all too few truly "special" programs, although the networks frequently prove that they can present quality programming well. But innovation is risky in series television.

The ratings show that Americans are watching television possibly more than ever before. This does not mean they are satisfied with what they are offered. It may even mean, as NBC's research expert Paul Klein suggests, that they are watching the "least objectionable" programs. Under the present network philosophy, the level of programs cannot change unless tens of millions of Americans simply turn off their sets.

"Paddy Chayefsky, who wrote the biting motion-picture satire of television, 'Network,' pessimistically described television as 'democracy at its ugliest.'"

Paddy Chayefsky, who wrote the biting motion-picture satire of television, "Network," pessimistically described television as "democracy at its ugliest." Television cannot be dismissed that easily or that cynically, for it is much too important to our society and our culture. And, besides offering an inordinate amount of mediocre entertainment, it does cover news events and sports well, it does give us entertaining hours of series shows, it does offer good as well as bad movies and occasionally presents a remarkable movie made especially for television. If, as seems to have happened, the medium has lost its excitement, it may be time for the networks to set aside a few prime-time hours a week to reach those who are becoming bored with routine television.

Red Skelton used to thank his audience each week for "permitting me to come into your home." The popular comedian, and many others in those adolescent days of the medium, considered television to be a guest in the nation's living rooms.

We put up with the clutter and the inanity of much of television because it serves our needs and the rewards are worth the discomfort they entail. ◆

TV FOR PROFIT

When you have finished reading the article, answer these questions in your notebook:

1. According to the first paragraph of the article, what is the purpose of TV?
2. What effects does the emphasis on profit have on what you see on TV?
3. What does the author think that TV does well?
4. According to the author, why do you continue to watch TV?
5. Based on the TV programs you watch, how accurate are the author's arguments? Does the age of the article account for any disagreement between you and the author and for the often sexist language in the article? Be sure to provide specific examples to support your points.

A NEW SHOW FOR NEXT SEASON

1. Look at the prime-time schedule examined by your group in Activities 2 and 3 and find a show that you think should be replaced.
2. Decide what category of program must go in this time slot to replace the existing show. Be sure to consider the need to block and blunt.
3. Write a one-paragraph summary explaining your argument for replacing the show. Refer to the Info-box on page 159 for a review of how to organize a summary.
4. Submit your summary to the chief programmer (your teacher) for comment and approval.

ACTIVITY 11 THE NEW PROGRAM

The chief programmer for your network agrees with your summary and your solution for a new program. You are therefore asked to create a program that is more realistic than many TV programs and that contains characters who have the same jobs and do the same activities as its audience. The chief programmer reminds you that the major roles played by men must be equal to those played by women during the entire evening of viewing.

1. Working alone, decide whether your prime-time evening has an equal number of major men and women characters. Also decide if their jobs reflect the real world of work.
2. In your notebook, briefly outline your new show using a chart form on which you indicate the following information:
   - the major characters
   - their jobs or roles
   - the location or setting
   - the lifestyle of the major characters
   - a brief outline of a typical situation in the series
   - any special features of the program that will give it audience appeal
3. Write a friendly letter to another programmer (a member of your group) to explain why you think your program will be a success. Use the model for a friendly letter on page 163 and the revision strategies suggested earlier in this unit.
4. Present your outline for a new show and your letter to your group. Ask the group for advice on how to improve both your outline and your letter.

ACTIVITY 12

SELLING YOUR IDEA

In order to get the chief programmer to buy your program idea, you will need to sell your program. In addition to your letter and outline, submit a dramatization of a five-minute segment of your program. This dramatization could take the form of a video clip, an audio clip, or a live presentation. To develop your dramatization, follow these steps:

1. Write the dialogue for your presentation. Try to include a section from the script that will emphasize the special features of your program. Then write an introduction for the dialogue so that the viewer will know what has gone on before.
2. Insert camera and setting information that will help to stage your scene. For example, indicate when the camera does:
   - a 'closeup' (screen filled with one thing, often a face)
   - a 'pan' (camera turns to show a wide area)
   - a 'medium shot' (usual distance for the camera from the subject)
   - a 'fade' (shot gradually gets fuzzy and disappears)
   - a 'cut to' (image changes instantly to a different picture)
3. Reproduce copies of your dialogue for all the actors in your dramatization.
4. Take turns role playing the scenes produced by the members of your group.
5. Rehearse your scene with the group.
6. Using the members of your group as actors, record and present your scene to the whole class – or act it out live.

END THOUGHTS

This unit has helped you to look at the way TV programs are planned and how they are organized into the prime-time week. You have learned about the way programs are presented on different networks and some of the techniques used to keep you watching. You have looked at a TV guide and thought about what it tells you. And you have looked into some TV programs and considered whether or not the view they present of people and reality is in fact true. From now on, your knowledge of how TV programs work should help you be more aware of and have more control over your TV viewing.

ACTIVITY 13

EXTENSION IDEAS

1. In your notebook, write a response to the ideas in this unit. If you need some help getting started, try responding to the following questions. Each question should form the basis of a paragraph. Be sure to explain why you feel the way you do, giving examples wherever possible.

   a) What new information did you learn in this unit?
   b) What information did you already know about TV programming?
   c) What was the most interesting information that you gained from this unit?
   d) What changes do you want to see in TV programming on any of the Canadian networks?

2. Prepare a bulletin-board display on jolts. Be sure to include a graph or chart comparing the jolts per minute in different kinds of TV programs.

3. Visit a local television station. Interview the station manager about the methods used to select programs at his or her station. Tape the interview and play it for the class. Before you go to the interview, plan and write out the key questions you need to ask.

4. Examine the schedule for Saturday morning television from 7:00 a.m. to noon on all available Canadian networks. Look for the programmers' techniques of blunting and blocking. Compare the use of jolts in three Saturday morning programs with those used on three prime-time programs. Summarize your results and write a report.

5. Write the dialogue that might occur in your house if the main characters from two different TV programs were to join your family for dinner. Ask members of the class to help with a reading of this scene.

6. Write a sixty-second television ad. Think carefully about how to create the appropriate number of jolts. If you can, videotape your ad and present it to the class. Explain the basis on which you made your decision about the number of jolts included in this ad.

7. Write to one of the Canadian television networks, asking for information about how programming decisions are made – and by whom. Think of several questions you could ask the chief programmer in your letter.

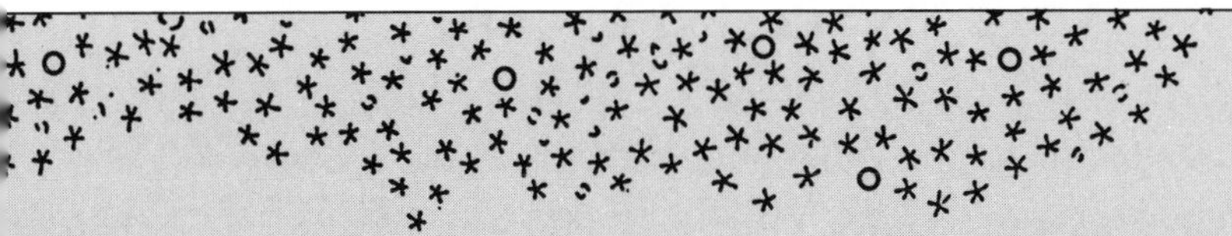

UNIT 9

★ ★ ★ ★ ★ ★ ★

AD APPEAL

INTRODUCTION

When you read a magazine, how much attention do you pay to the ads? Which ones do you look at? Which ones do you read? Why?

In this unit you will look closely at the images, the content, the language, and the appeal of magazine advertisements. Then you will use this information to prepare your own ad. When you are finished, you will be more aware of how ads are created and of how they are used to sell products.

MAGAZINES AND READERS

Magazines are aimed at a specific market; that is, each magazine is designed and written to appeal to a certain group of people. A company that places an ad in a magazine tries to make sure that the people who read this magazine are also the kind of people who will buy the company's product. As a result, you can tell a great deal about who reads a magazine from the ads that appear in it.

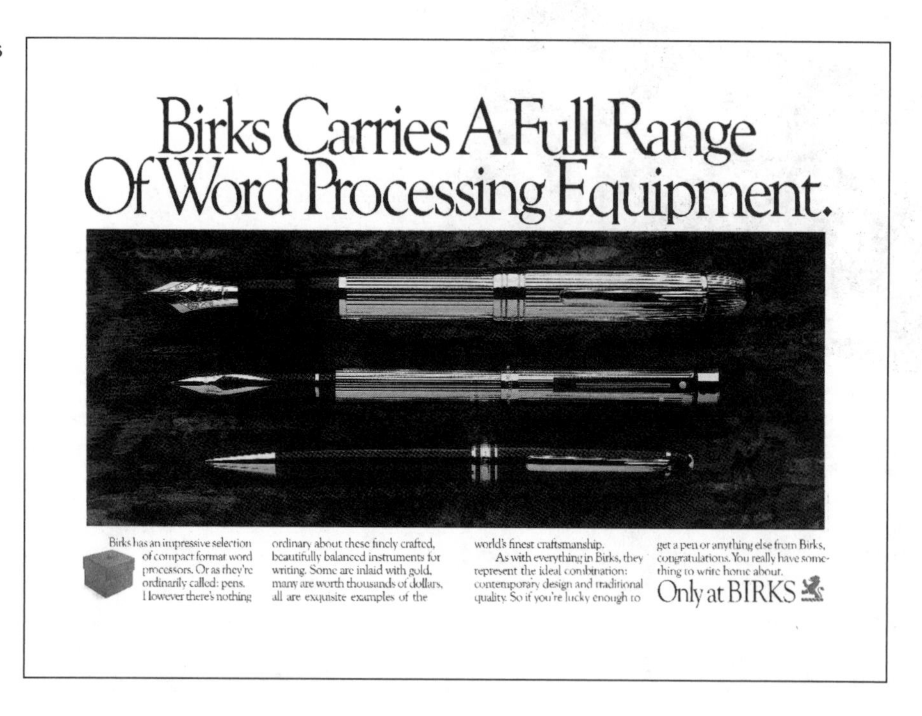

Figure 9-1 What clues can you find in this ad that suggest the kind of audience for which it is intended?

ACTIVITY 1 FIRST GLANCE

Figure 9-2 Are any stereotypes being encouraged in this ad?

Figure 9-3 Notice how colour is used in certain places in this ad.

1. Figure 9-2 and Figure 9-3 show two very different ads for two very different products. What can you tell from each ad about the audience for which they were prepared? Is the audience meant to be male or female? How old? How much money do they have to spend? What do they enjoy doing? What is important to them?

2. Look at a variety of magazines that you or your teacher has brought into the classroom. Pick one that you find interesting and examine it. Use the following tasks to guide your examination:

   a) Count the total number of pages in the magazine.
   b) Count the total number of pages containing ads.
   c) Calculate the percentage of pages containing ads. Refer to the formula in the following Info-box (p. 176) to calculate percentages.
   d) Make a list of the kinds of products that are advertised in the magazine (for example, food, clothing, cars, beverages, make-up, personal hygiene, and electronics).
   e) Count the number of ads for each kind of product that you see listed.

f) Pick an ad that catches your attention and in your notebook explain what interested you about this ad.
g) Look at what else in the magazine is located near the ad that you selected. What, if any, is the relationship between them?

3. When you have completed your survey, choose a partner who has looked at a magazine that is quite different from yours. Compare your findings in a chart using the following headings:

- number of pages in the magazines
- number of pages containing ads
- kinds of ads
- most common kind of ad
- kinds of readers of the magazine
- your favourite ads

4. After you have completed your comparison, discuss your findings with your partner. Use the following questions to focus your discussion:

a) What did you like or dislike about the ads?
b) What makes an ad effective?
c) How much do you think you are influenced by ads? Why?
d) How do ads affect what you buy?

5. Next write a brief journal entry expressing your thoughts about magazines and ads.

info-box

CALCULATING AD PERCENTAGES

Use this formula to calculate the percentage of pages containing advertisements:

$$\frac{\text{number of pages containing ads}}{\text{total number of pages}} \times 100 = \_\_\_\_\_ \%$$

IMAGES THAT SELL

Since most people leaf quickly through magazines, an advertiser has only a few seconds to catch your attention. You may not stop to look closely at an ad, but just your having seen it is enough for the advertiser. Most ads are designed to make an impact that you can absorb at a glance. Therefore, the visual appeal of an ad is very important. There are a number of visual elements that make up an ad. These elements are displayed in the following Info-box.

info-box

VISUAL ELEMENTS OF AN ADVERTISEMENT

- ***General Mood:*** the overall feeling that is conveyed by the ad (for example, a picture may convey a feeling of joy, nostalgia, fun, or satisfaction)
- ***Typeface:*** the size, shape, and style of the print used in the ad
- ***Logo:*** the sign, symbol, or lettering that stands for the company or the product
- ***Colour Scheme:*** the colours used in the ad and how they relate to each other
- ***Light:*** the brightness of the ad, the contrast between light and dark, and the relationship between them
- ***Shapes:*** the shape of the product, the shapes of the other components in the ad, the relationship between them, and what thoughts and feelings are conveyed by the shapes
- ***Overall Composition:*** the relationship of the above elements to each other and the ways in which they are arranged in the ad (for example, in an ad for motorcycles, the advertiser might convey meaning by using a bold typeface,bright colours, and sharply contrasting images)

ACTIVITY 2 WHAT DO YOU SEE?

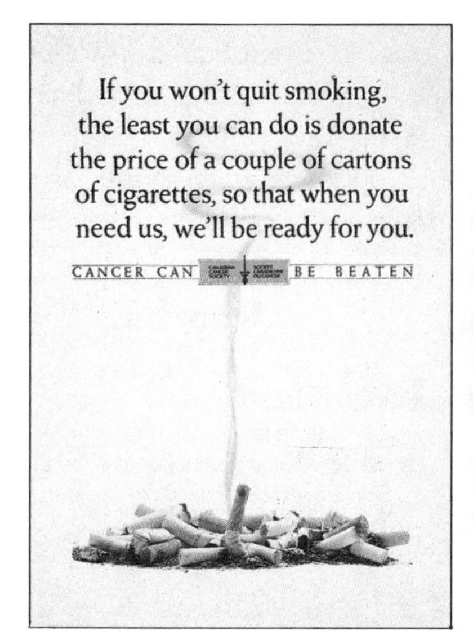

Figure 9-4 A Cancer Society ad

Figure 9-5 An ad for tourism

1. In chart form, compare the visual elements of the two ads. Use the following headings:

- general mood
- logo
- light
- overall composition
- typeface
- colour scheme
- shapes

2. When you have completed your chart, compare your findings with those of someone else in the class. Use the following questions to help focus your discussion:

a) Were your observations similar or different? In what ways?
b) How do you account for the differences?
c) Which ad did you each find more effective? Tell each other why you picked the one you did.
d) What would you have done differently if you had designed the ad?

3. In your notebook explain what you think makes an ad visually effective. Illustrate what you mean by including some examples from magazines or, even better, draw some yourself.

STORIES THAT SELL

If an advertiser has managed to get your attention visually, chances are good that you will look more closely at the content of the ad. Many ads have components that are similar to those of stories. These components are listed in the following Info-box.

info-box

STORY COMPONENTS IN ADVERTISEMENTS

- ***Characters:*** the people in the ad and the personalities they seem to have
- ***Plot:*** the event that is shown in the ad itself and the events that you imagine have occurred before, or will occur after, that moment
- ***Setting:*** where and when the scene shown in the ad takes place
- ***Symbols:*** an object that stands for something more than itself (spring flowers, for example, might be used to associate a soap product with youth)
- ***Sub-text:*** a meaning that goes beyond the surface meaning suggested in the ad (an ad for children's toys might, for example, contain a message about violence)

STORY ELEMENTS IN AN AD

1. Look carefully at the ad in Figure 9-6 and then answer the following questions:

a) What is happening in the ad?
b) What do you think happened immediately before the situation shown in the ad?
c) What do you think will happen next?
d) Who are the people in the ad? What can you tell about them from the way they are dressed, the expressions on their faces, and their body language?
e) What do you think the characters are saying to each other?
f) Where and when is this scene taking place?
g) What feeling or mood do you get from the ad? Why?
h) What are some of the main objects in the ad? What do they represent?
i) What is going on 'below the surface' of this ad?

2. Use the notes you made in response to the preceding questions and write a story based on this ad.

Figure 9-6 What story components does this ad use?

NEEDS THAT SELL

Another way that advertisers convince us to buy their products is by appealing to basic human needs. Consider the list of needs in the following Info-box.

info-box

NEEDS APPEALED TO BY ADVERTISERS

NEED:	*EXAMPLE:*
• to be physically healthy	"Take Vita-Plus for a well-balanced diet."
• to be physically attractive	"Are blemishes interfering with your social life? Be confident with Dermaclear."
• to be free from fear and anxieties	"Never be lonely again. Call Dial-a-Date today."
• to feel good about ourselves	"Buy Romance Perfume. You deserve it."
• to belong to a group	"Meet the gang at Mario's Restaurant – the place where friends gather."
• to have status	"Arrow – the car that says you have made it."
• to be informed	"The facts are clear – Whiteout cleans 50% better than the most popular detergent."
• to identify with people we admire	"Sue Supersport uses it, so why not you?"

ACTIVITY 4 WHAT FITS YOUR NEED?

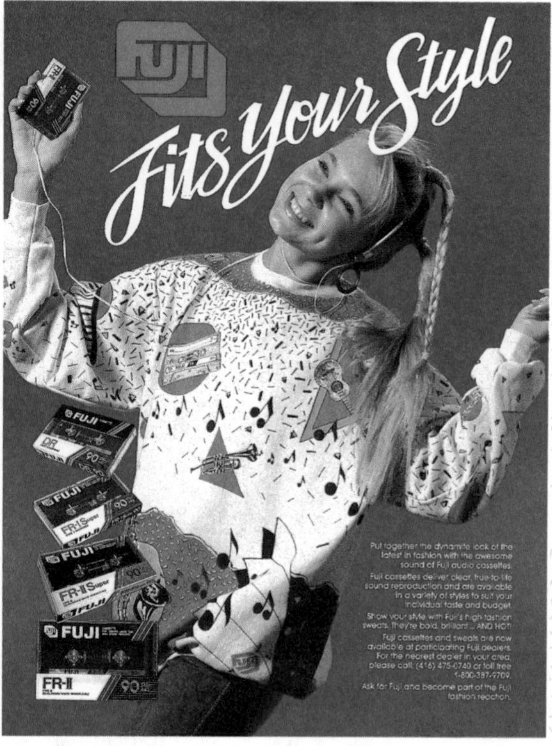

Figure 9-7 What do you think of the language in this ad?

Figure 9-8 What needs does this ad "fit"?

1. Look carefully at the ads in Figure 9-7 and Figure 9-8.
2. Consider Figures 9-7 and 9-8 using these questions to guide your thinking:
   a) For what audience were these ads prepared?
   b) What needs do they appeal to? Do you think the ads are effective? Why or why not?
   c) To what other needs might the advertiser of these products have appealed? Give some examples.
   d) What images of women and men do these ads present?
3. In a group of three or four people, compare answers to question 2. How were your responses to the ads similar? How were they different? How do you explain the differences?

WORDS THAT SELL

The words used in an ad are very carefully selected. They have to convey just the right message with just the right associations. The meanings that are associated with words are called connotations. The word *work*, for example, has both literal and connotative meanings. The literal meaning of *work* is a task or job, something that is usually done for money. The connotative meaning of the word depends on your feeling about work.

ACTIVITY 5

POWER LANGUAGE

Figure 9-9 Guess what the missing words are.

In the ad in Figure 9-9 several key words have been deleted. Look at the product being advertised and the image that the manufacturer is trying to convey. Then guess what the missing words are.

1. Write down the words that you think appeared in the original ad. What part of speech are they? What are the connotations of the words that you have chosen?

2. Compare your words with those of someone else in the class. What are the differences in the messages and feelings conveyed by the two sets of words?
3. Turn now to the last paragraph of End Thoughts on page 189 and look at the words that originally appeared in the ad. What are the connotations of these words?
4. Who do you think the advertiser was appealing to by using these particular words? Which selection of words do you find more effective – yours or those in the original ad? Why?

Figure 9-10 What are the connotations of the words chosen for this ad? What is your response to this choice of words?

A NOVEL APPROACH

The following excerpt is from Margaret Atwood's novel *The Edible Woman*. This novel tells the story of Marian McAlpine, a young woman whose consumer-oriented world falls apart as she begins to identify with what she consumes. The following excerpt occurs early in the novel, when Marian conducts interviews about people's reactions to ads. One of the people she interviews has a rather unusual reaction to the beer commercial that Marian is using in her survey.

HEALTHY HEARTY TASTE

Margaret Atwood

When we got to the telephone commercial he went to the phone in the kitchen to dial the number. He stayed out there for what seemed to me a long time. I went to check, and found him listening with the receiver pressed to his ear and his mouth twisted in something that was almost a smile.

"You're only supposed to listen once," I said reproachfully.

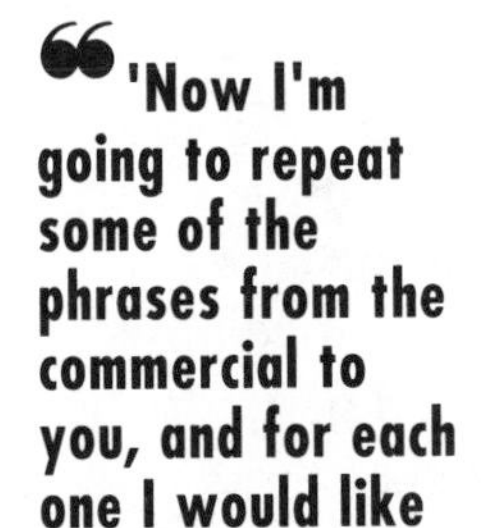

He put down the receiver with reluctance. "Can I phone it after you go and listen some more?" he asked in the diffident but wheedling voice of a small child begging an extra cookie.

"Yes," I said, "but not next week, okay?" I didn't want him blocking the line for the interviewers.

We went back to the bedroom and resumed our respective postures. "Now I'm going to repeat some of the phrases from the commercial to you, and for each one I would like you to tell me what it makes you think of," I said. This was the free-association part of the questionnaire, meant to test immediate responses to certain key phrases. "First, what about 'Deep-down manly flavour?'"

He threw his head back and closed his eyes. "Sweat," he said, considering. "Canvas gym shoes. Underground locker-rooms and jock-straps."

An interviewer is always supposed to write down the exact words of the answer, so I did. I thought about slipping this interview into the stack of real ones, to vary the monotony for one of the women with the crayons – Mrs. Weemers, perhaps, or Mrs. Gundridge. She'd read it out loud to the others, and they would remark that it took all kinds; the topic would be good for at least three coffee-breaks.

"Now what about 'Long cool swallow?'"

"Not much. Oh, wait a moment. It's a bird, white, falling from a great height. Shot through the heart, in winter; the feathers coming off, drifting down.... This is just like those word-game tests the shrink gives you," he said with his eyes open. "I always liked doing them. They're better than the ones with pictures."

I said, "I expect they use the same principle. What about 'Healthy hearty taste?'"

He meditated for several minutes. "It's heartburn," he said. "Or no, that can't be right." His forehead wrinkled. "Now I see. It's one of those cannibal stories." For the first time he seemed upset. "I know the pattern, there's one of them in the Decameron and a couple in Grimm's; the husband kills the wife's lover, or vice versa, and cuts out the heart and makes it into a stew or a pie and serves it up in a silver dish, and the other one eats it. Though that doesn't account for the Healthy very well, does it? Shakespeare," he said in a less agitated voice, "Shakespeare has something like that too. There's a scene in *Titus Andronicus*, though it's debatable whether Shakespeare really wrote it, or..."

"'Tang of the Wilderness' is obviously a dog, part wolf, part husky, who saves his master three times, once from fire, once from flood and once from wicked humans....'"

"Thank you." I wrote busily. By this time I was convinced that he was a compulsive neurotic of some sort and that I'd better remain calm and not display any fear. I wasn't frightened exactly – he didn't look like the violent type – but these questions definitely made him tense. He might be tottering on an emotional brink, one of the phrases might be enough to push him over. Those people are like that I thought, remembering certain case histories Ainsley had told me; little things like words can really bother them.

"Now, 'Tingly, heady, rough-and-ready?'"

He contemplated that one at length. "Doesn't do a thing for me," he said, "it doesn't fit together. The first bit gives me an image of someone with a head made out of glass being hit with a stick: like musical glasses. But rough-and-ready doesn't do anything. I suppose," he said sadly, "that one's not much use to you."

"You're doing fine," I said, thinking of what would happen to the I.B.M. machine if they ever tried to run this thing through it. "Now the last one: 'Tang of the wilderness.'"

"Oh," he said, his voice approaching enthusiasm, "that one's easy; it struck me at once when I heard it. It's one of those technicolour movies about dogs or horses. 'Tang of the Wilderness' is obviously a dog, part wolf, part husky, who saves his master three

times, once from fire, once from flood and once from wicked humans, more likely to be white hunters than Indians these days, and finally gets blasted by a cruel trapper with a .22 and wept over. Buried, probably in the snow. Panoramic shot of trees and lake. Sunset. Fade-out."

"Fine," I said, scribbling madly to get it all down. There was silence while we both listened to the scratching of my pencil. "Now, I hate to ask you, but you're supposed to say how well you think each of those five phrases applies to a beer – Very Well, Medium Well, or Not Very Well At All?"

"I couldn't tell you," he said, losing interest completely. "I never drink the stuff. Only scotch. None of them are any good for scotch." ◆

ACTIVITY 6

PICTURES IN THE MIND

1. What does each of the following images from the commercial make the young man think of?

- "deep-down manly flavour"
- "long cool swallow"
- "healthy hearty taste"
- "tingly, heady, rough-and-ready"
- "tang of the wilderness"

2. What does each one make you think of?

3. What are some other words or phrases that could be used in a beer commercial?

4. Write down some of the images that are used in television or radio ads. What does each image make you think of? Compare your responses with those of other people in your class.

PUTTING IT ALL TOGETHER

Appeal to a need, create a striking image, use catchy words, tell an interesting story – put these together and you have an effective ad. Now that you know what goes into the creation of an ad, it's your turn.

YOU AS ADVERTISER

1. Choose one of the following situations:

- a neighborhood event (for example, a garage sale)
- a school event (for example, a dance)
- a community event (for example, a winter carnival)
- a fund raising campaign (for example, for your students' council)
- the sale of a used item (for example, a bike, car, or stereo equipment)

2. Prepare an ad for the situation you've chosen by following these steps:

a) Select your market (the people who will buy your product).
b) Decide what visual elements you'll use in your ad. Remember to use what you've learned about mood, typeface, logos, colour, light, shape, and overall composition to create an effective visual message.
c) Think about the story that you are trying to tell in your ad. What do you want your reader to conclude about the events before and after the moment shown in your ad?
d) To what needs will you appeal in your ad? How will you convey these to your reader?
e) The written text of an ad is called the copy. Carefully pick the words that make up the copy of your ad. Think about both their literal and their connotative meanings.
f) Explore different ways of composing your ad. Take each of the components you have designed and try arranging them in different ways on the page. Pick the one you like best.

3. Display your ad. The test of your ad is whether or not it produces the results you want.

END THOUGHTS

This unit has shown you how ads are constructed. When you understand how ads are made you should be able to read and look at them more critically. Write a brief statement in which you describe your thoughts and feelings about ads. To help you write your statement, try completing some of the following:

- "I think that ads help people to..."
- "People are affected by ads in different ways. One way is..."
- "We need to be careful about how ads affect us because..."
- "I like ads that..."
- "I don't like ads that..."
- "I believe that what makes an ad effective is..."
- "I believe that the main goal of advertisers is..."

And by the way, the missing words in the ad in Figure 9-9 on page 183 are: scrunch, spike, flare, rake, sculpt, and studio.

EXTENSION IDEAS

1. Make a bulletin-board display of various ads. Label the components that make up the ads. Explain the techniques being used in them.
2. Collect several magazines that are aimed at readers of different age groups or those with special interests. Prepare a report on the products advertised, the techniques used, and what you learn about the readers on the basis of the ads found in the magazine.
3. You are an explorer from another planet and your only source of knowledge about earth people is the ads from a popular magazine. Prepare a report for your people about earth creatures as revealed in their ads.
4. Invite a commercial artist to speak to the class. Ask him or her to explain the process that is used to design an ad and to mount an advertising campaign.
5. Go to the library and look up back issues of a popular magazine. Go back ten, twenty, thirty, or more years. Compare the ads and how they have changed over the years. Write a report about how these changes reflect changes that have occurred in society.

6. Re-read the excerpt, "Healthy Hearty Taste" on page 185. The young man in the excerpt listened on the telephone to a beer commercial with these exciting phrases in it: "deep-down manly flavour;" "long cool swallow;" "healthy hearty taste;" "tingly,heady, rough-and-ready;" "tang of the wilderness." Write the commercial that the young man might have heard on the telephone.

7. Apply the principles that you have learned about advertising to the visual display of this unit.

a) How effective is this unit in communicating its message?

b) What is your opinion of the title of this unit? Can you think of a better one?

UNIT 10

EXAMINING STEREOTYPES

★ SURFACES AND REALITIES

★ THE MISUNDERSTOOD

★ THE SHORT STORY WRITING PROCESS

INTRODUCTION

The word *stereotyping* originally referred to the plates used in printing. This original meaning has changed over time. Today, a stereotype is a "fixed mental impression." In other words, stereotyping occurs when people unthinkingly categorize people.

We often have a tendency to see people in categories and to divide them into groups – young people and old people, rich and poor, female and male, black and white. Since these categories do exist, there is nothing wrong with them as long as they are just categories. But when people start to give a category certain qualities or meanings that are fixed in their minds, they are guilty of stereotyping. If you stereotype people, you may not understand them. This unit will help you explore the idea of stereotyping and will help you see what happens to people who are the victims of stereotyping.

SURFACES AND REALITIES

Examples of stereotyping exist all around you. It's all too easy, but not fair, to dismiss a person because of her or his physical appearance. Instead, try to suspend judgement by first asking yourself, "What is this person really like?" Stereotyping is wrong simply because it doesn't fit all the people in a category. Often it fits only a few of the people. For this reason, stereotypes are dangerous. If you see a person in school or on the street who seems to fit a category, you may make incorrect judgments about this person.

Figure 10-1 What stereotype about women does this cartoon support?

Wizard of Id

IN THE SHADOWS

Tina Kirkeby

In the shadows
lurk strange obscure things
like freakish creatures
floating in the wind

In the shadows
walk lonely depressed people
like leaves in the breeze
going nowhere special

In the shadows
a black man stands
like a stone in a field
never moving, always forgotten

In the shadows
is where I stand
like the black man
going through life unnoticed

ACTIVITY 1

RESPONDING TO A POEM

1. What is your opinion of the poem "In the Shadows"?

a) What word or phrase do you believe is the most important one in the poem? Why?
b) What other word or phrase do you think sums up this poem? Explain your choice.
c) What does this poem say about stereotyping?

2. What is your opinion of the cartoon in Figure 10-1 on page 192?

a) What does this cartoon say about stereotyping?
b) Do you think cartoons like this are harmful to women?

3. In what ways are the poem "In the Shadows" and the cartoon in Figure 10-1 similar?

CHART A STEREOTYPE

It's important to see the other side of stereotyping: the reality.

1. On a full page in your notebook, make a chart like the one in Figure 10-2. For each category, list the stereotype and the reality. The category of young people has been done for you.
2. Try to add at least ten more categories and their stereotypes to this chart.
3. In the third column, add what you believe these people are like.

CHART OF STEREOTYPES

CATEGORY	STEREOTYPE	REALITY
YOUNG PEOPLE	SILLY, CARELESS	SOME ARE BUT MANY ARE SENSIBLE AND CAREFUL
OLD PEOPLE		
FATHERS		
MOTHERS		
MOTHERS-IN-LAW		
TEACHERS		

Figure 10-2 Are you guilty of stereotyping others?

THE MISUNDERSTOOD

Have you ever been misunderstood by a parent, a teacher, a sister, or a brother? How did you feel? Were you angry or frustrated? People who are put into groups – or are stereotyped by others – are misunderstood. They have the same reaction that you have when you are misunderstood. The effects of stereotyping can be very harmful for some people.

In order to be understood, stereotypes need to be examined. Have you ever noticed that there always seems to be another side to a story, another way of looking at events, and another side to a person you know? When you understand someone, you see more clearly why that person acts as he or she does. In the short story "The Cardboard Room," a young girl comes to understand someone who seems very different from her.

THE CARDBOARD ROOM

Teresa Pitman

My parents hate a lot of people.

It's not like kids, not like your best friend when you were six, saying "I hate you" because you won't give her a ride on your new bike, and stomping away home and then tomorrow, you're best friends again. Kids can be mad at each other and then it's all over an hour later.

Adults aren't like that. They hate deeper, stronger, and they cover it all over with smiles and soft words.

Oh, my parents have their reasons. They don't like the Johnsons down the road because they're Americans and if they really cared about this country, they'd get their citizenship. And because Americans are trying to take over the country, not by fighting a war, but through secretly buying up all our property. The Johnsons' split-level is just one small step in somebody's master plan, I guess.

"Adults aren't like that. They hate deeper, stronger, and they cover it all over with smiles and soft words."

Figure 10-3 This illustration suggests the feelng of isolation that can occur when you are stereotyped.

And the Freedmans might be okay if they didn't drink so much. And the Archers have six kids when, as my mom says, "It's totally irresponsible to have more than two children in today's world."

It doesn't matter if the people try to be nice to them. I remember going to a meeting at the school, all of us together and Phil Martin's dad came over. We laughed at Phil, you know, because of his clothes, and now here was his father dressed no better.

"The Johnsons' split-level is just one small step in somebody's master plan, I guess."

He had this smile on his face that looked like it hurt him to keep it there and the skin on his forehead was streaked with sweat. When he asked my dad if there might be any jobs up at the plant, my father just smiled and said no, but he'd keep his eyes open.

Even before Mr. Martin had finished saying thank you, my parents had started to walk away and all the way home, they shook their heads over the man's nerve, asking right out like that.

They didn't hate me then. None of this would have mattered – everything would still be okay – if it hadn't been for Eric.

It started out, you know, as a physics project. Mr. Hennessy announced that he was assigning partners for this one because he was tired of the same people always working together. I don't see what difference it made to him: We like it that way.

For a few minutes I had dreams of doing the project with Mike McCann who sat in the back and was on the football team and always kept a bottle in his gym bag in case the class got boring. But Mr. Hennessy assigned me to Eric Nye.

"I don't see what you're complaining about," he said when I asked him, after the bell rang, if I could switch. "Eric's probably the best student in the class."

"I'd rather work with another girl." That wasn't completely true, but it would be better than Eric.

"Get out of here. You do the assignment with Eric or you get zero."

And my dad said, when I told him, that it was teachers like Mr. Hennessy who were the problem in the public school system. They had no choice but to let me go, the next Saturday, when

Eric asked me over to his house. He had some magazines and stuff Eric said that we could use for the project.

Maybe it was mostly curiosity that made me go. The Nyes were – well, even the people my parents couldn't stand avoided the Nyes. There was a war in their country and they had come here with no money and no job. Refugees, some people called them.

"The Nyes were – well, even the people my parents couldn't stand avoided the Nyes. There was a war in their country and they had come here with no money and no job. Refugees, some people called them."

My father had other names for them. They had come here, he said, to be supported by our welfare system – medical insurance and everything. When he found out that Eric's father was working two jobs, weekdays and weekends, he was even madder: "No wonder we've got so many Canadians unemployed."

That's the trouble with the school system," my dad said after that first Saturday at Eric's house, and my mother scowled at him.

"I told you we should have sent her to a private school," she said and then shrugged her shoulders in resignation. It was an old argument and nobody wanted to hear it again. She turned to me instead.

"What was their house like? Did you eat any of their food?"

I was afraid to admit I'd eaten anything. It was only an apple, but I'd probably have had to stay in bed the rest of the day with a thermometer in my mouth if my mother knew. And what could I say about the house?

"It's small."

All the way home – I had to walk. Eric's family only had one car and his father worked on Saturdays too – I thought about their house, thought about how my parents would laugh if I told them about it, how it would become a joke to share with Dad's friends from work when they came over. And all I could say was "It's small."

It *was* a small house for them, the parents and the four kids, and it wasn't until I was inside that I discovered Eric's grandparents lived there, too. And even though it was small, the rooms looked stark, half-empty. They had almost no furniture.

The kitchen had no space for eating and there wasn't a dining room at all, so their big table with eight mismatched chairs around it stood in the middle of the living room. I guess they figured they

might as well put it there, because they didn't have a sofa, only a faded armchair and a black-and-white TV set.

My parents would have laughed at that. And they would have laughed at the bedsheets hung in the bedroom windows and the jars of beans and pickles and home-canned fruit on the basement shelves.

"Hasn't she ever heard of grocery stores?" my mother would have said. "They'll probably all die of food poisoning." And they would have laughed at Eric's room.

"Once you get used to hating one person, one family, one group of people, somehow it seems to get easier and easier to expand that group to include more and more people in it."

Once you get used to hating one person, one family, one group of people, somehow it seems to get easier and easier to expand that group to include more and more people in it. Practice makes perfect or something like that.

When I knocked on the door, Eric let me in and introduced me quickly – I didn't remember any of the names – and took me down to the basement. The house had three bedrooms just like ours, but his grandparents had one and his parents another, and so that Eric could have a little privacy, a place to work, they gave him a corner of the basement.

It was just a regular, unfinished basement with a cold floor and cement walls and a bare light bulb in the middle with a string tied to the chain. And one corner was enclosed with cardboard. That was Eric's room.

His father had taken apart some of those big cardboard cartons that stoves and dishwashers come in (they must have picked them up from the back of a furniture store because the fridge and stove they had upstairs hadn't been new for years), and stapled them together to make walls.

It was like the houses little kids make out of shoeboxes, with a cardboard door cut on the side nearest the stairs. And when we went inside, all Eric had was a mattress on the floor and some boxes with clothes and books and papers in them. I couldn't see anywhere to sit.

Eric started rummaging through a box full of papers, but stopped when he noticed me standing there awkwardly.

"Just sit on the bed."

I pulled up the wrinkled sheet and smoothed out the blanket. If this had been me with Mike McCann, sitting side-by-side on his unmade bed, I might have been self-conscious, wondering about the possibilities.

But Eric wasn't the kind of person you could have fantasies about. He was so thin, for one thing, I could see the line of his collarbone poking through the worn material of his shirt, and the faint shadows of his ribs. But part of me wondered what it would be like to touch him, his golden-brown skin, wondered if it would feel different, wondered if it would be warm or cool, smooth or dry. Not fantasies. Just wondering.

"He was so thin, for one thing, I could see the line of his collarbone poking through the worn material of his shirt, and the faint shadow of his ribs."

"Here," he said finally, handing me a bundle of papers. "I photocopied these from some magazines at the library."

Before I could look at the articles, he took them back and read them out loud to me. It wasn't that the words he was reading didn't make sense. It was great material – we were going to have the best project in the class. It was the way he was reading it, the tone of his voice. This was physics, after all, school work.

"You really like this stuff, don't you?" I asked him and when he stared at me. I knew he couldn't even understand why I had asked.

After I'd been there three or four times on Saturdays, putting this project together, his mother invited me to stay for lunch (I told my parents I was going to Burger King with Sylvia). I ate the food without looking too hard, just swallowed everything quickly before I could taste it too much, and tried to smile at the grandparents who didn't speak English.

I was getting used to Eric's mother who was so quiet and seemed to spend almost all her time in the kitchen, and after lunch I offered to help with the dishes. And while we were sloshing around in the soapy water, I found myself asking her things I was afraid to ask Eric.

"What was it like to leave your own country and come here?"

Silence. I shouldn't have asked.

"Like being born."

Silence again. I clinked the glasses together under the water.

"The pains, you know, come stronger and stronger, closer and closer, until it becomes too much to bear. And finally you have no choice but to be born into this new country. The cord is cut. This is our home now."

She wasn't looking at me. I wanted to ask her if she knew that people here hated her, hated her family, but when I saw her face, I didn't need to ask. She knew. They all knew.

That was the beginning. And maybe everything would have been all right had I let it stop there. But I didn't.

We finished the project and handed it in. I just mentioned it to my parents. And on Saturday morning, I knocked again at Eric's door. He didn't ask me what I was doing there, just let me in. And we sat on his bed in that cardboard room and talked.

"'You don't see how fragile it all is, do you?' he said. 'You don't know how quickly everything can change and then nothing is ever the same again.'"

He didn't talk about the things Sylvia and the other kids did. He didn't care about clothes or music or long stories about getting stoned and driving around the city at twice the speed limit.

He talked about all the things he wondered about, like what colours looked like to different people, and whether God really existed, and about the things he was afraid of. And sometimes he would tell me stories about the country they had left behind, and about his two brothers who had died, the older one who was killed in the fighting and the baby who was sick when there was no room in the hospital.

I shook my head, not disbelieving him, but unable to make his stories fit into the world that I lived in, where there was always room for babies in the hospital and older brothers went off to college, not to war.

"You don't see how fragile it all is, do you?" he said. "You don't know how quickly everything can change and then nothing is ever the same again. Never the same again."

I went home that day thinking I'd never go back, but I did. It was like having a tooth with a cavity that you are trying to ignore, but your tongue keeps going back to that tooth and probing and pushing at it. Talking to Eric was like that. I needed to explore the exact dimensions of the cavity, find the depth of the pain.

> "Now I could see the walls my parents had built: solid brick and mortar, impenetrable."

But I thought I could do it without anyone knowing. It worked for awhile.

"You've been spending a lot of time with that Nye boy, haven't you?"

"Well, there's that physics project..."

"That's not what I mean."

I felt my face flush. They must have found out about the day we skipped school together. Eric wanted to show me a new exhibit at the museum, but we left by separate doors and met two blocks away from the school so that nobody would know. I hadn't told anyone. They must have found out.

But my mother flattened the paper she held on the table in front of me. Physics project. Graded A+, with "Excellent work" added in Mr. Hennessy's red ink.

"You finished this weeks ago." Calmly, coldly.

"Eric..."

"What have you been doing with that boy all this time? Are you sleeping with him? How could you do this to us?"

I knew it didn't matter what I said. Suddenly I knew what Eric meant about things changing. The rest of the conversation, the accusations and the threats were not important. It was just that everything had changed.

Now I could see the walls. It was as though I had taken a piece of photographic paper, completely blank, and dipped it into the developer and watched the picture spring into focus. Now I could see the walls my parents had built: solid brick and mortar, impenetrable. And now I was on the outside.

My parents hate a lot of people. Oh, they have their reasons. It doesn't matter if you try to be nice to them. It doesn't matter...

Eric knew, Eric knew all along how fragile things are, how easily destroyed. And nothing is ever the same again. ◆

ACTIVITY 3

RESPONDING TO A SHORT STORY

Answer the following questions about "The Cardboard Room."

1. What was your first reaction to this story? For example, did something in the story make you angry? Did something make you happy? What would you like to change in this story? Why?

2. The narrator of the story compares the way adults and younger people hate. She concludes, "Adults aren't like that [young people]. They hate deeper, stronger, and they cover it all over with smiles and soft words." Use these questions to focus your thoughts about this quotation:

a) What does the narrator mean? Do you agree with her?
b) Are the adults you know like the ones described by the narrator?

3. What is your opinion of this statement: "Once you get used to hating one person, one family, one group of people, somehow it seems to get easier and easier to expand that group...." Does this quotation from "The Cardboard Room" describe the community in which you live?

4. The narrator's parents react to her friendship with Eric by asking, "What have you been doing with that boy all this time? Are you sleeping with him? How could you do this to us?"

a) In what tone of voice would the narrator's parents speak these words?
b) What do you think of the parents' reaction to the narrator's friendship with Eric?

5. Write an explanation of the last two sentences of the story: "Eric knew, Eric knew all along how fragile things are, how easily destroyed. And nothing is ever the same again."

RECONSTRUCTING "THE CARDBOARD ROOM"

1. Draw the cardboard room with the narrator and Eric in it. Re-read the story for details.

2. Choose a character in the story with whom you sympathize. Write a letter to that character in which you explain why you are sympathetic. Be sure to give examples from your own experiences that can be compared to those of the character.

3. Choose a character in the story who you do not like. Write an entry in your notebook in which you explore your thoughts about this character. Be sure to include details from the story in your entry. Also try imagining other actions that the character might have done.
4. The narrator in "The Cardboard Room" describes how Eric talked about the way colours looked to different people, about God, and about his fears. He also told stories concerning his homeland and the death of his brothers. Find a partner and discuss Eric's way of looking at the world.
5. With at least one other person, write a scene in which the narrator in "The Cardboard Room" and Eric meet and talk in his room. Record the conversation on a tape cassette.
6. Choose a character in the story and write a journal entry exploring your concerns and feelings about hate and prejudice from the point of view of that character.

THE SHORT STORY WRITING PROCESS

Everybody likes to hear a story. You tell stories all the time to your friends – what you did last night, what your mother said when you got home, a joke you heard somewhere. The short story form is similar to the stories that you tell your friends in that all stories have a purpose – the teller wants to communicate an idea to an audience. The short story, however, tends to be more complex and the action covers a longer period of time than in the stories you tell your friends. For these reasons, you need to plan a short story thoroughly and spend time developing it into a form that reads well and that accurately expresses your theme.

The process described in the following pages should help you write a believable story dealing with the theme of stereotyping.

info-box

HOW TO WRITE A SHORT STORY

1. *Prewriting:*	getting the idea for the story
2. *Prewriting:*	the outline
3. *The First Draft:*	writing
4. *The First Draft:*	editing for content
5. *The First Draft:*	writing
6. *The First Draft:*	proofreading
7. *The First Draft:*	publishing

PREWRITING: THE IDEA

1. Think about an experience you – or others – have had that involves conflict as the result of stereotyping.
2. Talk with your friends, parents, or your teacher in order to clarify your idea.
3. Once you clarify your idea, go to the next stage in the writing process: the outline.

PREWRITING: THE OUTLINE

1. In your notebook, write a short plan or outline for your incident. The following headings may help you organize your ideas:
   - Title
   - Setting: time, place
   - Characters: names, ages, details
   - Plot
   - Conflict
   - The point made about stereotyping
2. You will also have to make a decision about narrative technique: who is going to tell the story? You can choose one of two options:
   - first person ("I")
   - third person ("he" or "she")

Here is a sample outline for a short story based on the theme of stereotyping:

- Title: "Decisions"
- Setting: time – the present
  place – a corner store
- Characters:
  – a six- to seven-year-old girl (the narrator)
  – her ten-year-old brother Jack
- Plot:
  – two kids go to the store to buy candy
  – the girl has the money
  – decision about what to buy
  – the girl discovers the money is missing
- Conflict:
  – argument over what to buy
  – is the girl old enough to carry money?
- The point: – young kids sometimes make mistakes, but they feel as badly about the mistake as anyone does
- Narrative technique: – first person narrative ("I")

THE FIRST DRAFT: WRITING

1. Using "The Cardboard Room" as a model, write your own story in your notebook. The following suggestions will help you develop your story:

- Write on every other line. It's then easier to add words or make corrections.
- Begin dramatically. "The Cardboard Room," for example, begins by immediately establishing what the theme of the story will be.
- Use conversation. It's always interesting to have your characters talk with each other.
- Let the reader see the story happen step by step. Don't summarize what happens – show it!
- Be descriptive – but make it short and vivid. For example, "It was like the houses little kids make out of shoeboxes, with a cardboard door cut in the side nearest the stairs."
- End your story in a way that makes your point about stereotyping very clear to the reader.

THE FIRST DRAFT: EDITING FOR CONTENT

1. Re-read your first draft from beginning to end. Don't be afraid to add or delete anything at this stage.
2. When you finish your first draft, show it to a writing partner, a friend, or your teacher. Look for the following:
   - Are the characters different from each other?
   - Is the problem in the story clear?
   - Can you see the events taking place?
   - Does the ending make the point clearly?
   - Look for vivid language, clear descriptions, and natural conversation.
3. Record your work on a tape cassette. You can often hear if the language you've used needs further revision.

info-box

NOTES ON WRITING DIALOGUE

- For each new speaker start a new paragraph. This tells the reader that the speaker is the other person.
- Indent each new paragraph five spaces.
- Words like "calmly, coldly" tell the reader in what tone of voice the mother spoke.
- Place quotation marks before the first words and after the last words in a conversation.
- Use a comma whenever 'he said' or 'she said' occurs. For example: "What have you been doing with that boy all this time," she said.

THE FINAL DRAFT: WRITING

1. After spending a lot of time improving the first draft of your manuscript by thinking about it, reading it, talking about it, and revising parts of it, rewrite it neatly. Use a typewriter or word processor if possible. As you copy your work, make further changes that will improve the effect of your writing.
2. Use the following rules for manuscript form:
   - Write on every other line.
   - Use only one side of the page.
   - Make it look neat and clean.
   - Make it accurate.
3. Try leaving your story for a while before you write your final draft. This way you will be looking at your writing with new eyes – and you might see problems with it that you didn't notice before.

THE FINAL DRAFT: PROOFREADING

1. Use the following suggestions to proofread your final draft:
   - Read your story carefully, this time looking for any mistakes in punctuation, grammar, spelling, and sentence structure.
   - Show it to someone else. Have the person focus on the correct use of language. Be a proofreader yourself and help a friend or partner. Use a dictionary.
2. Make a cover page that includes the title of your story and your name. Staple the cover to the story and add a blank page at the back.
3. Circulate your story among your classmates. This will give you an opportunity to read the stories written by others in your class. Use the blank sheet at the back to comment on other people's stories. Take your time. Think about other people's points of view. Initial your comments so the authors will know who wrote them.

THE FINAL DRAFT: PUBLISHING

Collect some or all of the stories and have them typed for publication.

1. Have two or three people type them on a word processor.
2. Have someone in your class illustrate the stories with line drawings.
3. Choose a vivid title for your collection.
4. Have someone design and draw a cover page.
5. Ask members of the class to contribute a poem, a journal entry, or another piece of imaginative writing. In this way your collection will have a variety of types of writing in it.
6. Type a table of contents and a preface that include an explanation of who contributed to your collection.
7. Have someone photocopy the collection so each person who contributed can have a copy. Give copies to other people, such as the principal of your school or people who visit the school. Show your own copy to your parents and friends.

REVIEW OF STEREOTYPING

1. Write a personal statement for each of the following topics:
    - your definition of stereotyping (for example, you could start with "To me the word stereotyping means....)
    - the effects of stereotyping on people ("Stereotyping affects people because....")
    - personal thoughts about putting others down ("I think that....")
    - personal feelings about this practice ("I feel that....")
    - a concluding statement about your own behaviour ("From now on I....")
2. Then put these paragraphs together to create a non-fiction piece of writing about stereotyping. Try to link each paragraph. In addition, it may be necessary to create a beginning and an ending paragraph.

END THOUGHTS

In this unit you've explored the harmful practice of stereotyping. You've become more aware of stereotyping in the world and of your own actions and words that may harm others. You've written a story on the theme of stereotyping and will be able to take pleasure in your work. You should now appreciate more deeply the short stories that you read since you're more aware of the hard work that goes into good writing.

EXTENSION IDEAS

1. With a group of students, do some research outside your classroom to pinpoint where and when stereotyping happens in your school, at home, and in your community.
2. In a small group, think about these words and decide how they are different from each other: prejudice, discrimination, stereotyping, bigotry, bias, racism.
3. What is your opinion of this statement: "Parents are a far stronger influence on teenagers than are their friends." Use this quotation as a basis for a small group discussion. Be prepared to report your group's conclusions to your class.
4. Interview at least two adults (for example, your parents) on the question of how parents should and should not act towards their children. Prepare a list of questions in advance. Record your interview to make analysis of their opinions easier.
5. Create a questionnaire of at least ten questions. The topic of the questionnaire should be closely related to the stereotyping that takes place in "The Cardboard Room." Ask at least ten people, both teenagers and adults, to answer your questions. Summarize your findings and draw conclusions.
6. Make a collection of poems on the topic of stereotyping. Look in books in the library to find songs or poems that are important to you. Copy the best four or five poems and make a booklet. Illustrate the cover page, add a table of contents, and write an introduction in which you explain why you chose the poems. You may also include poetry written by yourself or other people that you know.

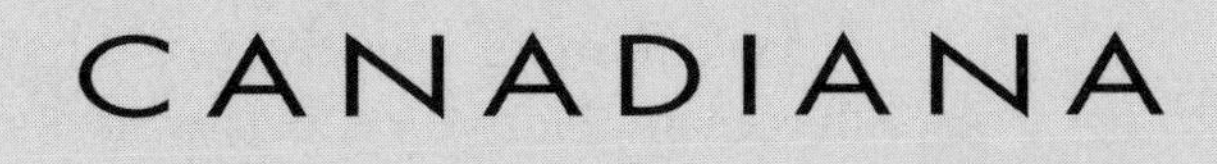

- CANADIAN ORIGINS
- FACES AND STORIES
- ANECDOTES
- FINDING AN ANECDOTE
- FROM ANECDOTE TO FICTION
- NATIVE CANADIANS

INTRODUCTION

This unit is a celebration of our Canadian cultural differences – of the people we are and the stories we have to tell. The activities in this unit will lead you to think and read about the experiences of Canadian immigrants. You will be invited to interview people from different cultural backgrounds and to use their stories or the ones you will be reading as the basis for your own writing.

CANADIAN ORIGINS

People from all over the world have come to Canada. As well Canada has many Native peoples whose ancestors have always lived here. To get some idea of the origins of Canadians look at the pictures below:

Figure 11-1 Canada is increasingly becoming a multi-cultural and multi-lingual society.

ACTIVITY 1

CANADIAN FACES

1. Look at the faces in the photographs in Figure 11-1. Although they are all very different, they have one thing in common: they are all Canadians. Pick one of the portraits. Think about the story of this person. In a brief paragraph, tell the story of this person. The following questions will help you think about what you should say in this paragraph:

- What is her or his country of origin?
- How old is this person?
- When and why did he or she come to Canada?
- What challenges were faced when she or he first came to Canada?

2. The word *ethnic* comes from the Greek word for nation. Look at the people in your class. Write down their names. Beside each name write what you think is his or her ethnic origin. When you have finished, have each person state his or her family's original nationality. How close were you in your predictions? Did any surprise you?

3. In small groups or with the whole class, share what you know about your family's ethnic background.

4. How does the ethnic representation of your school's population compare with that of Canada as a whole? To find out, use the following form to conduct a survey of the students in your school:

Student's Name: ______________________________
Ethnic Origin: ______________________________

Check one of the following:

_____ Native Canadian
_____ First Generation Canadian
_____ Second (or more) Generation

Note: Each student in your class could survey a different class in your school.

5. When you have finished your survey, summarize the results. To what extent is your school typical of the Canadian distribution? To what extent is it different? How do you explain the similarities and differences?

Figure 11-2 William Kurelek. *No Grass Grows on the Beaten Path.* Many of Kurelek's paintings depicted the life of Ukrainian farmers in western Canada.

FACES AND STORIES

Behind the faces in the photographs on page 212 lie many different stories – some sad, some humorous, all very human. The following are some experiences of young Canadian immigrants as described in their own words.

Figure 11-3 "My first impression of Canada was that it was all white."

I GOT LOST

Karin

I've been here one year and four months. My first impression of Canada was that it was all white – it was all snowy. It was colder than Jamaica. And I didn't know anyone. I felt good when I was going on the plane and when I was coming to the airport in Canada. I want to be a stewardess like my aunt when I grow up, 'cause I like riding on planes. I wouldn't mind being a pilot but I don't think I'll ever have enough money to buy a plane.

I feel funny when I start school because I don't know anyone. I got lost once and when I went back to school the next day, they started to tease me that I got lost and I didn't know the way. But that was the first time I was here and I went out on my own. That made me feel awful. I don't like when everyone teases me.

The school work here is easier than in Jamaica but the teachers shout at you. They don't do that too much in Jamaica. The kids are different here, too. If you're in a fight and someone beats you and you didn't run they tease you here that you can't do anything, and if they ask you to do something and you say "no" they call you "chicken." ◆

IT'S A SIN

Natalie

I'm eighteen years old and I can't do anything. I can't go out. If I do I have to lie about it. I have to be home around 7:00 or 7:30, and that's it. I'm not enjoying life. My parents just don't understand what it is to be with a guy or with friends. That you don't have to do anything wrong.

Figure 11-4 "Parents on TV do everything that your parents don't."

They believe that the guys are supposed to come to you. They're supposed to knock on the door and say, "You've got two daughters. Who's married and who's not?" They don't believe in going out on dates or dancing or going to social gatherings. They don't believe in that at all. I can do anything during the daytime up until seven o'clock or eight o'clock when the action really starts. Then I have to stay home. And that's why many a times my parents and I have arguments.

We went to Huntsville on a school trip and my Dad started teasing me and saying, "I still have to find out where you went. I still have to find out who you were with. I still have to find out who your friends are." He really got me upset. So I said to him, "Look Dad, I can't take it any more. If this goes on I'm going to run away from home and I'm not coming back." He didn't answer me. I was really surprised. He usually says to me that whatever he says is for my own good. But I told him that I didn't believe this was true, that I respected his ideas but he couldn't expect me to live by them. And I think I'm going to try him out. One day, if I really want to go somewhere with someone, whether it's a boy or a girl, I'm just going to go. Hopefully, I'll come back and find the door open. But it's a chance I'll have to take.

It's hard to have dates. Nobody asks you. Because of my background, because I'm Portuguese, guys tend to not look at me. They talk to me all right, but they don't get personal. They seem to think, "Oh, she's Portuguese. She won't be able to go out on dates."

My parents are always telling me that everything I do is a sin. If I talk bad, it's a sin. If I answer back, it's a sin. If I come in late, it's a sin. It's a sin. It's a sin.

It's hard to be a girl when your parents are not Canadian. People on TV do everything that your parents don't. ◆

Figure 11-5 "The colour of your skin really makes a big difference here."

THE COLOUR OF YOUR SKIN

Kamala

When you first realize you are not getting a fair chance because of your colour, it makes you depressed. You don't want to talk to anyone. Slowly you get very thick-skinned, then you become pushy. If anyone says anything to me about my colour, I can give an answer right back to them. My children don't agree with me about colour discrimination here. They say there is none. But they are young and attractive, and they have had their schooling here.

I remember when my son first started school here. He was 10. He really suffered. He didn't want his father to go to school to pick him up. The other children would tease him because his father had a turban and a brown skin. He said they teased him, too, about his skin and he would just give them a left and a right. But when they said it about his father he felt very bad. The colour of your skin really makes a big difference here. A very big difference. ◆

STORIES BEHIND THE FACES

1. In your notebook, state your reactions to one of the experiences narrated in the preceding anecdotes. Use these statements to help you get started:

- "This story made me feel __________ because ___________."
- "I especially like the part about _______ because ________."
- "It sounded true to me because ________________________."
- "It reminded me of ______________________________."

2. Get together with another student who picked the same story. Compare your reactions. Was there anything in your background and that of your partner that made you react differently to the same story? If so, what was it?

3. Get together with a student who picked a different story. Tell each other your reasons for picking the story you did.

ANECDOTES

The stories that you have just read are anecdotes. An anecdote is based on a real experience and real people. We all tell anecdotes regularly. Whenever you tell a friend about something that happened to you or that happened to someone else, you are telling an anecdote. People seem to have a basic need to tell their stories. Below is another example of such a story. We will use it to look more closely at what makes a successful anecdote.

THREE WORDS - YOU GOT JOB?

Antonio Aiello

I was a dumb kid of seventeen and I didn't know anything, no English, sure. My uncle said I had to get work, and I didn't know how it was done because I didn't have a job when I left Italy. I went by ship to England and then to Montreal and that's where my uncle met me, in Montreal, and he took me to Toronto by the train.

He said I was to go to places around, shops, little factories where they made clothes and shoes and other things, and I was to say, "You got job?" Those were the first three words in English I knew. He said say it after him, and I would say it, and he said no, not like "you got job," as though the boss had a job. I was to say it like it was me that wanted the job. Like, "You got job?" Raise my voice at the end. To make it a question.

“'This is Antonio Aiello, and he comes from a hill town in Italy and he is a good boy and a hard worker. He will work hard for you.'”

This was the trick, and I guess a lot of other guys did it. It was like you'd call it a game. You would smile at the boss and say those little words, coming out at the end with "job" like it was a squeak. The first day I got a job in a store unpacking fruit. I said my words, and when the man sort of smiled, I gave him the piece of paper my uncle had written out, and the paper told him about me. "This is Antonio Aiello, and he comes from a hill town in Italy and he is a good boy and a hard worker. He will work hard for you."

→

"Then when I paid that off, I didn't owe anything, and I could buy clothes, and I was learning English at night school when winter came, and that's how we did it."

I worked hard that afternoon, and when I went to my uncle's fruit stand and said I had got a job, he said good, and that he would go with me next morning and talk to the owner, a Mr. Faber. That happened, and they decided I was worth thirty-five cents an hour, and my uncle would get the money from Mr. Faber and he would take half and give the rest to me.

Sure, half. My pay came to about twenty bucks a week, and the ten he took, that went for my paying him back, my boat fare, the passage, sure. I gave him five dollars a week of my ten dollars for living with them, and I worked for him at nights at fifteen cents an hour, so I had five dollars for myself in a week, and I paid him ten for my boat fare and maybe three dollars came off it, too, for the money I earned working for him. That way I paid off my fare, which I think was about $170. Then when I paid that off, I didn't owe anything, and I could buy clothes, and I was learning English at night school when winter came, and that's how we did it. It was a good way.

Sure, I think it was a good way. I was working and paying off my uncle and learning English so I could get a good job. The job I had with Mr. Faber wasn't a good one. His son was in charge of the warehouse and he was a smart bastard, and he made it hard on me and the two other guys from Italy working there. He was a fat slob. Nothing good about him.

In two years I got a good job in Simpson's warehouse, and then I was driving a truck for them and making good money, and that's when I decided to bring my little brother out from Italy, so it started over again. He paid me back, and then my father died in Italy and we paid for the funeral, and next year we brought our mother out and a sister, and soon we had our own house. You see, we all worked together and we became Canadians.

More and more Italians came to Toronto and now there are a million. ◆

ACTIVITY 3

GETTING A JOB

1. Look at the advice Antonio got from his uncle. Do you think it was good advice? Why or why not? What advice have you been given about finding work? What advice would you give a newly arrived immigrant about finding work in Canada?
2. Do you think the arrangement that the uncle made with Antonio was fair? Why or why not? What would you have done if you had been in Antonio's position? What would you have done if you had been Antonio's uncle?
3. Look again at some of the problems faced by Antonio. How are they similar or different from problems that you have encountered in trying to find a job?
4. An anecdote is usually told orally. Even though this one is written down, what qualities make it seem like you are hearing it? In your answer consider the speaker's use of events, characters, dialogue, details, and language.
5. What aspects of the anecdote did you find effective? What made you want to keep reading it?
6. What is your opinion of the narrator who is telling this anecdote? Was he as dumb as he says he was?
7. Briefly describe how you got your first part-time or summer job.

FINDING AN ANECDOTE

Find an anecdote about the experience of someone who came to Canada from another country. A good way to get an interesting anecdote is to interview someone you know. Before you conduct the interview, there are several things you might want to keep in mind.

- Pick a person who has recently arrived in Canada and is willing to tell you about his or her experiences. It could be someone you know, but don't neglect other people in your community. If you need a translator sometimes younger members of the family will be happy to interpret what their parents or grandparents have to say. Consider going to a senior citizens' home and asking if any of the people there would like to share their stories with you.

Weak Questions:

Did you come to Canada by boat?

Did you enjoy the trip?

Better Questions:

How did you come to Canada?

What do you remember about the trip?

- Make an initial contact with your subject. Explain that you are working on a school project about the experiences of immigrants in Canada and that you would like to set up an appointment to interview them. If possible briefly discuss suggested topics for the interview. A day or so before the interview contact your subject to confirm your appointment.
- Prepare your interview questions ahead of time. Make most of your questions open ended. In other words, avoid questions that can be answered with a "yes," a "no," or another one-word answer.

ACTIVITY 4

INTERVIEW QUESTIONS

1. In groups of three or four prepare a list of questions that you could ask in an interview. The following is a list of topics about which you could ask your informant. You will probably be able to add others to the list.

- leaving home
- first impressions
- finding work
- discrimination
- arriving in Canada
- clearing customs
- a new language
- becoming Canadians

2. Often a good follow-up question will lead your subject to offer further interesting details. For example, a question about where someone lived when they first came to Canada could be followed up by questions such as these:

- What did you like or dislike about the place where you first lived?
- What do you remember about your neighbours? What did they do to help you and your family?
- What was life like for you and your family in your first home?
- How was life there different in winter and summer?

3. Pick several of the questions that your group has made up and add three or four follow-up questions to them. During the interview watch for appropriate moments to ask follow-up questions that will provide your subject with a chance to elaborate on what he or she is telling you.

info-box

CONDUCTING AN INTERVIEW

During the Interview:

1. Arrive on time. Briefly state again the purpose of the interview. Be polite and friendly throughout the interview.
2. Test the tape recorder before you start the interview. Check the sound level to see if the voices are being picked up clearly.
3. Turn on the tape recorder soon after you arrive and let it run through your preliminary comments so that your subject can become comfortable with the machine.
4. Tell your subject that you will also be taking notes on names, dates, and places during the interview. You should check correct spelling of these after your interview.
5. Establish a comfortable and relaxed tone with your first question. For example, you could say "Before we talk about your experiences when you first came to Canada, could you tell me a little about yourself? For example, where and when were you born?"
6. Be interested in what your subject is telling you. Don't get so wrapped up in your prepared questions that you miss opportunities to ask follow-up questions about interesting points raised by your informant.
7. Manage your time well. Ask your most important questions early in the interview. Be prepared to digress from your plan but try to come back to your main questions. Keep an eye on the amount of space left on your tape recorder.

After the Interview:

1. Write a brief thank-you letter.
2. Review your notes immediately after the interview to see if you need any additional information or clarification.
3. Listen to the tape.
4. Phone or contact your subject as soon as possible if clarification is needed.

ACTIVITY 5

IN ACTION

1. Listen to your tape recording and/or read over the notes that you took during the interview. Write down the parts that you want to use in your piece.
2. Read over your transcription. Cross out any repetitions, unrelated information, and parts that you do not want to use. Then look carefully at the order in which you have transcribed the information. Try rearranging the details in an order that is clear and appropriate.
3. Once you write a second draft, edit your story by looking carefully at the sentence structure. Often when people speak, they use long rambling sentences joined by 'and' or 'but'. At other times they may use incomplete sentences. Break the sentences that are too long into shorter ones and complete any fragments.
4. Consider the words used by the person you interviewed. Are any of them used incorrectly? Which ones do you want to keep in order to show the individuality of your speaker? Which ones do you want to change?
5. Write the edited draft and pass it to someone whose opinion you trust. Ask him or her to respond to it and make specific suggestions for improvement. Then write your final draft.

FROM ANECDOTE TO FICTION

The stories that you have collected for your projects are anecdotes. They are memories based on real experiences that happened to real people. Usually they are told in an informal, unpolished style.

A short story is a literary genre. It may be based on a true episode but the author has gone beyond the actual facts. Through her or his imagination the author has transformed fact into fiction, life into art.

The following selection is a short story about a young boy who immigrates from Holland to Canada. The story gives you an account of the emotional problems that someone who comes from a different culture has in adjusting to our culture.

SPELLING

John Terpstra

They were in the city and the reporter stood, waiting. "This is your chance," the mother said. "Tell him your name is John. If they print that, it will make it easier to get them to start calling you that from now on. Tell him your name is John Veenstra." Then, there it was in the *London Free Press*, not on the front page mind you nor was the picture of him but of the dark-haired Greek girl, the one who had been the winner, but it did mention clearly that a number of the finalists had been born outside of Canada and were recent immigrants, and his name was one of them. To be in Canada less than three years, be the St. Peter's school spelling champion, and then participate in the Sixth Annual Southwestern Ontario Spelling Competition held at Catholic Central High School in London was heady stuff for a ten-year old.

"In the farming community where his father had inexplicably placed them, they were always being gawked at, their appearance a source of never-ending snickers and asides."

This should show Wilfred Chapman. If they couldn't be friends, at least this should shut him up and stop the endless taunting of "D.P., D.P., You're nothing but a skinny D.P."[1] and "What'd you eat for breakfast, eh? Boiled tulip bulbs, eh?" The taunt was picked up by even the timid and the whole playground it seemed reverberated with "Tulip bulb, tulip bulb, German is a tulip bulb" until once more those scalding shameful tears would come and his body would shake with waves of hatred.

But now he'd changed his name and he'd been mentioned in the newspaper. Surely respect would be given. He might even make them understand that not all immigrants were displaced people, whatever that meant, and that not all Dutch people

[1] Displaced Persons, or "DP's as they were often called in a derogatory manner, were those people who are displaced from their homes as a result of war. These people endured hard times in refugee camps. After the Second World War countries such as Canada needed people to work in construction, road building, logging, mining, fishing and farming. Many of the people who were displaced during the war filled these demanding jobs and worked hard for little pay. The Veenstra family were Displaced People from Holland.

These Displaced People encountered prejudice as they tried to adjust to their new country. Their children, too, had to deal with discrimination.

lived in windmills and posed in baggy pants for smiling tourists. He'd never even owned a pair of wooden shoes. And what was so special about tulips. Weren't they primarily for export to other countries such as Canada?

Canadians still puzzled him, particularly in terms of their humour, which he found corny and rather mean. They got so much fun out of teasing people and playing practical jokes. In the farming community where his father had inexplicably placed them, they were always being gawked at, their appearance a source of never-ending snickers and asides. And at school, life was a constant war: they were always stealing his lunch or his books and they got a special pleasure out of pushing and tripping him, someone forcing a finger into his stomach pushing him backwards while someone else crouched behind, with the inevitable dust-bath a result. Sister St. Thomas had never seemed to be present then. The time he had hurled a handful of stones in self-defence, she had seen all, of course, and the strap had shamed him further. The more furiously he fought them off, the more he tried to defend himself, the more they laughed.

"His new home, out in the country, exposed to such extremes of heat and cold, made the other world, the place of his birth seem so much more appealing."

And always in the lead was Wilfred. Bigger than most boys, blessed with brawn and surprisingly and irritatingly also with brains, he swaggered around the playground, his shock of straight black hair and dark brown eyes setting him apart from all the others. He was the cock of the walk, calling the nuns crude words that John had never heard before. Wilfred was as normal as the Scotch thistles in the playground; it seemed to John that Wilfred was the key to his acceptance. John had tried to befriend Wilfred; he worked hard, perhaps too hard, even sharing the gifts of chewing gum and candies the French-Canadian boy had given him, but all to no avail. Wilfred was lord and German, as they called him, was simply "that damned Dutchman," the alliteration even conspiring against him.

And yet, despite all this, there was the kindness of the older people, their gentle prying to know all about them, their generosity and sharing. When they had arrived there were boxes of second-hand clothes and offers of used furniture; at Christmas there was food and boxes of games and puzzles. What difference did it make if there were a few pieces missing? "It's the thought that counts," his father intoned. And maybe he was right. Certainly Mr. Middleton, the neighbour who had taught them their first few words of English as he had rebuilt parts of the house they were renting; which still smelled of the apples that had been stored there the previous winter, was a man who sincerely and liberally had taken on sponsoring their welfare. There were also those warm crinkle-eyed ladies, the ones who had helped out with the church-basement Thanksgiving dinner, the school Halloween party, and the Christmas pageant, the same kind matrons who sang with gusto those strange songs of allegiance to a foreign king and called themselves Imperial Daughters of the Empire, their voices choked with emotion by "maple leaves forever."

"She had learned to do without running water and electricity, forgotten the luxuries of bathrooms and got used to the smelly outhouses where you sometimes had to use paper torn from old Eaton's catalogues."

He struggled with that contrast and with the others. His new home, out in the country, exposed to such extremes of heat and cold, made the other world, the place of his birth seem so much more appealing. The city where he had been born seemed so cosmopolitan, so exciting, perhaps somewhat cold, yes, and very impersonal, but somehow safe; this new place was claustrophobic and cloying, both kind and cruel, assaulting him and making him feel visible and vulnerable.

His mother knew his fears, saw his embarrassment and confusion. She too shuddered at the way his name was being mocked, not purposely she understood but nevertheless sullied in some way. She knew it was too much to expect the average Canadian to make the unusual guttural sound for "g," the sound inelegant but even a gentler "g" would be acceptable. "Ggggermen" could become "German." Why should they pronounce it as "German" as if it were that shameful nationality, misspelling the name into the bargain. German Jan Veenstra was to her beautiful and meaningful, a name with a long lineage. She knew her son's pride, which was like hers, and therefore, took more time with him encouraging him to relax. She counselled him: "Learn to adapt. Learn what's expected and do what's necessary to be the best. It's a good country," she had added, bravely forgetting the nausea and the horror of the transatlantic crossing and the months of tears with which she had tackled the shack called home on the dusty sideroad. She had learned to do without running water and electricity, forgotten the luxuries of bathrooms and got used to the smelly outhouses where you sometimes had to use paper torn from old Eaton's catalogues. She had learned to adjust. "Things will get better," she had said with hope and determination. "Learn the language, work hard, be successful in school, and you won't be stuck here forever." And she had put into practice what she preached. She went into town and worked as a cleaning lady, turning coffee and tea breaks into spontaneous language classes. His mother wasn't too proud; she may have been considered needy but her greatest need, she felt, was to learn to speak the language.

"He memorized list after list of words, observed some patterns, and worked out schemes for all the exceptions."

Thus it was she who had supported him when the spelling bee was first announced. That was the day he had come home humiliated because he hadn't been able to hit the ball with that silly round bat and Wilfred had blackened his eye when he, with tears of anger, had taken exception to the aside, "What can you expect from a D.P.?" She had first washed his face, applied something cold to the swollen eye, and then listened as he explained what was meant by a spelling bee. She had already learned about quilting and preserving bees, knew about barn-raising bees, but this was a new one. His father only cast him a quizzical eye and more so when the hours of preparation became a happy routine. He memorized list after list of words, observed some patterns, and worked out schemes for all the exceptions. His father's repeated hints that Mr. Middleton was looking for young boys to pick strawberries went unnoticed and finally to get his father's approval his mother came to his defence.

He had a knack for spelling, first winning the grade six competition and then making the school finals. His only rival had been Wilfred and the moment had been confusing. He wondered what would happen to his conflict with Wilfred? But then the competition had begun, the battle had been fierce, and John had won.

“But then the competition had begun, the battle had been fierce, and John had won.”

What a moment that had been. Even the fact that Mr. Worsnop, the grade eight teacher, had been sympathetic to Wilfred and comforted him on the way out to the baseball diamond couldn't take away John's pleasure. "Spelling bees are cruel and unusual punishment," he had heard the teacher say. "They don't prove anything. It's a dubious victory," whatever that meant.

But then there had been the trip to London, his mother beside him on the bus and the excitement of being away from dust, back in the warm womb-like comfort of a city. There he found safety and anonymity; the crowds of smartly dressed people were too busy to gawk, look him up and down and spit sideways in judgement. The restaurant afterwards dwarfed the actual competition, which was really not a glorious occasion. He had done well in the written part of the spelling competition but failed to spell the first word correctly during the oral part. He had added an extra "s" to "disappointing." But then there had been the reporter who had wanted to talk to him and the journalist's interest and delight had made John forget the sudden defeat.

They had returned from the city and been followed with the newspaper report. He was now no longer German Jan Veenstra but John Veenstra and armed with pride he entered the playground. Rather arrogantly he sought acceptance but Wilfred simply ignored him. No taunts, no fights, no insults. He might just as well not have been there. He could feel the glory of his victory fade away. And later, much later that night, as he passed the carefully cut newspaper article in the red photo album with the fine white parchment dividers, he felt curiously empty. Was it really as Mr. Worsnop had stated, "a dubious victory," that's true, but then, snatching at straws, he reminded himself that he had got a new name out of it and perhaps if he couldn't find acceptance as German Jan, he might find himself less visible as John. ◆

JAN OR JOHN

1. Discuss with a partner your reactions to "Spelling."

- How do you feel about the ways in which the boy was treated?
- Does this story remind you of any experiences that you or people you know have had? Describe one of them.
- If you had been in the class with "John" when you were younger how would you have acted toward him?
- If you had been on the receiving end of the taunting and teasing how would you have reacted?
- What advice would you have given to "John" if you had known him?
- What are other situations in which prejudice occurs? What do some of these situations have in common? In what ways are they different?
- What do you think can be done about prejudice that arises in school, the community, or the work place?

2. After your discussion, write a response in one or two paragraphs to one of the following:

- If John were in your class at school, what advice would you give him about how to survive in Canada?
- Describe what you would have done if a bully such as the one described in the story picked on you.
- Write about a similar incident that you have experienced or heard about.

Figure 11-6 Inglis Sheldon-Williams. *The Landmark.*

NATIVE CANADIANS

A Native Canadian is a person of North American Indian or Inuit ancestry. These people have lived in Canada for a long time. They met the boats that brought the first Europeans to Canada. There are many different groups of Native Canadians, all the way from the Inuit in the North to the Haida on the West Coast and the Micmac on the East Coast. In all, the Native Canadians speak some three hundred different languages, some of which are as different from each other as English is from Chinese.

Wayne Keon, whose mother is Algonquin and father Iroquois and Irish, wrote the following poem as a tribute to the rich variety of people of Indian and Inuit ancestry:

HERITAGE

Wayne Keon

AlgonkinAssiniboineAthapaskanB
eaverBellaCoolaBeothukBlackfoo
tCarrierCaughnawayaCayuyaChilk
atChilcotinChipewyanCreeCrowDe
lewareDogribEskimoFlatheadFoxG
rosVentreHaidaHareHuronIllinoi
sIroquoisKickapooKitwancoolKoo
tneyKoskimoKutchinKwakiutLake
LilloetMaleciteMalouinMenomine
eMetisMiamiMicmacMississaugaMo
hawkMohicanMontagnaisMuskoeeN
ahaniNaskapiNeutralNicolaNipis
singNootkaOjibwayOkanaganOneid
aOnondagaOttawaPequotPetunPieg
anPotawatomieSalishSarceeSaukS
aulteauxSekaniSenecaShawneeSho
shoniShuswapSiouxSlaveStoneySu
squehannaTagishTalhltanThompson
TlinkitTsetsautTsimshianTuscar
oraWinnebagoWyandotYellowknife

Life in Canada for these Native peoples has not been easy. The European explorers and settlers disrupted their culture and way of life. Their story is the struggle to find a place in a foreign culture that was imposed on their native land. Unlike the other ethnic groups in Canada who can point to a homeland where their language and original culture continue, Native Canadians must work at maintaining their cultural identity within Canada.

The following poem express the frustrations that the Native Canadians have felt in finding themselves in the ethnic and cultural mosaic that is Canada. It was written by Mireille Sioui, a Huron from Quebec, who writes poetry in both English and French.

MIXED BLOOD

Mireille Sioui

There have been wars, bitter, brief encounters
Yet also times of peace and planting
Time for tender friendships – intimate.
When Indian blood mixed with the flood of the white river
I am born of all, of peace and war
Of hate and love. I am union
Of the red sun setting and the white moon rising.
Indian by name, spirit and heart
And Canadian, descendent of nations
Of this warm blood, proud I walk through the land
Indian in soul, clothed in brightness.

It hasn't been easy for the Native Canadians to "walk through the land/Indian in soul, clothed in brightness." They have had to locate their own identity within their ethnic heritage, and to find out how they fit in with the culture of the dominant ethnic groups in Canada. John Amagoalik, an Inuit writer, talks about this concern for the survival of his culture. Although he writes about the Inuit in the North West Territories, he speaks for all Native people in Canada.

WE MUST HAVE DREAMS

John Amagoalik

Will the Inuit disappear from the face of this earth? Will we become extinct? Will our culture, our language and our attachment to nature be remembered only in history books? These questions bring a great sadness to me. To realize that we Inuit are in the same category as the great whales, the bold eagle, the husky and the polar bear brings me great fear. To realize that our people can be classified as an endangered species is very disturbing. Is our culture like a wounded polar bear that has gone out to sea to die alone? What can be done? There does not seem to be one single answer to these questions.

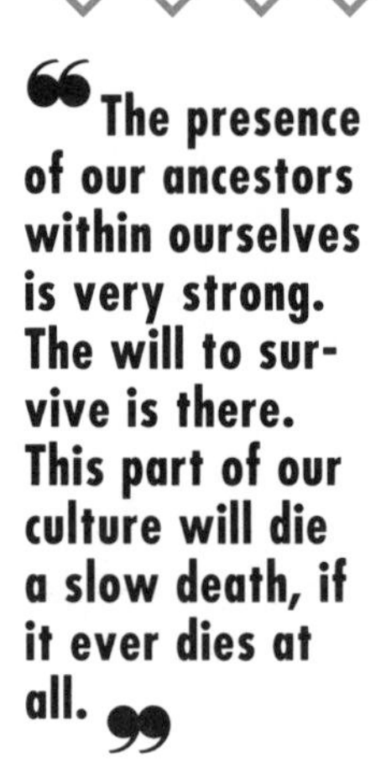

It may be true that the physical part of our culture has been eroded to the point where it can never return to its full potential. But the non-physical part of our culture – our attitude towards life, our respect for nature, our realization that others will follow who deserve the respect and concern of present generations – are deeply entrenched within ourselves. The presence of our ancestors within ourselves is very strong. The will to survive is there. This part of our culture will die a slow death, if it ever dies at all. If we are to survive as a race, we must have the understanding and patience of the dominant cultures of this country. We do not need the pity, the welfare, the paternalism and the colonialism which has been heaped upon us over the years.

We must teach our children their mother tongue. We must teach them what they are and where they came from. We must teach them the values which have guided our society over the thousands of years. We must teach them our philosophies which go back beyond the memory of man. We must keep the embers burning from the fires which used to burn in our villages so that we may gather around them again. It is this spirit we must keep alive so that it may guide us again in a new life in a changed world. Who is responsible for keeping this spirit alive? It is clearly the older people. We must have the leadership which

they once provided us. They must realize this responsibility and accept it. If the older people will remember, the young must listen.

In a world which becomes more complicated with each passing year, we must rely on the simple, gentle ways of our people to guide us. In a world so full of greed, we must share. We must remember that, of all the things in this world, nothing belongs to us. Of what we take, we must share.

A lot of people tell me that we must forget the past, and instead, look to the future. To me it would be a mistake to completely ignore the past because the past determines the present and the present determines what will be in the future. Sometimes it is necessary to look to the past to make decisions about the future. When I talk about the future and try to describe what I would like for my children, some people sometimes say to me that I am only dreaming. What is wrong with dreaming? Sometimes dreams come true, if only one is determined enough. What kind of world would we live in if people did not have dreams? If people did not strive for what they believe in? We must have dreams. We must have ideals. We must fight for things we believe in. We must believe in ourselves. But there are also realities we must face. We can only attempt to make the best of any given situation or circumstances. If we are not successful, we must not give up hope. We must tell ourselves that we can only try a little harder the next time.

“We must have dreams. We must have ideals. We must fight for things we believe in. We must believe in ourselves.”

Over the past few years, in my visits to Inuit communities, I have had many private conversations about what is happening to our people and what the future holds for us. I have become more and more concerned about the angry words which some of our people are starting to use. I cannot really blame them for their feelings. Their feelings towards the white man are easy to understand. It is very easy to blame the white man for the predicament we find ourselves in today. But anger and hate are not the answers. We need the patience and understanding of our white brothers. If we are to expect that from them, we must offer the same in return. The Inuit, by nature, are not violent people. This is one of our virtues which we must not lose.

Figure 11-7 An Inuit scene by Alootook Ipellie

It disturbs me a great deal to hear about native organizations squabbling with other native organizations. If we are to achieve anything, we must not fight among ourselves. We can agree to disagree, but we must sort out our problems together. We must be of one mind and of one voice. This is not always possible among human beings. But we must not let petty disagreements divide us.

The Inuit were once strong, independent and proud people. That is why we have survived. That strength, that independence, and that pride must surface again. We must prove to Canada that the original citizens of this country will not lie down and play dead. After all, the Inuit have been described by the United Nations as a people who refuse to disappear. ◆

THE WOUNDED POLAR BEAR

1. What do the following sentences from "We Must Have Dreams" mean?

a) "It may be true that the physical part of our culture has been eroded to the point where it can never return to its full potential."

b) "If we are to survive as a race, we must have the understanding and patience of the dominant cultures of this country. We do not need the pity, the welfare, the paternalism and the colonialism which has been heaped upon us over the years."

c) "We must keep the embers burning from the fires which used to burn in our villages so that we may gather around them again."

2. John Amagoalik writes: "What kind of world would we live in if people did not have dreams?" What is his answer to this question?

3. Examine the drawing of an Inuit scene by Alootook Ipellie in Figure 11-7. What message does Ipellie give to his viewers?

4. John Amagoalik is concerned about the Inuit people and writes about their situation. In what ways do Amagoalik's ideas describe your life and your situation as a member of an ethnic group living in Canada?

END THOUGHTS

In this unit you have read, written, and talked about Canadian ethnic origins. Now that you have considered some of the experiences of Native and new Canadians, take a few moments to summarize your thoughts and reactions. What can we do to help immigrant people adjust to their new land? How can we eliminate the prejudice that some newcomers experience? And how can we overcome the prejudice that some Native peoples experience? What can you as a student do to help?

ACTIVITY 8

EXTENSION IDEAS

1. Invite some of the people interviewed by members of the class to tell their stories to the class as a whole. Encourage them to bring pictures or objects of interest with them.
2. Prepare a class publication of the most interesting excerpts from the various projects and share them with family, friends, and members of your community.
3. View a production of a play or film based on oral history, for example *Ten Lost Years, The Farm Show,* or *Billy Bishop Goes to War*. Prepare your own stage or video show based on the material collected by the class.
4. Pick a theme of particular interest to your community such as farming, fishing, industry, family, or local history and use the techniques that you have learned in this chapter to prepare another project.
5. Survey the members of your community to discover some aspects of local culture that are in danger of becoming lost. These might include stories about the old days, recipes, superstitions, historical memories, lost arts, folk arts, and specialized knowledge. Collect as many of these as you can and use them to prepare a class booklet or a show based on them.
6. View the movie *Little Big Man*. Talk to your class about this movie. What does this movie say about the life of Native Canadians? How does it encourage Native Canadians, and others, to have a dream?

UNIT 12

★ ★ ★ ★ ★ ★ ★

BETWEEN YOU AND ME

- ★ BUILDING TRUST
- ★ TABLEAUX
- ★ DIALOGUE
- ★ IMPROVISATIONS
- ★ WRITTEN DIALOGUE

Figure 12-1 Trusting involves taking some emotional risks – but it's worth it.

Love consists in this,
that two solitudes protect,
and touch, and greet each other.
– *Rainer Maria Rilke*

INTRODUCTION

Each person is different. Because of this difference, you may find that understanding another person can sometimes be a challenge. One of the places you can step into another person's shoes, however briefly, is in drama class. Through drama you can begin to break down the barriers between you and another person. In this unit you will be introduced to some of the techniques of drama that will enable you to explore the movements, mannerisms, emotions, actions, behaviours, and expressions of another person. The emphasis will be on developing confidence through working in pairs. When you feel confident in working with a partner, try some drama activities in larger groups.

BUILDING TRUST

Getting to know someone new involves a willingness to take risks. If you are going to offer your friendship to someone or to work with another person, you need to be able to trust that person. Since actors work closely with each other, they especially need to have confidence in each other. Actors use 'trust activities' to achieve a high level of confidence in others. You will need to work closely with a partner to complete the activities in this unit. The following trust exercises will help you gain confidence in your partner.

IN STRICT CONFIDENCE

1. Tell your partner your life's story in two minutes. Then listen while your partner tells you the story of his or her life.
2. Interview each other. Ask each other five to ten questions about topics such as growing up, favourite places, family, likes and dislikes, school, work, and the future.
3. Tell your partner a story. Begin the story and at a signal from the teacher stop, even if you're in the middle of a sentence. Then have your partner continue where you ended. Take turns telling the next part of the story. Each time start where the other finished.
4. Mime a game to music. Pick a game that takes two people to play, such as checkers, tennis, handball, or judo. Listen to music that is sometimes slow and sometimes fast. As the music changes, change the speed of the game. Remember to react to each other's movements.
5. Toss a make-believe balloon back and forth between you and your partner. Move in slow motion.
6. Pretend that your partner is your mirror image. Start moving and have your partner follow your movements at the same time. Once you are together, take turns leading. See if you can take the lead without actually telling each other and still stay together.
7. Blindfold your partner. Take him or her on a tour around the room. Make sure that your partner does not bump into anything. Let him or her feel confident in your leadership; then switch roles.

ACTIVITY 2

ABOUT TRUST

Writing often helps to clarify your thoughts and feelings. Keep a 'learning log' to record your reactions to some of the activities in this unit. As you write in your log and think about what you learned, you will find yourself becoming increasingly aware of how you learn best.

1. After trying some of the trust exercises in Activity 1, take a few minutes to write your reactions to the following questions:

   a) What thoughts went through your mind as you participated in Activity 1?
   b) How did you feel? What made you feel this way?
   c) Did you feel you could trust the person you were working with? Why or why not?
   d) What made you feel confident? What made you feel unsure?
   e) How could your confidence in the other person have been increased?

TABLEAUX

A tableau is a living picture, a moment frozen in time. Like a picture, a tableau captures an action, an event, or an emotion –and holds it. In drama classes, a tableau is used to focus the attention of the actors on expressing an emotion through gesture. An effective tableau has all the elements of a good photograph. The Info-box on page 241 describes what makes a photograph effective.

info-box

ELEMENTS OF AN EFFECTIVE PICTURE

Subject:	the people, things, setting that make up the content of the picture (for example, a picture of a horse and a girl in a field)
Composition:	the way the parts of the content are arranged to create an effect (for example, the horse and girl are in the foreground of the picture, and the field serves as a backdrop and frame)
Levels:	some parts of the content may be low, some high, others in between to create interest and variety (for example, the girl is sitting on the horse's back or standing beside its head)
Focus:	one part of the content is selected for particular interest (for example, the lines in the photograph draw the viewer's attention to the horse's head)
Body Language:	the way a subject assumes a posture or uses a gesture (for example, the girl might be standing close to the horse and stroking its nose)
Facial Expression:	the look on the subject's face conveys a message about her or his thoughts or feelings (for example, the girl might be gazing affectionately at the horse)

Figure 12-2 One picture can be worth a thousand words.

ACTIVITY 3

THE COUPLE

1. 'Read' the photograph in Figure 12-2 using the questions below:

a) Subject: What can you tell about the two people from their appearance? their clothes? What kind of work do they do?
b) Composition: How are the two people and the setting arranged in the picture? What is the effect created by this arrangement? How is this effect created?
c) Levels: Where do you think the camera was located when the picture was taken? How has the photographer's choice of camera eye affected the levels in the picture?
d) Focus: When you look at the picture what or who gets your attention first? Where do your eyes go next?
e) Body language: What does the way the people sit and the position of their arms and legs tell you about them?
f) Facial expressions: Look closely at the faces of the two people. What can you tell about them from their expressions? What are they thinking about?

2. In your learning log, write your response to the picture. Use the preceding questions to focus your response.

You can 'read' a great deal of information from a picture. In the following activity you will use the elements of a picture to create a tableau. When you create a tableau, assume a position that will best convey your message. Then 'freeze' the picture while others look at and discuss your tableau. Use the information in the Info-box outlining the "Elements of an Effective Picture" on page 241 to look at and understand tableaux.

ACTIVITY 4 A LIVING PICTURE

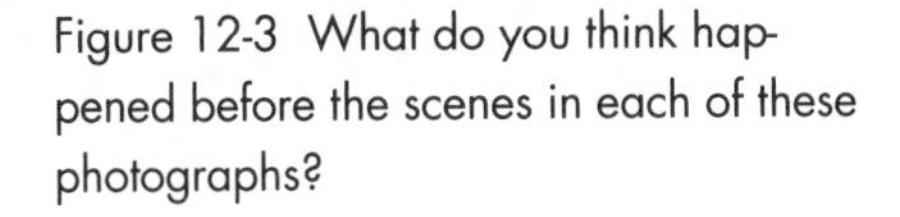

Figure 12-3 What do you think happened before the scenes in each of these photographs?

1. With a partner, pick a picture from Figure 12-3 (p. 243). Make a tableau that re-creates the scene. Then make a tableau that shows an event that preceded the scene in the picture. Create a final tableau that shows an event that occurs after the scene in the picture
2. Present your three tableaux in sequence. Ask your viewers to comment on the composition and message in your tableaux.

DIALOGUE

The following excerpt is from a collection of short stories called *Digging Up the Mountains*, by Neil Bissoondath. "Arrival" is the story of Sheila James, a young woman from Trinidad who immigrates to Canada. In this excerpt, she arrives at the airport, is greeted by members of her family, and is taken to her sister Annie's home. Through the conversation she has with her sister you learn a great deal about Sheila.

ARRIVAL

Neil Bissoondath

There I was, hands hurting like hell from suitcase and boxes and bags and I couldn't find the door handle. My head was still full of cotton wool from the plane and my stomach was bawling its head off for food. I just wanted to turn right round and say, "Take me back. The doc was right. I ain't going to be able to live in a place where doors ain't have no handle." But then a man in a uniform motion me to keep walking, as if he want me to bounce straight into the door. Well, if it have one thing I fraid is policeman, so I start to walk and, Lord, like the Red Sea parting for Moses, the door open by itself.

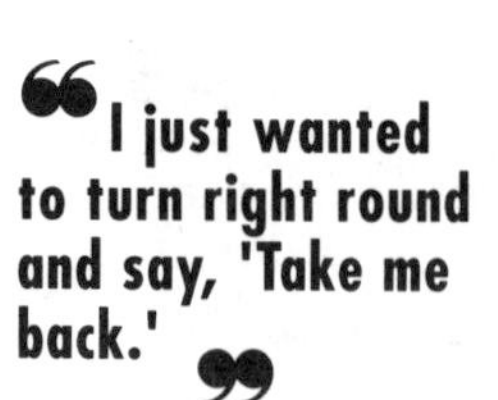

This make me feel good. I feel as if I get back at the customs man who did ask me all kind of nasty questions like, "You have any rum? Whiskey? Plants? Food?" as if I look like one of them smugglers that does ply between Trinidad and Venezuela. I thought, I bet the doors don't open like that for him!

As I walk through the door I start feeling dizzy-dizzy. Everything look cloudy-cloudy, as if the building was just going to fade away or melt. I was so frighten I start to think I dreaming, like it wasn't me walking there at all but somebody else. It was almost like looking at a flim in a cinema.

Then I hear a voice talking to me inside my head. It say, Sheila James, maid, of Mikey Trace, Trinidad, here you is, a big woman, walking in Toronto airport and you frighten. Why?

"They was mostly white. My chest tighten up and I couldn't hardly breathe. I was surrounded by tourists. And not one of them was wearing a straw hat."

I force myself to look around. I see faces, faces, faces. All round me, faces. Some looking at me, some looking past me, and some even looking through me. I start feeling like a flowers vase on a table.

Then all of a sudden the cloudiness disappear and I see all the faces plain-plain. They was mostly white. My chest tighten up and I couldn't hardly breathe. I was surrounded by tourists. And not one of them was wearing a straw hat.

I hear another voice calling me, "Sheila! Sheila!" I look around but didn't see nobody, only all these strange faces. I start feeling small-small, like a douen. Suddenly it jump into my head to run headlong through the crowd but it was as if somebody did nail my foot to the floor: I couldn't move. Again like in a dream. A bad dream.

And then, bam!, like magic, I see all these black faces running toward me, pushing the tourists out of the way, almost fighting with one another to get to me first. I recognize Annie. She shout, "Sheila!" Then I see my brother Sylvester, and others I didn't know. Annie grab on to me and hug me tight-tight. Sylvester take my bags and give them to somebody else, then he start hugging me too. Somebody pat me on the back. I felt safe again. It was almost like being back in Trinidad.

Sylvester and the others drop Annie and me off at her flat in Vaughan Road. Annie was a little vex with Syl because he didn't want to stay and talk but I tell her I was tired and she let him go off to his party.

Annie boil up some water for tea and we sit down in the tiny living room to talk. I notice how old Annie was looking. Her face was heavy, it full-out in two years. And the skin under her eyes was dark-dark as if all her tiredness settle there. Like dust. Maybe it was the light. It always dark in Annie's apartment, even in the day. The windows small-small, and she does keep on only one light at a time. To save on the hydro bill, she say.

She ask me about friends and the neighbours and the pastor. It didn't have much family left in Trinidad to talk about. She ask about the doc. I tell she about his advices. She choops loud-loud and say, "Indian people bad for so, eh, child."

"I notice how old Annie was looking. Her face was heavy, it full-out in two years."

She ask about Georgie, our father's outside-child. I say, "Georgie run into some trouble with the police, girl. He get drunk one evening and beat up a fella and almost kill him."

She say, "That boy bad since he small. So, what they do with him?"

"Nothing. The police charge him and they was going to take him to court. But you know how things does work in Trinidad. Georgie give a police friend some money. Every time they call him up for trial, the sergeant tell the judge, We can't find the file on this case, Me Lud, and finally the judge get fed up and throw the charge out. You know, he even bawl out the poor sergeant."

Annie laugh and shake her head. She say, "Good old Georgie. What he doing now?"

"The usual. Nothing at all. He looking after his papers for coming up here. Next year, probably."

Annie yawn and ask me if I hungry.

I say no, I did aready eat on the plane: my stomach was tight-tight.

"You don't want some cake? I make it just for you."

I say no again, and she remember I did never eat much, even as a baby.

"Anyways," she say quietly, "I really glad you here now, girl. At last. Is about time."

What to say? I shake my head and close my eyes. I try to

smile. "I really don't know, Annie girl. I still ain't too sure I doing the right thing. Everything so strange."

Annie listen to me and her face become serious-serious, like the pastor during sermon. But then she smile and say, "It have a lot of things for you to learn, and it ain't going to be easy, but you doing the best thing by coming here, believe me."

But it was too soon. With every minute passing, I was believing the doc was righter.

"'I really don't know, Annie girl. I still ain't too sure I doing the right thing. Everything so strange.'"

Annie take my hand in hers. I notice how much bigger hers was, and how much rings she was wearing. Just like our mother, a big woman with hands that make you feel like a little child again when she touch you.

She say, "Listen, Sheila," and I hear our mother talking. Sad-sad. From far away. And I think, Is because all of us leave her, she dead long time but now everybody gone, nobody in Trinidad, and who going to clean her grave and light her candles on All Saints? I close my eyes again, so Annie wouldn't see the tears.

She squeeze my hand and say, "Sheila? You awright? You want some more tea?"

She let go my hand, pick up my cup, and went into the kitchen. She say, "But, eh, eh, the tea cold aready. Nothing does stay hot for long in this place." She run the water and put the kettle on the stove. When she come back in the living room I did aready dry my eyes. She hand me a piece of cake on a saucer, sponge cake, I think, and sit down next to me.

She take a bite from her piece. "You know, chile," she say chewing wide-wide, "Tronto is a strange place. It have people here from all over the world – Italian, Greek, Chinee, Japanee, and some people you and me never even hear bout before. You does see a lot of old Italian women, and some not so old, running round in black dress looking like beetle. And Indians walking round with turban on their head. All of them doing as if they still in Rome or Calcutta." She stop and take another bite of the cake. "Well, girl, us West Indians just like them. Everybody here to make money, them and us." She watch me straight in the eye. "Tell me, you ketch what I saying?"

I say, "Yes, Annie," but in truth I was thinking bout the grave and the grass and the candles left over from last year and how lonely our mother was feeling.

"Is true most of them here to stay," she continue, "but don't forget they doesn't have a tropical island to go back to." And she laugh, but in a false way, as if is a thing she say many times before. She look at my cake still lying on the saucer, and then at me, but she didn't say nothing. "Anyways," she say, finishing off her piece, "you see how I still talking after two years. After two years, girl, you understanding what I saying?"

"So I mustn't forget how to talk. Then what? You want me to go dance shango and sing calypso in the street?"

"I don't think you ketch what I saying," Annie say. She put the saucer down on the floor, lean forwards and rub her eyes, thinking hard-hard. "What I mean is... you mustn't think you can become Canajun. You have to become West Indian."

"What you mean, become West Indian?"

"I mean, remain West Indian."

I think, Our mother born, live, dead, and bury in Trinidad. And again I see her grave. I choops, but soft-soft.

Annie say, "But eh, eh, why you choopsing for, girl?"

"How I going to change, eh?" I almost shout. "I's a Trinidadian. I born there and my passport say I from there. So how the hell I going to forget?" I was good and vex.

She shake her head slow-slow and say, "You still ain't ketch on. Look, Canajuns like to go to the islands for two weeks every year to enjoy the sun and the beach and the calypso. But is a different thing if we try to bring the calypso here. Then they doesn't want to hear it. So they always down on we for one reason or another. Us West Indians have to stick together, Sheila. Is the onliest way." Again her face remind me of the pastor in the middle of a hot sermon. You does feel his eyes heavy on you even though he looking at fifty-sixty people.

"'Look, Canajuns like to go to the islands for two weeks every year to enjoy the sun and the beach and the calypso. But is a different thing if we try to bring the calypso here. Then they doesn't want to hear it.'"

My head start to hurt. I say, "But it sound like if all-you fraid for so, like if all-you hiding from the other people here."

I think that make she want to give up. I could be stubborn

"But lemme tell you one thing, and listen to me good. You must stick with your own, don't think that any honky ever going to accept you as one of them."

when I want. Her voice sound tired-tired when she say, "Girl, you have so much to learn. Remember the ad I tell you bout in my letter, the one with the little girl eating the banana pudding?"

"Yes. On the plane I tell a fella what you say and he start laughing. He say is the most ridiculous thing he ever hear."

Annie lean back and groan loud-loud. "Oh Gawd, how it still have fools like that fella walking around?"

"The fella was colored, like us."

"Even worser. One of we own people. And the word is black, not colored."

It almost look to me like if Annie was enjoying what she was saying. And I meet a lot of people like that in my time, people who like to moan and groan and make others feel sorry for them. But I didn't say nothing.

All the time shaking her head, Annie say, "Anyways, look eh, girl, you going to learn in time. But lemme tell you one thing, and listen to me good. You must stick with your own, don't think that any honky ever going to accept you as one of them. If you want friends, they going to have to be West Indian. Syl tell me so when I first come up to Tronto and is true. I doesn't even try to talk to white people now. I ain't have the time or use for racialists."

I was really tired out by that point so I just say, "Okay, Annie, whatever you say. You and Syl must know what you talking bout."

"Yeah, but you going to see for yourself," she say, yawning wide-wide. "But anyways, enough for tonight." She get up, then suddenly she clap her hands and smile. "Oh Gawd, girl, I so happy you here. At last." She laugh. And I laugh, in a way. She pluck off her wig and say, "Come, let we go to bed, you must be tired out."

Before stretching out on the sofa, I finish off my cake. To make Annie happy. ◆

ACTIVITY 5 READING AND RESPONDING TO ARRIVAL

1. After you have read the excerpt, complete the following statements about "Arrival":

a) "As I was reading the story, I thought about ..."
b) "As I read the story, I saw pictures of ..."
c) "The story made me feel ..."
d) "I think Sheila is ..."
e) "I think Annie is ..."
f) "I didn't understand the part about ..."
g) "One thing that bothered me was ..."
h) "This excerpt reminded me of ..."
i) "This is what I think will happen to Sheila ..."

2. Share your written responses to "Arrival" with someone in your class. Talk about the similarities and differences in your responses. How do you explain your different reactions?

3. Use the following questions to think about "Arrival":

a) In what ways are the two sisters similar? How are they different?
b) To what extent do they understand each other?
c) Sheila's thoughts are often different from her words. What is she not telling Annie about what she thinks and how she feels?
d) What might you do in a situation similar to Sheila's?

4. In a small group, create a tableau to express your reactions to this short story. This tableau should show others what your group felt about the story of Sheila James's arrival in Canada as an immigrant.

IMPROVISATIONS

In drama, an improvisation is a short scene or skit that has not been rehearsed but is made up by the actors as they go along. Whereas a tableau is one scene caught in time like a photograph, an improvisation is a continuing reaction like a television program. As they improvise, actors try to think, act, and feel as their characters would. Actors do this by making up the dialogue and action as they act and respond to the situation.

ACTIVITY 6

THE PICTURES SPEAK

Figure 12-4 Try to imagine what the people in each picture might say to each other.

1. Get together with a partner. Pick one of the pictures from Figure 12-4.
2. Briefly discuss what is happening in the picture, what might have happened just before it was taken, and what may happen next.
3. Discuss what you feel is revealed about the people in the picture. What might they say to each other?
4. Re-create the picture in a tableau.
5. From your tableau do several improvisations, and record one of them on audio tape. Save the tape to use in Activity 8.

WRITTEN DIALOGUE

The dialogue between Sheila and Annie in "Arrival" is part of a short story. In a story, the author is able to provide the reader with much more than just the actual words that are spoken. He or she can present the thoughts of the characters and the actions that are occurring around them. The author of a play, on the other hand, is much more limited in the ways in which he or she can convey information. Except for a few stage directions, the author has to rely entirely on the words of the characters.

ACTIVITY 7

FROM STORY TO SCRIPT

1. Change "Arrival" into a dramatic dialogue. The first part has been done for you. As you complete the scene, remember to include any appropriate stage directions such as those in brackets in the following dialogue.

    [Sheila James, a woman from Trinidad, has recently arrived in Canada. She is visiting with her sister, Annie, for the first time. As the scene opens, they are in Annie's apartment.]
    Annie: (pouring tea) Have you hard anything about Georgie, Sheila?
    Sheila: (upset) Georgie run into some trouble with the police ... girls. He get drunk one evening and beat up a fella and almost kill him. (She spills her tea.)

FROM TAPE TO SCRIPT

1. Listen to the tape recording of the improvisation you did with a partner in Activity 6. Transcribe the recording.
2. Revise your transcription, using these suggestions:
    - Add words, phrases, and sentences to make the dialogue clear.
    - Write it as a play with the speakers identified and stage instructions included.
3. Edit your script by checking your spelling, punctuation, usage, and sentence structure.
4. Write or type your final draft.
5. Perform your script by taping it or presenting it to your class.

END THOUGHTS

Getting to know new people means being willing to take a chance. It involves taking time to get to know them, recognizing their uniqueness, and acknowledging them for who they are. Take a few minutes to write your thoughts and feelings about relationships between people by completing one of the following:

- Write a note to someone you know recommending that he or she take a class in drama as a way of developing self-confidence and the ability to work with others.
- Write a note to your future grandchildren giving them advice about how to survive relationships with teachers, parents, and their fellow students when they will be teenagers.
- Explain how a movie, play, or television program that you have seen helped you understand other people better.
- Describe how participating in a sport, a play, or another school activity can help you learn about other people and how to work together with them.

EXTENSION IDEAS

1. Prepare a class show using the dialogues that have been written for this unit.
2. Use the entries in your learning log as the basis for a journal entry in which you explain how drama can be used as an effective preparation for writing.
3. Continue the work begun in this unit on improvisation by trying this activity. Have each person in the class write on a slip of paper an interesting character, job, or role. Include an age for the person (for example, a fifteen-year-old astronaut). Place all the suggestions in a box. Ask students, two at a time, to select one slip of paper each from the box. Take a few minutes to think about your character's situation. In pairs, improvise a scene in which the two characters meet, experience conflict, and work out a solution.

4. Use a selection of interesting pictures from magazines as the basis for a series of group tableaux or improvisations. Write a skit on the basis of the improvisations.
5. Cut out a selection of articles or stories from newspapers. Pick pieces that include several interviews. Turn your selections into dramatic skits.
6. Find some interesting photographs from magazines or your family album. Pick pictures that demonstrate techniques of effective photography. Use the pictures to create a series of tableaux showing scenes from family life.

UNIT 13

★ ★ ★ ★ ★ ★ ★

THE WRITING PROCESS

- PREWRITING
- DRAFTING
- REVISING
- POLISHING YOUR WRITING
- PUBLISHING YOUR WRITING

INTRODUCTION

From the time you started school, you have been writing. Your early drawings with a few words carefully etched underneath, the stories you wrote in grade school, the notes you passed to your friends, the letters you wrote, and the essays in your social studies or science classes – all these have contributed to the way you developed as a writer.

You can improve your writing skills if you learn what happens as a piece of writing develops. In this unit you will write about going out with someone. You might not know at this time what you will say about this topic. Each of the activities in this unit will help you discover what you might say, how you will say it, and your reason for writing it. You will be able to use this process to help you write your assignments in all of your classes – not just in English.

PREWRITING

Before you write you need to spend some time at the prewriting stage collecting and creating ideas, clarifying what you already know, and getting more information about your topic. There are a number of techniques that you can use to help you develop ideas for your topic.

Brainstorming Diagrams: A quick way to develop your ideas is to use a brainstorming diagram. In the centre of a blank piece of paper, write a key word that expresses your main idea. Draw lines from this word and at the end of each line write a key word for any related ideas you think about. Since this is a brainstorming activity, don't judge or reject any ideas. Rather, write down key words and related ideas as quickly as you can. As you work, you will find that one new idea may suggest another. The lines that you draw between ideas will remind you of how they are connected.

Figure 13-1 A brainstorming diagram

Timed Writing: A famous writer once said, "How do I know what I think until I see what I wrote?" You too may not know what you think until you see what ideas surface in your writing. The technique of timed writing is an excellent way to uncover ideas by writing about them.

To do timed writing, set yourself a specific length of time (for example, four minutes). During this time, write everything you can think of about your topic. Don't stop to correct, erase, or change. Just keep writing. If you can't think of anything to write, continue writing your key word until a new idea occurs to you.

When you have finished your first timed writing, read it over. Underline the most interesting phrase or idea. Then try a second four-minute timed writing, starting with the interesting idea or phrase as the first key word or words.

Gathering Information: Another kind of prewriting activity is to gather information. Try reading stories and articles, or try doing research in a library on your topic. Also try conducting interviews or surveys. Films and videos are another source of information about your topic.

PREWRITING TECHNIQUES

Choose one or more of the prewriting techniques to develop your ideas on the theme of going out with someone.

1. Create a brainstorming diagram. Put the words "going out" in the centre of a blank piece of paper. Collect your ideas, as you think of them, on this diagram. You may find it helpful to complete more than one brainstorming diagram. To do this, look at your first diagram, choose the most important idea there, and use that idea as the centre of a new diagram.
2. Do two or three timed writing experiments on the theme of going out with someone.
3. Choose two of the following ways to collect information about your topic:
   - Read books, articles, magazines, or other print sources.
   - Conduct an interview with one or two people, or poll several people for a survey.
   - Look at non-print sources such as film or video.

DRAFTING

When you begin your first draft, don't look for the perfect word or phrase or consider the mechanics of writing – you'll be working on these later. Instead, what you need are words and ideas. One author has called words and ideas the "rough lumber" of writing. If you plan to build a piece of writing, you need to have a pile of lumber to work with.

Audience, Purpose, Form: As you write, you need to make some decisions about your writing. Sometimes you make these decisions yourself. At other times, they are part of the writing assignment that you have been given.

Your writing will be read by someone else. Your audience is the person who reads your writing. Try writing in a way that is appropriate for your audience. Here are some possible audiences:

- yourself
- an adult
- a teenager
- a child
- a teacher
- a friend

Your writing will also have a purpose. If you have a clear purpose, you will be more direct and forceful in your writing. Here are some possible reasons for writing:

- to inform
- to persuade
- to entertain or amuse
- to give directions

Finally, you need to decide what form your writing will take. Often you don't make this decision yourself because you are assigned a particular form. But when you do choose, try to find a form that will connect with your audience and convey your purpose. Here are some possible forms:

- a newspaper article
- a fictional diary
- a dialogue
- a paragraph
- a short story
- a speech
- a pamphlet
- a poem
- an essay
- a journal
- a report

SORTING IT OUT

1. In your notebook, number a chart from one to fifteen down the side of the page. Then create three columns and label them Audience, Form, and Purpose.
2. Fill in the chart with different combinations of audiences, forms, and purposes.

Figure 13-2 Choose a form of writing appropriate for your audience and purpose.

WRITING CHART

	AUDIENCE	FORM	PURPOSE
1.	My mother	a letter	to explain why going out is important to me
2.	Teens	magazine article	to point out teen problems with going out
3.	Teens	short story	to show the kinds of pressures on teens who aren't going out

3. Review your chart of audiences, forms, and purposes.
   a) Choose an item from each column that you wish to use in your writing.
   b) Write these items at the top of a new sheet of paper.
4. With this specific audience, form, and purpose in mind, write a first draft on the theme of going out with someone. As you write, try to change and develop the material from your prewriting stage so that it connects with your choice of audience, form, and purpose. Be sure to double space this draft.

REVISING

Revising is extremely important in the improvement of your writing. When you revise, re-examine the ideas in your previous drafts and the way you have presented those ideas. Use the *SOAR* principle to help you revise your writing.

Substitute: What other words or phrases could you use to explain your ideas more accurately?

Omit: What words and phrases are unnecessary?

Add: What other information could you include to make your ideas clearer or more informative?

Rearrange: What happens if you rearrange your information or ideas? Which order is most effective?

REVISING YOUR WORK

1. Use a pencil to revise your first draft. Use the *SOAR* principle as a guide to make your changes.
2. Give your revised draft to a writing partner. Ask her or him to apply the *SOAR* principle to make suggestions for revisions and additions. Ask your writing partner to comment on the following:
   - the information you are presenting
   - whether you have written for your audience and used your form correctly

POLISHING YOUR WRITING

The final stage in developing your writing is to polish it. In this stage, you are concerned with accuracy. Use a dictionary, a thesaurus, and a book on language usage to check your work for the following:

- spelling
- word choice
- capitalization
- punctuation

An important part of the polishing process is the preparation of a publication copy of your writing. Readers are always influenced by how a piece of writing looks. Keep your audience, purpose, and form in mind as you make decisions about the physical layout of your writing. Most handwriting looks best single spaced and written on one side of the page. Always strive for your neatest handwriting, typing, or word processing. You want your reader to think about your words and ideas, not how difficult your work is to read because of the errors in it.

Having prepared your publication copy, you're ready for a final proofreading to catch all of the copying errors. A useful proofreader's trick is to read backward from the end of the piece one sentence at a time, stopping at the end of each sentence to check capitalization, punctuation, and spelling.

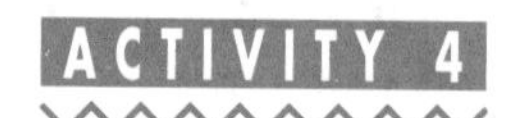

POLISHING BY EDITING

1. Re-read your draft, checking carefully for errors in spelling, punctuation, word choice, and capitalization. Make your changes directly on your second draft.
2. Give your draft to a writing partner for editing.

POLISHING THE PUBLICATION COPY

1. Prepare a publication copy of your writing, using your best handwriting and spacing.
2. Decide whether your writing needs a title and a cover page.

PROOFREADING THE PUBLICATION COPY

1. Slowly proofread your publication copy one sentence at a time from the end to the beginning. Then read your writing one final time from beginning to end.
2. Have your writing partner also carry out a final proofreading of your publication copy.

PUBLISHING YOUR WRITING

The purpose for most writing is to celebrate and publish it. If you are writing with a clear audience and purpose in mind, publication is easy.

Most often, you write to complete a class assignment. Your teacher, or some other marker, becomes your audience. But there are other audiences for your writing, too.

Send your work to a friend, a senior in a special care home, or even a pen pal in Antarctica. Or collect your work from class assignments and compile a book to leave in your school library. One grade seven class from Regina, Saskatchewan, once inserted their paragraphs into a helium balloon, and one student received a reply from Synder, Texas. School newspapers and local newspapers are also places were your writing can be published and celebrated.

There are some unusual things that you can do to share your writing with others. You might, for example, set your writing to music and perform it for someone. You could insert your writing in a collage and display it. Or you could convert your writing into a script and read it over your school's public address system.

PUBLISHING AND CELEBRATING

1. Now that you have finished and polished your writing, publish it using one of the following suggestions:
   - Collect the pieces written in your class and publish them in a class anthology for your school library.
   - Put on a readers theatre by having several class members read dramatic excerpts from their short stories or letters.
   - If you wrote a letter, send it and see if you get a response.

- Make a bulletin-board collage using pieces written by students in your class, pictures from magazines, and illustrations by students in your class.
- Share your writing with members of other groups in your class.
- Present your writing orally to your class. Tell them what you were trying to do with the audience and purpose in the piece and then read a section from your writing that will show how you have handled these issues.
- Send your work to a trusted reader outside the class. Ask this person to read your writing and then to write a letter back to you in which he or she comments on the ideas you have presented.
- In a small group, read a number of pieces of writing on going out with someone and then develop a list of do's and don'ts for going out. Publish your list on chart paper and hang it in your classroom.

END THOUGHTS

If you think about the writing process whenever you write, you will improve your writing skills. The suggestions in this unit will help you with any kind of writing you may want to do. But remember that the writing process is a guide only, not a lock-step method that you must follow in an exact way. Good writers may be in the middle of drafting a piece and then stop to revise or they may run out of ideas and go back to the prewriting stage to gather more information. Different kinds of writing may demand a switching of stages. Try to develop your own writing process by finding the most comfortable way for you to write.

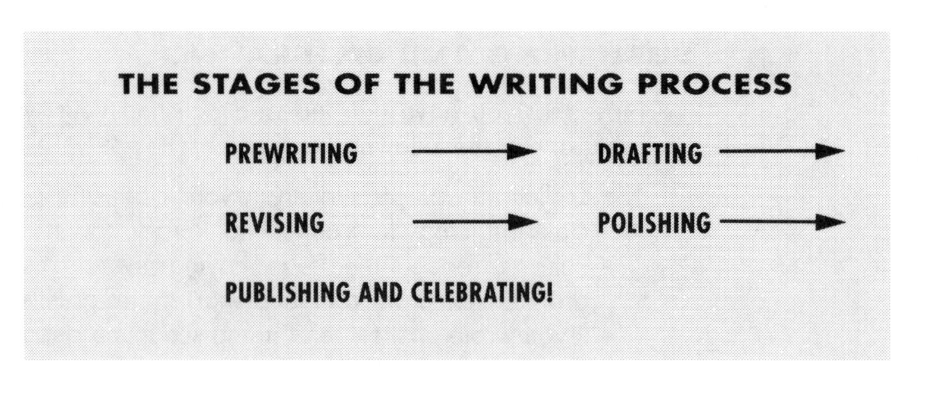

Figure 13-3 Use these stages of the writing process as guidelines to help you develop your own writing process. Remember, each person develops his or her own writing process.

UNIT 14

★ ★ ★ ★ ★ ★ ★

GROUP WORK

- BRAINSTORMING
- GROUP DISCUSSION
- PARTICIPATION

A RESOURCE UNIT

INTRODUCTION

Whether it's in the cafeteria, at home in your living room, or with friends in the classroom, small-group talk is a natural activity. Through talk, you learn new information, sort out how to think and feel about issues, and identify the information and ideas you already have. Although talking in groups is very natural, you can make it even more effective. This resource unit will help you think about small-group skills such as brainstorming, group discussion, and participation.

BRAINSTORMING

The technique of brainstorming allows you to work effectively in a small group. Brainstorming is a means of generating as many ideas as possible on a topic before making a decision. At this stage, no ideas should be judged or discarded. Often the most unusual ideas can help you to solve problems in a creative way. When brainstorming, have one person record the group's ideas. Once your group has listed as many ideas as possible, or has used up its allotted time for brainstorming, you can begin to assess the ideas in front of you.

GETTING STARTED

What will life be like in the twenty-first century? In a group of four or five, use the brainstorming technique to answer this question.

1. Brainstorm to produce a list of at least ten answers to the question.
   a) Have every member of your group contribute to the discussion.
   b) Ask one member of your group to record the ideas as they are suggested. Try to generate as many ideas as possible.
2. Brainstorm to produce a list of at least ten answers to this question: What should we do to prepare for life in the twenty-first century?
   a) Ask each member of the group to contribute an idea, one person at a time.
   b) Again, appoint a recorder to list the ideas.
   c) Then allow any member to add to the list.

3. List your final ideas for the first question on chart paper and report them to your class. Working as a group compare your lists with those produced by other groups. Add to your list any good ideas from the lists of the other groups.
4. Repeat question 3 to find possible solutions to the question of how we should prepare for life in the twenty-first century.
5. On your own, write a journal entry entitled "Me and the Twenty-First Century!"
6. Write a journal entry in which you comment on the brainstorming technique you used in this activity. Use these questions to guide your thinking:
   a) What role did you play in the group discussion?
   b) What role did the other members of your group play in the discussion?
   c) What is the purpose of this brainstorming technique? Is it more valuable as a way to solve problems than people working alone?
7. Share your journal response to question 6 with your group members to compare thoughts on the value of brainstorming.

GROUP DISCUSSION

Group discussion helps you to brainstorm ideas. Group discussion also helps you to clarify your opinions by saying them aloud and by hearing how others state their ideas and react to yours. This next activity will help you to think about group discussion and to understand how people participate in groups. Before you begin Activity 2, appoint one member of your group to act as group observer. *Have the observer read the instructions on page 269*. When the group observer has read the instructions, your group can begin this activity.

"I THINK!"

Many teenagers wish that adults would treat them as mature individuals and give them more responsibility.

1. In your group, talk about the extent to which you *are* treated as adults, and to what extent you *should be* treated as adults. Spend about fifteen minutes on this topic. As you work:
   - ignore the group observer
   - join in the discussion – don't take notes
   - try to keep the group on topic
   - help the group out with a new idea if it seems to be getting bogged down
2. After your group has completed its discussion, look at the instructions for the group observer on page 269 to see the role he or she was playing. Then ask the observer to show you the diagram she or he created. As a group, discuss what you think this diagram reveals about the way each member participated in the group. The observer's diagram can show information such as:
   - how much each person participated
   - who talked with the whole group and who held conversations with individual members of the group
   - how certain comments contributed to the discussion
   - who dominated the group and who participated little
3. Based on this diagram, make one positive suggestion to each group member about the way he or she participated in the group discussion.
4. Think back to the discussion your group had about the way teenagers are treated and should be treated. In your journal, record how you feel about this topic. Be sure to include a number of points raised in the group discussion to support your opinion. Save this record for use in a later activity.
5. In your journal, record what you learned about small-group discussion from this activity.

Instructions for Group Observer (Activity 2): Don't show these instructions or your work to the other group members until they have finished their discussion.

1. On a piece of paper, write the names of the members of your group in a large circle on your page. List the names in the order that the group members are sitting.
2. Every time a group member speaks draw an arrow to indicate the target for his or her speech.
   - If the person speaks to the whole group, draw the arrow to the centre of the circle.
   - If the person speaks directly to another individual, draw the arrow to the person addressed.
   - If the person speaks to a member of another group or makes a comment that is off topic, draw the arrow away from the circle.

Your finished diagram might look something like this:

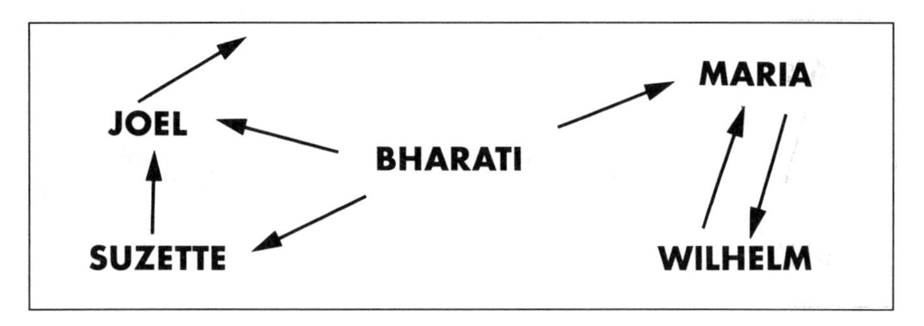

Figure 14-1 An action diagram

PARTICIPATION

An effective group member tries to make certain that her or his contribution is aimed at the whole group and not just at one or two other group members. The diagram in Activity 2 showed how much you participated in the group discussion and to whom you spoke. It doesn't show how constructive your participation was. Did you contribute new ideas to the group? Did you clarify ideas that were confusing? Did you help to keep the discussion going? Did you help to make other members of the group feel comfortable? Did you take on a leadership role in the group?

ACTIVITY 3

ROLES

Appoint a new group observer and have her or him look at page 271 for instructions for this activity. The rest of the group should not look at the group observer's directions. As well, try to ignore the observer during your group discussion.

1. When your group observer has finished preparing for this activity, meet as a group to suggest ten pieces of advice to parents about how their teenage children should be treated. As a group, rank your advice from the most important to the least important. Have everyone in the group record the information that is developed in your group discussion. To help you begin, read your journal entry from Activity 2.
2. After your group has completed question 1, read the instructions to the group observer on page 271 and ask the observer to show you the chart he or she developed. Ask the observer to explain why each decision was made.
3. As a group talk about what individual members can do to make others feel comfortable in the group, to take on a leadership role, or to sort out confusing ideas.
4. In your journal, reflect on what you learned from this discussion about participating in groups. Think, too, about a specific aspect of working in small groups that you might work on to improve your participation.

info-box

GROUP WORK

Working well in groups means suggesting ideas and also taking on roles to help:

- give leadership
- sort out ideas
- make the group comfortable

Instructions for Group Observer (Activity 3):

1. Draw a chart on a piece of paper. Down the side of the page put the names of your group members. Across the top put these column headings: "Helps group members feel comfortable," "Sorts out confusing information," "Takes on leadership role."
2. Position yourself so that you can hear the group but they can not see your chart. Each time one of the group members says something that falls into one of the three categories on your chart, put a check mark in the correct space. (Not all the comments will fall in one of these categories. Many comments will be idea or information giving. Ignore these because they are not directly related to the process of group interaction.)

END THOUGHTS

As you work in groups, remember these key elements for effective group work:

- Use brainstorming as a way of finding new ideas.
- Think about the importance of positive participation in groups.
- Think about the roles you can take on in group work.

UNIT 15

INDEPENDENT STUDY

A RESOURCE UNIT

- POSSIBILITIES
- CHOOSING A TOPIC
- RESEARCHING
- MAKING NOTES
- ORGANIZING THE FINDINGS
- REPORTING
- A SCRAPBOOK
- AN ANTHOLOGY

INTRODUCTION

An independent study project allows you to apply your many language and learning skills as you gain the time to discover interesting aspects about your topic. As well, you become much more involved in your work because you choose your own area of study and design the approach you take. When you do an independent study project, try to demonstrate your ability to work on your own.

In this unit you will develop your independent learning skills by learning how to find a topic of interest, how to develop a plan of action and carry it through to the final stage, and how to create a final report on your findings. You will also gain confidence in your ability as a learner as you see the results of your own decisions and hard mental work.

POSSIBILITIES

There are three characteristics of an independent study project:

- you have a choice of goals
- you select the methods to achieve the goals
- you choose the way to report your findings

There are also various kinds of activities that you can engage in for your study project. For example, you can complete:

- a research project for which you choose a topic, do research, make notes, organize the findings, and do a final report
- a scrapbook for which you collect material on a topic, including commentaries and conclusions
- an anthology for which you read a variety of poetry, songs, stories, or articles to make a collection on a particular topic and add commentary and conclusions

The following sections will outline the independent study process. Most of the ideas in the next sections apply to writing a report, but they may also be used to create a scrapbook or an anthology.

The following Info-box contains an outline of the stages of a research project. These stages can also be applied to other independent study activities such as a scrapbook or an anthology.

info-box

AN INDEPENDENT STUDY PROJECT

The research process consists of:

1. choosing a topic
2. researching
3. making notes
4. organizing your findings
5. reporting your findings

CHOOSING A TOPIC

The first step in the research process is choosing a topic. Try to select a topic that is large enough to allow for flexibility in your treatment of it. If you find that the topic you've chosen is so wide that you don't know where to start researching it, don't worry. At this stage it's more important to choose a subject you are personally interested in. Ideally, it will be related to the themes of your English course. You can narrow – or broaden – your research later.

Where to Look for Ideas: Look at the table of contents for this book. It is full of ideas. Maybe the units that you have completed will suggest ideas for further investigation. As you read the table of contents, ask yourself these questions:

- What idea appeals to me?
- What would I like to know more about?
- Do I know where there is more information on one of these interesting ideas?
- Who might know something about the topic?

Your topic could be very general at this time (for example, stereotyping, friendship, or television advertising). Or it could be very specific (a particular author, a book suggested in one of the units, how to make a television commercial). When you have decided on a possible topic, make a list in your notebook using the headings in the following Info-box.

In this chart, include notes on what you have decided so far about your topic. These notes will help you think about your project. Also try asking a friend if he or she has any ideas that might help you.

info-box

PREPARING A TOPIC PROPOSAL

- your name
- your topic (in two or three words)
- what you know about this topic (three or four points)
- what you would like to find out about this topic (two or three points)
- where you might find out more (two or three places)
- who you might talk to about your topic (one or two people)
- where you might go on your own time to find out more (one or two places)

If your teacher accepts your proposal and the process you have outlined, plan your time for the next few days. Plan, for example, to talk, read and think about your topic outside of class time. After all – this is an independent study project.

RESEARCHING

There are several ways you can research a topic. Try asking people about your topic and use their opinions and information as a source of ideas. Another method of research is to go to your school library and consult books, magazines, and other media sources such as videotapes and computer data bases. When you do an independent study project in which you look only in the library for information, you are doing a library research paper. When you want to combine both asking others and working in the library remember to include information from all your sources.

info-box

METHODS OF CONDUCTING RESEARCH

Asking Others for Information

- Surveys: A survey is usually a form that is distributed to a number of people. Collect the answers to your survey questions, analyze them, and then draw your conclusions.
- Interviews: Ask someone who knows a lot about your topic. This person may not have all the answers, but he or she may help you get started. Turn to page 222 to find out how to conduct an interview.

Using the Library to Find Information

- Encyclopedias: These collections of knowledge are a good starting point. Sometimes just the list of topics in the index is thought provoking.
- Dictionaries: Knowledge is recorded and communicated in words. Look up the words related to your topic to see how they are defined.
- Books: The card catalogue in your school library is organized by title, author, and subject. Look up your topic and write down the titles and call numbers of all the books listed there. You can then move on to any relevant authors' names or ask the librarian to recommend some names based on your list of books.
- Vertical files: Folders with newspaper clippings, brochures, photographs, and other loose materials will be in a special cabinet in the library.
- Magazines: Back issues of magazines are collected in the library. Sometimes there are valuable articles in them. You might also find this kind of material on microfiche or microfilm.
- Computer search: Find information by accessing a computer data base.
- Almanacs: An almanac contains a wealth of details on many different topics. They are also interesting to dip into for a few fast minutes of trivial pursuit.

MAKING NOTES

A good way to begin your independent study project is to collect the books on your topic on a table and look them all over. You will usually find two or three that seem useful. Discard the material that is too complex, too simple, or otherwise unsuitable.

Write your topic clearly across the top of a piece of paper. List your sources and then jot down ideas about your topic from each of your sources. Use point form only – don't write in sentences or paragraphs. These are just ideas about your idea. Once you have a well-defined topic, start making notes in an organized way.

info-box

MAKING NOTES FOR RESEARCH

- Use a separate page for each source.
- Write the title and the author's name at the topic of the page.
- Use headings to indicate main ideas.
- Write in point form only.
- Do not copy sentences from books and magazines.
- Keep the information safely in your notebook.

ORGANIZING THE FINDINGS

The more information you collect, the more difficult it is to organize it. But if your notes are neat, you can make the overall arrangement with confidence. But it does take time! Organizing takes advanced thinking skills: you need to think hard, think long, think logically.

There are two useful systems to help you organize your material: the web and the outline.

The Web: The purpose of a web is to help you think freely while beginning to organize your topic. Make a web by writing your topic in the middle of a page. Put a square around it. Pick four or five sections that the topic falls into and write them circles or boxes attached by lines to the main topic. Then break each of these sections into smaller parts, each tied to the subheading by lines. The great advantage of this system is that you can add to it any time – and there is no particular order to the items, just connections.

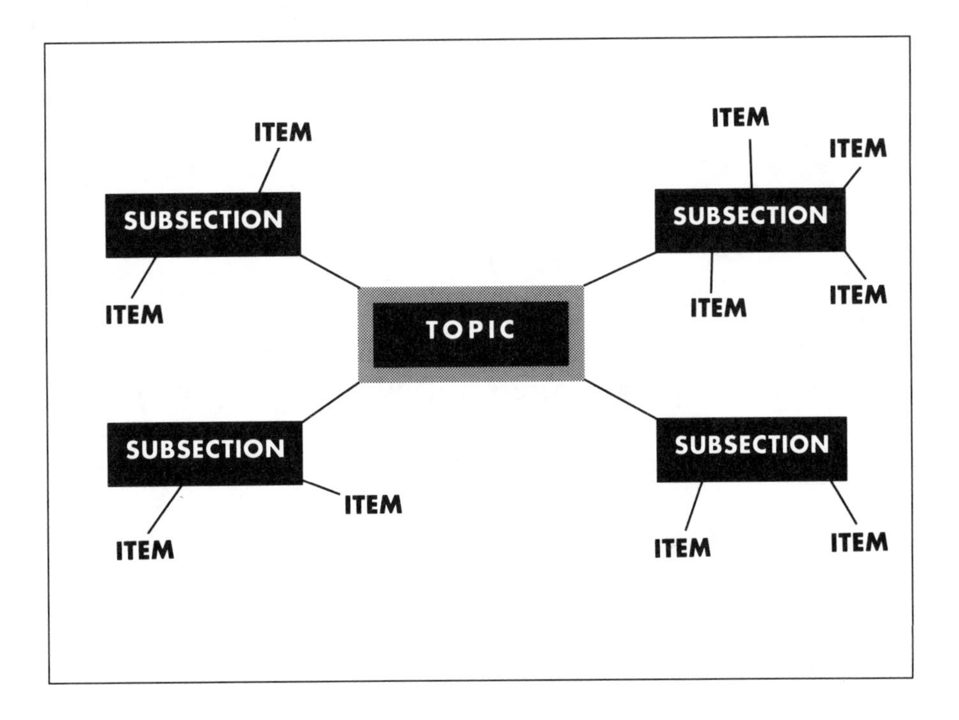

Figure 15-1 A web diagram

The Outline: An outline gives you an overview of your project and helps you organize the parts in a logical way. Because this stage is important, you should plan carefully.

Look at your web and simply number the subheadings, write them on a page, and add the connected items attached to each subheading in a logical order. Or think through the material in your notes and arrange it on an outline without using a web. Use the following format for your outline:

Topic of the Report

1. Heading
   a) subheading
   b) subheading
   c) subheading
2. Heading
   a) subheading

To the right of your subheadings, write the relevant page numbers from your sources, and other useful details, to help you write your report.

In the remaining sections of this unit you will find out how to collect the research information that you have gathered to produce a written report. You will also find information here to show you how to make a scrapbook or to create an anthology.

REPORTING

There are two types of reports: oral and written. But remember that researching and organizing your findings are the same, no matter what form your report will finally take.

The Oral Report: If you present your material orally you avoid the hard work of writing a report in several drafts to make it clear and complete on paper. However, the oral report must also be clear and complete, but the presentation to a group takes the place of writing.

The Written Report: If you have organized your findings well, writing them in a report should be a straightforward activity. Keep the stages of the writing process in mind as you do your independent study project. These stages are designed to help you take your idea from a first, sketchy thought about your topic, all the way to a published report. If you are uncertain about these stages, see page 264 in Unit 13.

When you use information from a book, be sure to use your own words – do not copy from books. The only exceptions to this rule may occur when you find a person's words that you wish to quote directly, or when you give a definition of a term. In both cases, you must use quotation marks and let your reader know your sources. You can do this in several ways. You can put the source material in parentheses after the quotation. You can create a footnote at the bottom of the page. Or you can place this information at the end of your report in an endnote. Look in a style manual for help in setting up footnotes or endnotes. An example of a such manual is *The Canadian Writer's Handbook*, second edition, William E. Messenger and Dan de Bruyn (Prentice-Hall Canada: Scarborough, Ontario, 1986).

All reports – both oral and written – require a conclusion that clearly expresses what you have learned from your independent study project.

info-box

FORMAT FOR A WRITTEN REPORT

- Include the headings in your outline.
- Write about each item under the headings following your plan.
- Write in correct sentences and paragraphs.
- Double space your report and write on only one side of the page.
- Use a word processor if possible. With a word processor, you can easily reorganize material and add new material.
- Include a list of your sources and add a cover page.

A SCRAPBOOK

Another way to report information for an independent study project is to make a scrapbook. The procedures for constructing a scrapbook are very much like those that you use for a report. Here are some basic steps for making a scrapbook:

- find a topic
- search for material
- organize the findings
- comment on the material
- draw conclusions
- design a format

Find a Topic: In order to simply your search, you need to identify a subject. Follow the procedure for choosing a topic that is outlined on page 275.

Search for Material: The library sometimes has material – usually old magazines or newspapers – that you can cut up. If not, you can make photocopies of material that is central to your project. It may be necessary to get permission from the person who holds copyright on this material before you can photocopy it.

Look for material at home. Newspapers, magazines, and other sources will provide current pictures, news stories, editorials, letters, and articles. You might also check at the homes of relatives and neighbours.

When you find something related to your topic, cut it out or photocopy it and put it in a large envelope until you have a lot of material. You might want to clip a note to each item to remind you later of how you would like to use it. Be sure, too, to keep an accurate record of where you found this material. Refer to this record when you cite your sources.

Organize the Findings: Read through the material carefully and select the items that are most suited to what you wish to show. Discard items that are inappropriate. Place the material on a large table. Sort it into piles of items on related aspects of your topic. Place these piles into an order that makes sense to you. For example, you could organize your material according to opposing sides of the topic, or according to the past, present, and future. Make an outline of the way you've organized your material based on a piece of paper. Use the headings from your outline and list the items under each heading.

Comment on the Material: Write your reaction to each item in your scrapbook. You can do this in two ways:

- glue the items into a notebook or scrapbook and write on the page
- type or use a word processor to write your reactions and then cut up and glue these on the page with the items

In either case, make the reactions thoughtful and personal.

Draw Conclusions: Write an introduction to your scrapbook that summarizes your ideas about the topic. Ask yourself what you learned about your topic. Refer to the items in your scrapbook when you write your introduction.

Design a Format: The way you arrange the material in your scrapbook and your presentation in general will determine how your work will be received. Will it have the effect you want it to have? Be creative! Some elements to consider when designing your format are noted in the following Info-box.

info-box

FORMAT FOR A SCRAPBOOK

- Use a notebook or scrapbook, or make one by stapling paper together.
- Design a cover sheet that contains the title of your collec tion, your name, and the date. Add an illustration of the topic to give it graphic appeal.
- Inside include a table of contents, your introduction, and your material.
- Make the whole package neat. Remember this is an inde pendent learning activity, so the final product should reflect the way you wish to be seen.

AN ANTHOLOGY

Another type of independent study project is an anthology. An anthology is a collection of material that relates to the same topic or theme. How do you go about collecting an anthology? Here is a suggested procedure:

- find a topic
- search for material
- organize the findings
- comment on the material
- draw conclusions
- design a format

Find a Topic: To create a literary anthology, read a number of poems, songs, short stories, essays, and articles and select several items that relate in some way to your central theme. Follow the procedure for choosing a topic that is outlined on page 275.

Search for Material: Your teacher can make suggestions and point out books for you to start with. The library is a good place to spend time on this project. Don't forget to take material home to read.

Take your time at this stage. Don't be too hasty about choosing material. Later you'll need to decide what your final collection will include. Stories are hard to reproduce on a word processor and are expensive to photocopy. You might consider including an excellent story, essay, or article and several poems and songs. Also look for pictures, sayings, or quotations by famous people to spice up your collection. During this stage, you might wish to write something yourself on the topic.

When you photocopy material for your anthology, you must ask for permission to reproduce this material. Permission is required by Canadian copyright law. To seek permission, write a letter to the publisher of the work, requesting permission to reproduce this material and to include it in your anthology. If you explain in your letter that you are completing a school project and will not be selling your anthology, it is unlikely that the publisher will charge you a fee for reproducing the work. The identification of the publisher is usually found on the front pages of the book. You may have to ask your librarian for help in finding the address of the publisher.

Organize the Findings: Choose carefully. There may be some natural order to your material. Create a list of items in the order that they may appear in the anthology.

Comment on the Material: Write your reaction to each item you wish to include.

- explain the point of each original poem, story, or article in a brief introduction
- explain what each item means to you
- explain what each item says about the topic of the collection

Draw Conclusions: Write an introduction to your anthology explaining what you learned. Have your ideas on the topic changed? Do you agree with all the authors?

Design a Format: Make your collection readable by typing it (ideally on a word processor). This material will be read by many people in your class, so present yourself well as an editor and commentator. Design an effective cover page, include a table of contents, and your introduction. You might want to include short biographies of the authors whose work appears in your collection.

END THOUGHTS

Whatever activity you choose to work on independently, remember that you learn best by being involved with the project emotionally as well as logically. Remember, too, that learning is a lifetime occupation. No one can do it for you. So take advantage of the opportunity to make some decisions for yourself. Take pride in your independent study project and do it well.

UNIT 16

★ ★ ★ ★ ★ ★ ★

READING AND RESPONDING TO LITERATURE

- ★ WHERE DOES MEANING LIE?
- ★ MEANING-MAKING IN LITERATURE

A RESOURCE UNIT

INTRODUCTION

Consider any work of literature. It might be a story, a play, a novel, a poem, or an essay. Think about what happens in your mind as you read it. How do you get meaning from what you are reading?

To understand a piece of literature is not a matter of guessing what is in your teacher's mind and of writing that information down in your notebook or on a test. A piece of literature probably has as many meanings as it has readers. What it means for you may be quite different from what it means for your teacher, for the person who is setting next to you, or for the person who wrote it. This unit will show you how the meaning of a selection of literature depends on how you look at it.

WHERE DOES MEANING LIE?

The diagram in Figure 16-1 shows the different ways of getting meaning from a poem, story, essay, or play. Let's look at each component of this diagram and see how you can read a selection of literature in different ways.

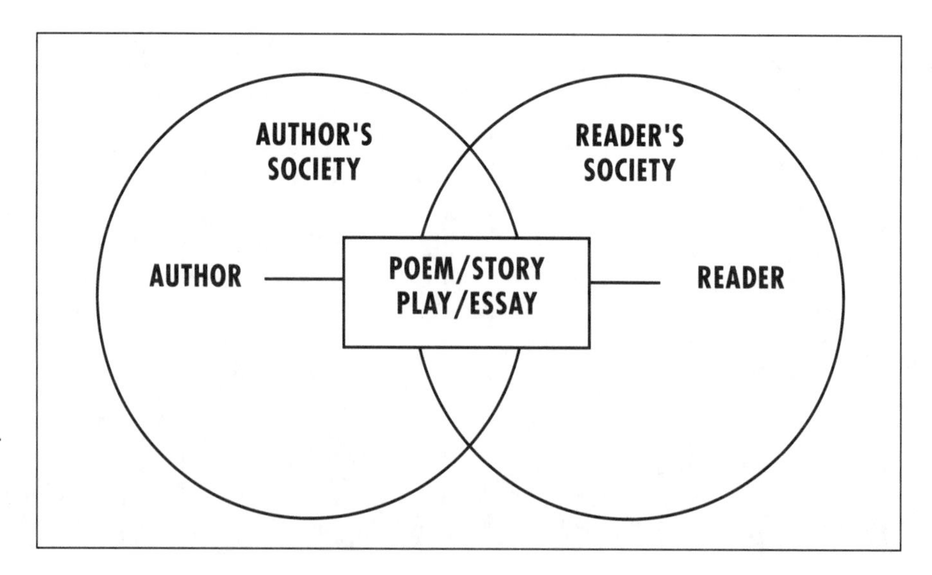

Figure 16-1 The components that shape meaning in literature

The Author: The author is an important source of information about what a particular poem or story means. Many writers talk or write about their creations and what they tell us is often helpful and sometimes surprising. If we rely too much on the author's explanation, however, we lose confidence in our own ability to read and understand a text.

The Text: Many writers refuse to comment on their creations. Once a writer is finished his or her work, it can take on a life of its own. What it means may not be what the author thought it meant. The act of creation can be quite mysterious and even the author is sometimes at a loss to explain a piece of literature that he or she has written.

The Reader: Every reader is different. Because readers bring a wide variety of experiences to the text, each reader will get somewhat different meanings from what he or she reads.

The Society: Who we are is greatly influenced by the society of which we are a part. The beliefs, values, economics, politics, and education of the social group to which they belong shapes what writers write and how readers read. The diagram in Figure 16-1 on page 288 shows how the society of the writer and that of the reader may overlap to some extent, but may also be quite different. If the reader and the writer come from two entirely different cultures, there may be significant variations in their interpretations of a particular work.

Figure 16-2 Different readers will interpret a piece of literature in different ways.

DAVID'S RABBIT

Dirk J. Verhulst

I realize now
that I had four years
to prepare you for this moment,
four years of days
begun with morning rituals
of food and water
brought faithfully
if not always cheerfully.

But now,
on this Sunday morning
when frost startles
the November trees
you have brought
the food and water
for the last time.

How do I tell you
that for every November death
there is a December birth,
when each time
seems like the first time
that a pet dies
and a child cries
and the time for tears
is forever?

What is the meaning of this poem? We can use the components of the diagram to answer this question in different ways.

The Author: The person who wrote "David's Rabbit" explains the poem in this way: "My son had had a number of pets – all of which had died. After each death, I tried to comfort him, but after the death of his rabbit, a pet of which he was particularly fond, I started thinking about how difficult it was to explain death to a child. The poem is my attempt to deal with this problem that most parents have to face."

The Text: For some readers the poem may not be about a rabbit at all; perhaps the loss of a dog is more vivid in their minds. For some readers the poem is about parents and children more than it is about pets. For others, it is about losses of all kinds, not just animals.

The Reader: The person who reads the poem may not share the same cultural background as the author. The poem may, therefore, mean something quite different to such a reader. The age of the reader will also influence the interpretation of the poem. A child might react differently to the poem than an adult; an adult with children might interpret the poem differently than one without children; and a person who has lost a pet may read the poem differently from someone who hasn't.

The Society: How we explain death is often closely related to the beliefs of the society we are part of. The author of the poem grew up in a Christian culture and it is natural that he explains the cycle of life and death in Christian terms. Words such as *ritual, faithfully, Sunday morning,* and *December birth* have religious significance. Although it is not stated directly, the poem suggests that just as Christ lived and died so all things go through a cycle of life and death.

MEANING-MAKING IN LITERATURE

The activities in this section will show you how the meaning of a literary selection varies according to your perspective. The first four activities will help you examine your own feelings about a story. The remaining activities examine other ways of obtaining meaning. The following short story – by Roch Carrier, a Canadian writer from Quebec – has been divided into three sections. Begin by reading the first part of the story.

“He touched each branch of the bush, one at a time, with religious care.”

A SECRET LOST IN THE WATER

Roch Carrier
Translated by Sheila Fischman

(Part 1)

After I started going to school my father scarcely talked any more. I was very intoxicated by the new game of spelling; my father had little skill for it (it was my mother who wrote our letters) and was convinced I was no longer interested in hearing him tell of his adventures during the long weeks when he was far away from the house.

One day, however, he said to me:

"The time's come to show you something."

He asked me to follow him. I walked behind him, not talking, as we had got in the habit of doing. He stopped in the field before a clump of leafy bushes.

"Those are called alders," he said.

"I know."

"You have to learn how to choose," my father pointed out.

I didn't understand. He touched each branch of the bush, one at a time, with religious care.

"You have to choose one that's very fine, a perfect one, like this."

I looked; it seemed exactly like the others.

My father opened his pocket knife and cut the branch he'd selected with pious care. He stripped off the leaves and showed me the branch, which formed a perfect Y.

"You see," he said, "the branch has two arms. Now take one in each hand. And squeeze them."

I did as he asked and took in each hand one fork of the Y, which was thinner than a pencil.

"Close your eyes," my father ordered, "and squeeze a little harder... Don't open your eyes! Do you feel anything?"

"The branch is moving!" I exclaimed, astonished. ◆

ACTIVITY 1

THE BEGINNING

Answer the following questions in your notebook – be sure to consider these questions before you read the next section.

1. What did you see as you were reading this first part of the story? What did it remind you of?
2. What memories did you recall? Describe them briefly.
3. What do you think will happen next?

A SECRET LOST IN THE WATER

(Part 2)

Beneath my clenched fingers the alder was wriggling like a small, frightened snake. My father saw that I was about to drop it.

"Hang on to it!"

"The branch is squirming," I repeated. "And I hear something that sounds like a river!"

"Open your eyes," my father ordered.

I was stunned, as though he'd awakened me while I was dreaming.

"What does it mean?" I asked my father.

"It means that underneath us, right here, there's a little fresh-water spring. If we dig, we could drink from it. I've just taught you how to find a spring. It's something my own father taught me. It isn't something you learn in school. And it isn't useless: a man can get along without writing and arithmetic, but he can never get along without water."

Much later, I discovered that my father was famous in the region because of what people called his "gift": before digging a well they always consulted him; they would watch him prospecting the fields or the hills, eyes closed, hands clenched on the fork of an alder bough. Wherever my father stopped, they marked the ground; there they would dig; and from there water would gush forth.

Years passed; I went to other schools, saw other countries, I had children, I wrote some books and my poor father is lying in the earth where so many times he had found fresh water. ◆

“Beneath my clenched fingers the alder was wriggling like a small, frightened snake.”

THE MIDDLE

Before reading the end of the story, answer these questions in your notebook.

1. What feelings did you have as you read the second section of "A Secret Lost in the Water"? What do you think caused these feelings?
2. What other thoughts or memories came to you as you were reading this section? What do you think caused these thoughts and memories?
3. What questions came into your mind as you were reading?
4. How do you think "A Secret Lost in the Water" will end?

A SECRET LOST IN THE WATER

(Part 3)

One day someone began to make a film about my village and its inhabitants, from whom I've stolen so many of the stories that I tell. With the film crew we went to see a farmer to capture the image of a sad man: his children didn't want to receive the inheritance he'd spent his whole life preparing for them – the finest farm in the area. While the technicians were getting cameras and microphones ready the farmer put his arm around my shoulders, saying:

"I knew your father well."

"Ah! I know. Everybody in the village knows each other ... No one feels like an outsider."

"You know what's under your feet?"

"Hell?" I asked, laughing.

"Under your feet there's a well. Before I dug I called in specialists from the Department of Agriculture; they did research, they analyzed shovelfuls of dirt; and they made a report where they said there wasn't any water on my land. With the family, the animals, the crops, I need water. When I saw that those specialists hadn't found any I thought of your father and I asked him to come over. He didn't want to; I think

he was pretty fed up with me because I'd asked those specialists instead of him. But finally he came; he went and cut off a little branch, then he walked around for a while with his eyes shut; he stopped, he listened to something we couldn't hear and then he said to me: "Dig right here, there's enough water to get your whole flock drunk and drown your specialists besides." We dug and found water. Fine water that's never heard of pollution."

"I closed my eyes and, standing above the spring my father had discovered, I waited for the branch to writhe."

The film people were ready; they called to me to take my place.

"I'm gonna show you something," said the farmer, keeping me back. You wait right here."

He disappeared into a shack which he must have used to store things, then came back with a branch which he held out to me.

"I never throw nothing away; I kept the alder branch your father cut to find my water. I don't understand, it hasn't dried out."

Moved as I touched the branch, kept out of I don't know what sense of piety – and which really wasn't dry – I had the feeling that my father was watching me over my shoulder; I closed my eyes and, standing above the spring my father had discovered, I waited for the branch to writhe. I hoped the sound of gushing water would rise to my ears.

The alder stayed motionless in my hands and the water beneath the earth refused to sing.

Somewhere along the roads I'd taken since the village of my childhood I had forgotten my father's knowledge.

"Don't feel sorry," said the man, thinking no doubt of his farm and his childhood; "nowadays fathers can't pass on anything to the next generation."

And he took the alder branch from my hands. ◆

THE END

When you have finished the story, answer these questions in your notebook:

1. How did the ending make you feel?
2. What did the ending remind you of?
3. What memories of your own father, or some other significant person in your life, did the short story make you recall? What memories of any other person, perhaps your mother, came to mind?
4. How was the ending of this short story different from what you had predicted?

PERSPECTIVES

Form groups of three. Refer to the notes that you took in Activities 1 to 3 and answer the following questions:

1. What did each member of your group *see* as he or she read the story?
2. What memories did each member of the group recall as he or she was reading the story?
3. What predictions did the members of the group make about how the story would end?
4. In what ways were the answers of the members of your group different? In what ways were they similar? How do you explain the similarities and differences in your answers?

ACTIVITY 5

MORE MEANINGS

Use these questions to obtain further meanings from this short story.

1. "A Secret Lost in the Water" takes place in two time periods: one when the narrator was a child and the other when the narrator returns as an adult. How has the narrator's attitude toward his father and his ability to find water changed?
2. From the perspective of your life and your culture, what object would you use in place of a divining rod? Why?

3. What movie or TV program that you have seen has a similar message to this story?
4. What does the neighbour mean when he says, "nowadays fathers can't pass on anything to the next generation"? How is the society to which the father belonged different from that of his son? How have these differences affected the lives of the father and the son?

In Activities 1 to 5, you considered how the meaning of a story can vary according to the personal response of each reader. Sometimes you can respond to a piece of literature by trying to recreate all or part of it. Such a task requires you to think about and to understand the piece of literature and then to use your imagination to create a new component for it.

IMAGINE THAT

1. Write a new ending for "A Secret Lost in the Water," one that is set in the place where you live and reflects your thoughts and feelings about the older generation.

END THOUGHTS

The author, the reader, the text, and the society of which they are a part, all contribute to the meaning of a selection of literature. The meaning of any medium – from a movie to a television program – varies according to the perspective of the creator, the audience, and the society in which it was produced.

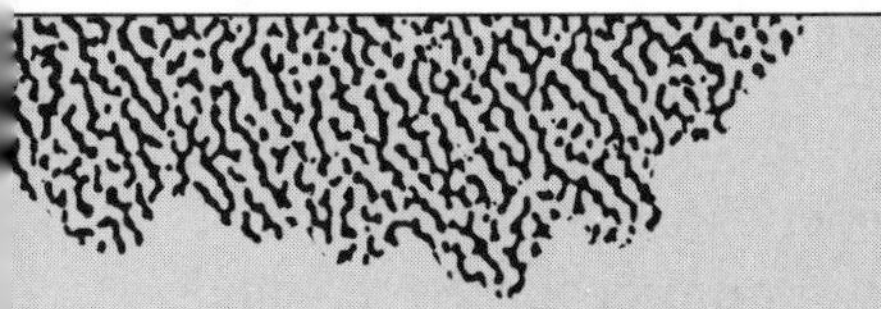

UNIT 17

★ ★ ★ ★ ★ ★ ★

SPEAKING AND LISTENING

- THE DAMAGE ISN'T EAR-REPAIRABLE
- EAR-RADICATE YOUR LISTENING PROBLEMS
- SPEAK TO ME
- TWISTING AND TURNING

A RESOURCE UNIT

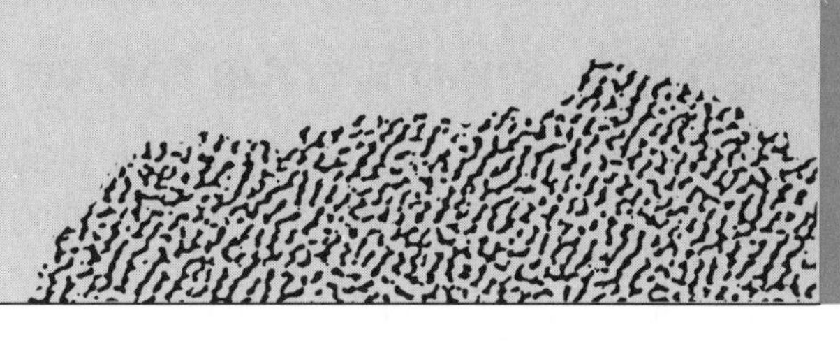

INTRODUCTION

Have you ever made an embarrassing comment in class, on a date, or when talking to a friend? Like everyone else, you probably have – and not because you are a poor speaker. It may, however, be that you need to work on your listening skills. You may have said something wrong because you didn't hear someone right. This unit will help you reduce the number of times you say "Why did I say that?" by giving you opportunities to practise your speaking and listening skills.

Figure 17-1 This ad is commenting on the viewing, listening, and speaking skills of politicians.

ACTIVITY 1

WHAT'S YOUR EAR-Q?

1. Assess your listening skills by completing in your notebooks the quizzes from "Your Listening Profile."
2. How does your Ear-Q stack up against that of your classmates?

YOUR LISTENING PROFILE

Lyman K. Steil, Ph.D.

How Well Do You Listen?

Here are three tests in which we'll ask you to rate yourself as a listener. There are no correct or incorrect answers. Your responses, however, will extend your understanding of yourself as a listener and highlight areas in which improvement might be welcome – to you and to those around you.

When you've completed the tests, see the "Profile Analysis," to see how your scores compare with those of thousands of others who've taken the same tests before you.

Quiz 1

1. State the term that best describes you as a listener.

Superior	Excellent	Above Average
Average	Below Average	Poor
Terrible		

2. On a scale of 0-100 (100 = highest), how would you rate yourself as a listener?

Quiz 2

On a scale of 0-100 (100 = highest), how do you think the following people would rate you as a listener?

Your Best Friend	Your Boss
Your Teacher	Your Parents

Quiz 3

As a listener, how often do you find yourself engaging in these 10 bad listening habits? Write the number of each question in your notebook. Then beside the number, describe your response using one of the following descriptions:

Almost Always Usually Sometimes Seldom Almost Never

1. Calling the subject uninteresting ____________
2. Criticizing the speaker's delivery or mannerisms ____________
3. Getting *over*-stimulated by something the speaker says ____________
4. Listening primarily for facts ____________
5. Trying to outline everything ____________
6. Faking attention to the speaker ____________
7. Allowing interfering distractions ____________
8. Avoiding difficult material ____________
9. Letting emotion-laden words arouse personal antagonism ____________
10. Daydreaming ____________

Scoring Key for Quiz 3
Use the following key to determine your total score:

For every Almost Always listed, give yourself a score of	2
For every Usually listed, give yourself a score of	4
For every Sometimes listed, give yourself a score of	6
For every Seldom listed, give yourself a score of	8
For every Almost Never listed, give yourself a score of	10

Profile Analysis

This is how other people have responded to the same questions that you've just answered.

Quiz 1

1. In response to the first question, eighty-five percent of all listeners questioned rated themselves as average listeners or less than average listeners. Fewer than 5 percent rated themselves as superior or excellent listeners.

2. When people rated themselves as listeners on a scale of 0-100, with 100 being the best rating, the lowest score was 10 while the highest score was 90. People generally rated themselves between 35 and 85, with most people rating themselves at 55.

Quiz 2

When asked who they thought would rate them best as a listener –their best friend, their boss, their teacher, or their parents –most respondents believed that their best friend would rate them highest as a listener. They also believed that their best friend would rate them higher as a listener than they rated themselves in Quiz 1, where most people rated themselves as listeners at 55 on a scale of 1 to 100.

Why do people think that their best friends would rate them so highly as listeners? We can only guess that best-friend status is such an intimate, special kind of relationship that it's hard to imagine that a person could become your best friend unless you were a good listener. If you weren't a good listener, you would not be best friends to begin with.

Quiz 3

The average score for poor listening habits was a 62, 7 points higher than the 55 that average test-takers gave themselves in Quiz 1 where they rated themselves as listeners. This difference in rating suggests that when listening is broken down into specific areas of competence, we rate ourselves better than we do when we rate ourselves on our listening abilities as a whole.

Of course, the best way to discover how well you listen is to ask those to whom you listen most frequently. Your boss, best friend, and so on. They'll give you an earful. ◆

THE DAMAGE ISN'T EAR-REPAIRABLE

After completing the quizzes in "Your Listening Profile," many people find that their listening skills are a little shaky. In all likelihood, you have never thought much about listening. You have taken this skill for granted. Yet there are several very simple skills that you can learn to improve your listening habits. When you become a good listener, you improve your interpersonal relationships at the same time. Almost everyone likes a person who will listen.

SET UP YOUR LISTENING LADDER

Jane Kvasnicka

Did you know that on the average we spend more time listening than any other human activity except breathing? Yet, although we spend up to 45 percent of our waking time listening, 75 percent of all oral communication is ignored, misunderstood or forgotten. Obviously listening is the weak link in the chain of human communication.

How does this happen? According to Robert L. Montgomery in the book *Listening Made Easy: How to Improve Listening on the Job, at Home, and in the Community* (New York: AMACOM, 1981), "Poor listening is a result of bad habits that develop because we haven't been trained to listen."

"The way we listen can influence the quality of friendships, family relations and school interactions."

We learn to improve our speaking skills in speech classes and our writing skills in composition classes. Yet rarely are we taught specifically about developing our listening skills.

Nevertheless, listening skills are vital because they help determine how we relate to others. The way we listen can influence the quality of friendships, family relations and school interactions. Poor listening habits thus undermine these relationships.

But don't give up hope! Montgomery says we can improve our listening skills. He lists six rules, geared to interpersonal communication, for learning how to listen effectively. It's easy to remember these rules, because they spell out the word LADDER. The six rules are:

1. **Look.**

Look at the person who is talking to you. Concentrate on the other person in order to judge the intent of the message as well as the content. Project genuine, active attention.

2. **Ask questions.**

This is the best way for anyone to quickly become a better listener. To encourage the other person to open up, develop the reporter's art of asking questions.

Remember that it's easier to build rapport with someone when you relate your questions sensitively to their background or

> “People are entitled to their opinions and the right to be heard.”

frame of reference. Asking open-ended questions helps draw the other person out.

3. Don't interrupt.

Let other people complete their sentences or ideas. This may take some practice! But keep in mind that none of us likes to be cut off when we're trying to express ourselves. Work at letting others finish what they have to say.

4. Don't change the subject.

Although this is a little different from rule three, both are sure ways to alienate people – fast. In either case, the other person gets the message that you don't care at all about what they're saying – or about them, either.

5. Emotions should be kept in check.

It doesn't pay to overreact to what others say. People are entitled to their opinions and the right to be heard.

Give others the chance, then, to explain their points of view. It's wise to hold off your judgement until then. And even wiser to hold off your reply.

Furthermore, getting overly excited causes us to fail to concentrate fully on what the other person might actually be saying.

6. Responsiveness pays off.

If you are unresponsive, the speaker will assume that he or she isn't getting across and may give up the effort.

Therefore, as you listen, look at the other person and show some sign of understanding. For example, smile, nod, frown in sympathy – whatever's appropriate. Although most of these cues are nonverbal, interjections such as "oh," "yes" and "hmmm" work well, too.

By the way, feel free to interrupt the speaker – cautiously, of course – when you need clarification about something he or she's said.

By following these six rules you can improve your listening skills. You can then expect improvement in your interpersonal skills as well.

Remember the words of the Greek philosopher Epictetus who said, "Nature has given us one tongue, but two ears, that we may hear from others twice as much as we speak." ◆

STEP BY STEP

1. Alone or as a shared activity, read the article, "Set Up Your Listening Ladder."

a) In your journal, list each of the six skills discussed in the article. Beside each one, write a journal entry in which you consider each skill.
b) With these six skills in mind, listen to a conversation to see how appropriate these skills are to what happens in real life.

2. For three days, practise the first skill: look at the person with whom you are talking. At the end of three days, write a journal entry summarizing what happened when you concentrated on this skill.

3. For the next three-day period, practise the second skill: ask questions. Write a journal response. Then practise each of the other skills for a three-day period and write in your journal about what happened.

4. Find a person who has never read the article "Set Up Your Listening Ladder," preferably someone younger than yourself. Talk with this person about one or two of these listening skills and help him or her practise them. Does your student improve his or her listening skills?

EAR-RADICATE YOUR LISTENING PROBLEMS

Now that you're aware of your listening abilities, it's time to reinforce your strengths and to strengthen your weaknesses. You can learn to be a better listener. And when you're a good listener, other people tend to find you a better person to be around.

IT'S THE TRUTH, TEACHER – HONEST!

1. Imagine that you have arrived late for class and must explain your tardiness to your teacher and the rest of the class. Your explanation should be between thirty and sixty seconds in length. Here's an example of such an explanation:

"I'm sorry I'm late, but just as I was leaving the house, our neighbor, Ms. Brown, who just turned ninety-three, came to the front door of her house and asked me to retrieve her pet budgie, Rudolph. It was terrible. Her budgie had flown into the cold air vent and was trapped. I had to get some tools from our other neighbor, Mr. Blackstone, who also turned ninety-three just recently. It took me a long time to explain to Mr. Blackstone what I wanted and why."

2. Test your class's listening skills by asking five questions about the content of your excuse. Here are some questions, based on the example excuse in question 1:
    - What was the budgie's name?
    - Who were the tools borrowed from?

SPEAK TO ME

According to Patricia Sternberg in her book, *Speak to Me* (Lothrop, Lee and Shepard Books, New York, 1984), how you say something is as important as what you say. Sternberg says that in addition to using the proper volume and speed as you speak, a good speaker's voice has these characteristics:

- it's articulate (clear and distinct)
- it's expressive (portrays different shades of meaning)
- it's pleasing (the tone is pleasant to the ear)
- it's relaxed (free from tension and affectation)
- it's personalized (appropriate to the age, sex, and image you desire)

The activity on page 308 will give you practice in using speaking styles. The style you choose will help you communicate your intent.

WHAT YOU SAY OR HOW YOU SAY IT?

1. Silently read the following conversation a number of times:

   A. Where are you going?
   B. Nowhere special.
   A. I want to know exactly where you're going to be.
   B. Why do you have to know that?
   A. Well, what if something happens?
   B. What could possibly happen?
   A. Lots of things. You could get sick or something.
   B. C'mon. How likely is that to happen?
   A. You don't know. Anything could happen.
   B. You're not really answering the question.
   A. I am answering the question. You can't predict when an accident will occur.
   B. Has anything ever happened before?
   A. No, but there's always a first time.
   B. You worry too much.

2. With a partner, decide who will say what part.
3. Decide which style each of you will use to read the lines to your class. You need not use the same style. Some possible styles that you might choose from include whining, calm and reasonable, sarcastic, or hostile and angry.
4. As you and your partner say your lines to the class, the class should decide which speaker has communicated his or her intent more effectively.
5. In a class discussion, ask the class members to give reasons to support their choices.
6. Ask the members of your class to guess the identity of each of the speakers based on the tone of delivery each has used.

TWISTING AND TURNING

How you say something depends on many things, including the time, the place, and the people to whom you are speaking. If you change one or more of these items, your conversation can take some unusual twists and turns. Imagine, for example, how a conversation in which you explain what you did at last night's party might change if your audience were your best friend, your mom or your dad, or a person in a position of authority.

ACTIVITY 5

SAY IT AGAIN, SAM

1. Have each student in your class choose a different personality (for example, a grandparent, a high-school student, or a doctor).
2. In pairs, begin a discussion at the front of the class on a mutually agreed upon topic. For example, a ten-year-old and a high-school student could discuss hockey.
3. At the end of one minute, appoint another class member to join the conversation (for example, a grandparent).
4. After another minute has passed, have another personality (for example, a biker) join the conversation.
5. After one minute, ask a fifth and final class personality (for example, a business person) to join the conversation.
6. As each person is added to the conversation, describe in your notebook the changes to the conversation that occur. Include changes in content, tone, and style. Here is an example of what you might observe:

   "When the grandparent joined the ten-year-old and the high-school student, the vocabulary became more formal and the high-school student's tone became more serious. The high-school student's style also changed. She spoke more loudly and more slowly."
7. After each group is finished, share your observations with your class.

END THOUGHTS

Speaking and listening are important everyday skills that go hand in hand. As you become a better listener, you become a better speaker. And as you become a better speaker, others become better listeners. So the moral of the story is: hear what is said and say what you want to be heard!

UNIT 18

★ ★ ★ ★ ★ ★ ★

VIEWING SKILLS

- EDITORIAL CARTOONS
- GAG CARTOONS
- CREATING CARTOONS

A RESOURCE UNIT

INTRODUCTION

The cartoon is a recent arrival in the world of media. During the 1980s, it became an influential form of mass communication. There are several kinds of cartoon forms. You are probably most familiar with the animated cartoons on television, the comic strips or "funnies" in your local paper, and the comic book. Cartoons are also of great commercial value. Cartoon characters appear on T-shirts, greeting cards, children's lunch kits, stationery, and posters. Although they consist of simple drawings, cartoons are much more complex than they might seem, and often comment on important social and political issues. As part of a growing trend in contemporary mass media, cartoons are quick-paced and communicate both through pictures and words.

This unit invites you to look at one form of the cartoon: the single-panel cartoon. These cartoons appear on editorial pages in newspapers and throughout magazines. Editorial cartoons are usually humorous treatments of political situations and personalities. The humour is often based on exaggeration, and carries a pointed message. The cartoons that appear in magazines are called gag or social cartoons. Like editorial cartoons, gag cartoons use humour to comment on life.

EDITORIAL CARTOONS

The single-panel editorial cartoon has become an effective way for newspapers to make a political statement or to comment on society. Editorial cartoons try to make viewers think and try to keep them informed. The relationship between Canada and the United States, for example, is a concern that appears again and again in Canadian politics – and occurs often in editorial cartoons. The cartoon in Figure 18-2(a), drawn thirteen years before Confederation in 1867, makes a statement about the trading relationship between Canada and the United States. The cartoon in Figure 18-2(b) shows that the Canadian election of 1988 focused on the same issue: free trade with the United States.

Figure 18-1 This editorial cartoon by Brian Gable is about the post office in Canada, a common target of editorial cartoons – even though the postal system moves millions of pieces of mail each year.

a)

b)

Figure 18-2 Free trade – a hot topic in 1854 a) and 1987 b).

Figure 18-3 Published in August, 1978, this cartoon by Duncan Macpherson comments on the problems facing Canada as an election draws near.

Figure 18-4 This complex cartoon by Duncan Macpherson comments on both the leadership of former Prime Minister Pierre Trudeau and on the Canadian public.

ACTIVITY 1

VIEWING CARTOONS

1. Look carefully at the cartoon in Figure 18-1 on page 313.

a) What does the cartoonist say about the Canadian postal system?
b) How does he make you chuckle?
c) Is the cartoonist fair in his treatment of the post office system? Why or why not?

2. Look at the cartoons in Figure 18-2 on page 313.

a) What does the cartoonist in Figure 18-2 (a) say about the issue of trade between Canada and the United States? What does the cartoonist in Figure 18-2 (b) say?
b) How are these two cartoons, created in different centuries, alike and how are they different? Do they communicate the same message? Has the cartoonist used the same or different techniques to capture viewer attention?

3. What does the cartoon in Figure 18-3 on page 314 say about Canadian problems in 1978?

a) Which politicians shown in this cartoon can you identify?
b) Does Canada have to consider these same problems today? Which problems are no longer pressing? What new problems have appeared on the Canadian scene?

4. Look carefully at the cartoon about former Prime Minister Trudeau in Figure 18-4 on page 314.

a) What does this cartoon say about Trudeau?
b) What does the cartoon say about Canada and the Canadian public?

EDITORIAL CARTOON CONTEST!

Complete this activity in a group of three to five people. Once you have completed your study of editorial cartoons, prepare a short report for your class in which you relate your findings about political cartoons.

1. Look through newspapers or magazines such as *Maclean's* and *Saturday Night* and collect at least twenty editorial cartoons.

2. Have a look at your cartoon collection.

   a) What messages do these cartoons communicate?
   b) What techniques of visual communication do the cartoonists use?

3. Carefully examine what you think is the best cartoon from your collection.

   a) Why did your group choose this cartoon?
   b) What message does this cartoon communicate to its viewers?
   c) What techniques does the cartoonist use?

4. Use your answers to questions 2 and 3 to prepare a brief report in which you tell the class what you found out about editorial cartoons in general and about one specific cartoon in particular.

GAG CARTOONS

The gag cartoon often appears in magazines and newspapers. Like the editorial cartoon, it is a single-panel cartoon. Whereas the editorial cartoon always appears on the editorial page, the gag cartoon can appear anywhere in a newspaper or magazine. And while political cartoons make a statement about a particular situation or person, gag cartoons are more general. They usually make a statement about humans as a group, rather than individuals.

The gag cartoon represents one of the most sophisticated levels in cartooning. Gag cartoonists work within very limited restraints. They must communicate their entire message using one picture and perhaps a short caption written beneath it. Everything in the cartoon must direct the reader to the cartoonist's message. The characters are few and the drawings are stylized. That is, the drawings represent the character or situation by presenting only essential details. Sometimes gag cartoonists are able to communicate their message without using words at all. Instead, they present all the action in the drawing itself.

Figure 18-5 In this gag cartoon by Len Norris, the characters are acting 'in character' but are placed in a ridiculous situation.

September 3, 1959

". . . and whereas said group comprising six males, hereinafter known as the party of the first part, and presently occupying a common carrier, to wit, an elevator, do charge and require said operator, hereinafter known as the party of the second part, to take all necessary procedures, with due regard for life and limb, to transport the party of the first part to a floor as designated by said party, to wit . . . convention floor."

Figure 18-6 This gag cartoon uses exaggeration to communicate its message.

Figure 18-7 This gag cartoon takes an ordinary situation and uses the viewer's knowledge of Mickey Mouse to make its statement.

Figure 18-8 Gag cartoons – like this one – often make a statement about contemporary social concerns.

ACTIVITY 3

A GAGGLE OF GAG CARTOONS

Respond to questions 1 and 2 in your journal.

1. Look at the cartoons in Figures 18-5 to 18-8 and answer these questions:

a) What makes the cartoon in Figure 18-5 on page 317 humorous?
b) What is the meaning of this statement about Figure 18-5: "Norris's cartoon is a caricature of lawyers."
c) What makes Figures 18-6 (p.317), 18-7 (p.318), and 18-8 (p.318) humorous?

2. In groups of three, make a collection of twenty or more gag cartoons.

a) Examine your cartoons and classify them into groups.
b) Choose one group of cartoons and make a display on this theme for your classroom bulletin board. You may find it convenient to trade cartoons with other groups to get the right cartoons for your theme.

3. In the same group you formed in question 2, analyze your collection of gag cartoons and then write a journal entry in which you respond to these questions:

a) How do the cartoons present male figures? Are they stereotypically masculine, weak, or sensitive?
b) How are the female characters shown? Are they stereotypically female, weak, or sensitive?
c) What roles are the characters playing? Do the cartoons tend to stereotype males and females? Who tends to be the leader – a male or a female?
d) Do the cartoons stereotype young people and old people?
e) What other stereotypes do you find in these cartoons?

4. Prepare a group report and present your conclusions for question 3 to your class.

CREATING CARTOONS

Cartoons are simple line drawings. Yet their message may be complex and powerful, capable of shaping the thoughts of millions of people. Cartoonists communicate in two ways. They simplify their subject, reducing it to simple and basic lines. They also exaggerate their subject, drawing the viewer to the one aspect that is being commented on. One writer has referred to a cartoonist's art as working with a microscope and a magnifying glass. In this section, you will have the opportunity to create some of your own cartoons.

Like real people, cartoons communicate much of their information through facial expression. Figure 18-9 shows the basic elements of the human face. The drawing in the upper left corner is a typical adult face. The eyes are in the middle of the head and the corners of the mouth are below the pupils of the eyes. The face beneath it represents a young child. Very young children have a dome-shaped head and the facial features seem further from the crown. As well, the eyes are larger than the mouth. The other drawings in Figure 18-9 create the appearance of sadness, smugness, and bewilderment.

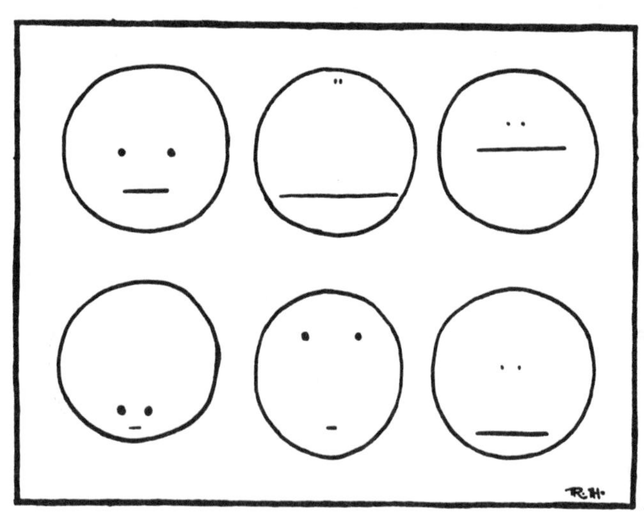

Figure 18-9 Typical faces

Figure 18-10 Basic expressions

Figure 18-10 shows you how cartoonists use the mouth, the eyes, and the eyebrows to create expression – perhaps because these are the facial features that move. The faces in Figure 18-10 show some universal expressions. The happy face is shown by curving the corners of the mouth up and making the eyes into an upside down crescent. The next face shows sadness by turning the corners of the mouth down and lifting the centre of the brow. You can show anger, as in the next face, by turning the corners of the mouth and the middle of the brow down.

To suggest surprise, as in the lower left face in Figure 18-10, lift the eyebrows and open the eyes. You can create a look of fear by adding hair that stands straight up. The middle face in the bottom row suggests fear – the eyebrows are raised in the centre, the eyes are open, and the mouth is curved down and back. In the last face, the cartoonist represents the feeling of disgust by sticking the tongue out of the corner of the mouth.

There is much more that you can learn about drawing cartoons. If you are interested in cartooning, you should be able to find a how-to book in your school or local library.

DRAWING CARTOONS

1. Use a thin piece of paper to trace the facial features of several cartoon characters. Change the shape of their basic facial features such as the mouths, eyes, or eyebrows. What difference do these changes make in the expression on the faces of the characters?
2. Look in a mirror and try expressing some of the basic emotions such as happiness, sadness, anger, fear, hate, and disgust. Use the same basic circle that you see in Figures 18-9 and 18-10 and draw your own face in various poses.
3. Create your own gag cartoon. Use stick figures if necessary and refer to Figures 18-9 and 18-10.

END THOUGHTS

This unit has introduced you to the world of cartoons. You looked specifically at the form of the single-panel cartoon as used in editorial and gag cartoons. Cartoons have become an important part of the popular media. They are easily understood, but at the same time they can be complex. As you browse through magazines, read the funny papers, or read a comic book, you should now have a greater appreciation for the ability of the cartoonist – and the cartoon as an art form.

UNIT 19

★ ★ ★ ★ ★ ★ ★

LANGUAGE STUDY

- GRAMMAR AND USAGE
- ADJECTIVES
- ADVERBS
- ADJECTIVES, ADVERBS, SENTENCES
- USAGE PROBLEMS WITH ADJECTIVES AND ADVERBS

A RESOURCE UNIT

INTRODUCTION

Why study grammar? It's not easy to answer this question – in fact parents, students, and teachers often disagree.

Language is our most powerful tool. It's what makes us human. Although a knowledge of grammar will not necessarily make you a more effective writer, it will help you share a common language, or terminology, with your teacher and fellow writers. This common language will help you talk about your writing with others.

GRAMMAR AND USAGE

You've probably heard this complaint: "Kids today don't use good grammar!" It's quite likely that people making this statement don't mean grammar at all. They often confuse grammar with usage. The word *grammar* refers to the study of the structure of a language, or how the language works. Grammar includes the sounds, syllables, words, and sentences that make up a language. The word *usage* refers to how that language is used by speakers in different situations. In some situations it might be appropriate, for example, to say "That pie was real good." Elsewhere, however, it might be inappropriate.

The focus of this unit is on adjectives and adverbs, but before considering some of the ways in which these parts of speech are used and misused, read the Info-box on page 325 to review your knowledge of nouns and verbs.

info-box

REVIEW: NOUNS, VERBS, SENTENCES

You will probably remember these definitions from your study of grammar in earlier grades:

- A noun refers to a person (Suzanne), a place (an office), or a thing (a ball).
- A verb expresses an action (run) or a state of being (is).
- The main noun in a sentence is called the subject (Suzanne).
- The main verb in a sentence is called the predicate (runs).
- Together a subject and a predicate form a basic English sentence (Suzanne runs).

NOUN + VERB = SENTENCE

This exercise will help you review your understanding of nouns and verbs.

1. Make a list of animals (for example, *coyote*) and a list of actions that describe how each animal moves (for example, *prowls*). Combine a word from the first list with one from the second list to make a simple sentence (*The coyote prowls*).

2. Do the same with each of the following combinations:

a) Combine nouns that indicate a job (*soldier*) with verbs that state what people do (*march*).
b) Combine nouns that name foods (*hamburger*) with verbs that state what food do (*satisfy*).
c) Combine nouns that name vehicles (*car*) with verbs that state what vehicles do (*zoom*).
d) Combine nouns that name a source of entertainment (*music*) with verbs that state what it does (*blasts*).

Try to create some unusual or humorous combinations.

ADJECTIVES

What Are Adjectives? Nouns and verbs are the meat and potatoes of the English language. Alone they can make a good basic meal. If we want to add some zest to the meal, however, we use adjectives and adverbs. Adjectives describe or modify nouns.

Inflection of Adjectives: Another way to consider adjectives is to think about what an adjective looks like. They are any words that take an adjective ending or are preceded by *more* or *most*. The following inflections create the three forms of adjectives:

Positive	**Comparative**	**Superlative**
big	bigger	biggest
joyful	more joyful	most joyful

The comparative form is used to compare two things. The superlative form is used to compare three or more things. Look at the advertisement in Figure 19-1 and see how the advertiser has made clever use of adjectives and the forms of adjectives.

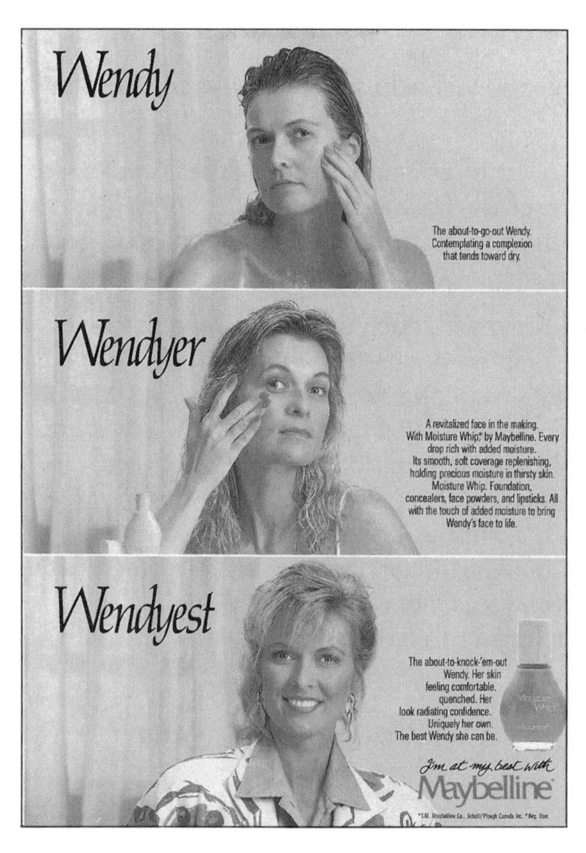

Figure 19-1 Is Wendyest an adjective?

EXPLORING ADJECTIVES

1. In the following paragraphs, all the missing words – except the last one – are adjectives. In your notebook, complete the paragraphs as part of a horror story. Then repeat this activity so that the paragraph would seem to come from each of the following kinds of story:

a) a humorous story
b) a romantic story
c) an adventure story
d) a sad story

The last word in the two paragraphs is a noun. In each case, choose one that is appropriate to the kind of story you are writing.

"The _________ man approached the _________ house. As he lifted the _________ latch, the _________ door opened revealing a _________ hall. He stepped over the _________ threshold and entered the _________ interior. In front of him, a _________ stairway curved to a _________ second floor. Above the landing hung a _________ chandelier.

When he began to climb the _________ steps, a _________ cat scurried past him. He followed the _________ animal into one of the _________ rooms. It was a _________ bedroom. There was a _________ bed, ___________ dresser, with a _______ layer of _______ dust. On the bed was a _________."

2. The adjectives in the following travel advertisement have been deleted. In your notebook, rewrite this paragraph using effective adjectives to make the place being advertised sound very attractive.

"Discover Erehwon!
_________ days and _________ nights await you. Feel the _________ breezes. Taste the _________ food. Smell the _________ flowers and _________ trees. See the _________ sights and _________ people."

3. Write a radio advertisement for one of the following products: a car, a motorbike, perfume, makeup, jeans, a sweater, a carbonated drink, stereo equipment. In your ad, use adjectives to catch the buyer's interest and attention.

4. Find a paragraph in a novel that contains a description of a person or a place. List all the adjectives contained in it. What feelings do your get from these adjectives? How would removing these adjectives affect your reading of the paragraph?

5. From a magazine, select a picture that you find especially effective. List the items shown in the picture. Beside each item write several adjectives to describe it. Using these adjectives, write a brief paragraph about the picture.

6. The following adjectives get used over and over again:

   - nice
   - great
   - pretty
   - wonderful
   - good
   - funny

   A thesaurus is a dictionary of synonyms. Look up some of these overused adjectives and list some interesting alternatives that you could use instead. Write pairs of sentences, one of which has the overused adjective; the other, the synonym that you found in the thesaurus.

ADVERBS

What Are Adverbs? Like adjectives, adverbs are describing words. But while adjectives describe nouns, adverbs describe or modify verbs, adjectives, or other adverbs. The following examples show the uses of adverbs.

- An adverb describes a verb:

  Run quickly
  verb adverb

- An adverb describes an adjective:

  That was an incredibly delicious dinner.
  adverb adjective

- An adverb describes another adverb:

  She ran extremely quickly.
  adverb adverb

Inflection of Adverbs: Like adjectives, the form of some adverbs changes. Most adverbs, too, have positive, comparative, and superlative degrees. For example:

Positive	**Comparative**	**Superlative**
quickly	more quickly	most quickly
fast	faster	fastest

Other adverbs, however, such as *there*, *here*, *now*, and *then* cannot be compared and therefore do not have inflected endings. Still other adverbs are irregular. The adverb *well*, for example, becomes *better* in the comparative form and *best* in the superlative form.

Kinds of Adverbs: Adverbs are usually divided into several categories. Adverbs of time answer the question of *when*. *Today*, *tomorrow*, *yesterday*, and *forever* are examples of time adverbs. Adverbs of place answer the question of *where*. *Here*, *there*, and *everywhere* are examples of place adverbs. Adverbs of manner answer the question of *how*. *Quickly*, *slowly*, *backwards*, and *sideways* are examples of manner adverbs.

ACTIVITY 3

EXPLORING ADVERBS

1. The adverbs have been omitted in the following paragraph. In your notebook, fill in the missing words:

"The hockey player skated _________ down the ice. She _________ looked down the ice, began to circle _________, cradling the puck _________ in the _________ constructed hockey stick. _________ out of the left corner of her eyes she saw an _________ fast skater come up _________ beside her. She wheeled _________, stopped _________, and shot the puck _________ at the _________ bewildered goalie."

2. A word game called "Tom Swifty" uses adverbs to create a pun. For example:

"Please clean the window," Tom asked *painfully*.
"Make sure that your hands are dry when you turn on the light," Tom said *shockingly*.

Create some of your own Tom Swifties.

3. Find a section in a story that contains a lot of action. Select sentences that include effective adverbs. Write the sentences in your notebook, but leave a blank space where the adverbs were in the original paragraph.

    a) Exchange your sentences with a partner and supply the missing adverbs in each other's sentences.
    b) Compare your choices with the original adverb. Which do you find more effective. Why?

4. Make a list of ordinary action verbs. Beside each one write three adverbs that would make the action more vivid. Use some of the verb-adverb combinations in sentences.

5. Make a chart with three columns, one for each form of the adverb: positive, comparative, superlative. List the following adverbs under the positive column:

    - quickly
    - correctly
    - suddenly
    - steadily
    - wildly
    - softly
    - loudly
    - carefully
    - cautiously

    Then fill in the other two columns.

ADJECTIVES, ADVERBS, SENTENCES

Modifiers such as adjectives and adverbs can be used to add important information to a basic sentence. The following sentence has a simple structure:

The	singer	sang	a	song.
	noun (subject)	verb (predicate)		noun (object)

You can hear and see the singer better if you use a more vivid noun and verb and add two colourful adjectives and an adverb. For example:

The nervous vocalist painfully warbled a dreadful ballad.

VIVID SENTENCES

1. Rewrite each of the following sentences by adding interesting adjectives and adverbs. Use more effective nouns and verbs where appropriate.

   a) A man rode into town.
   b) The girl hit the ball.
   c) The child ate dinner.
   d) The boy left class.
   e) A father cooked the meal.
   f) A teenager played music.

USAGE PROBLEMS WITH ADJECTIVES AND ADVERBS

Good/Well: *Good* is an adjective. *Well* can be either an adjective or an adverb. As an adjective well refers to health, as in this sentence: *He is not feeling well.* As an adverb, well describes how something is done: *She plays basketball well.* Use *good* when referring to the senses: *Steak tastes good.*

Fewer/Less: *Fewer* and *less* are both adjectives, but they are used in different ways. Fewer refers to a countable number, as in this sentence: *John has fewer pets than Maud.* Less refers to an amount or degree that is not countable: *Juanita spends less time at work than Ida does.* (But note this sentence: *Juan spends fewer hours on the job than I do.*)

Real/Really: *Real* is an adjective meaning genuine: *Deborah is a real athlete.* *Really* is an adverb meaning very or extremely, as in this sentence: *Agatha plays hockey really well.* In informal, spoken English, real is sometimes used as an adverb, as in this sentence: *Agatha plays hockey real well.*

Dropping the 'ly' in Adverbs: One of the trends in modern usage is the increasingly frequent tendency to drop the '*ly*' ending for some adverbs. Consider these examples: *Go slow. He drives slow.*

USAGE PROBLEMS

1. Your younger brother has asked you to check a paragraph that he has written. He has some problems with his adjectives and adverbs. Rewrite the paragraph for him in standard English.

   "Last Wednesday we had a real good game of hockey. It started kind of slow but the pace picked up real quick. I played gooder than last time and scored a real nice goal. The coach said I done super! That made me feel awful good."

END THOUGHTS

An awareness of grammar and usage helps you to use one of our most powerful tools – language. A knowledge of grammar allows you to express yourself in a way that others can understand. And a knowledge of usage allows you to choose words that are appropriate to the situation in which they're being used.

UNIT 20

★ ★ ★ ★ ★ ★ ★

STUDY SKILLS

- ★ ANSWERING QUESTIONS
- ★ READING ON THE LINES
- ★ READING BETWEEN THE LINES
- ★ READING BEYOND THE LINES

A RESOURCE UNIT

INTRODUCTION

Poor grades, poorly done assignments, incomplete work, indifference – all result from a lack of understanding of what is expected. In this unit you will look at ways to help you answer questions effectively and think clearly.

ANSWERING QUESTIONS

Look at the following questions:

- "List four reasons why teenagers drink."
- "Discuss four reasons why teenagers drink."

Both questions ask you why teenagers drink. However, there are different expectations for the two answers. The first question asks you to simply list four reasons. An appropriate answer might be:

1. Everyone else is doing it.
2. Teenagers drink out of curiosity.
3. It's "adult" to drink.
4. Ads on TV, in newspapers, and in magazines encourage teenagers to drink.

The second question asks for more information than merely listing reasons provides. A reasonable answer might be:

1. Teenagers drink because they think everyone else is doing it. They feel a great deal of peer pressure if they're with a group that drinks, and thus drink for fear of being left out or being called chicken if they don't.
2. As teenagers grow older they are anxious to try out new things and gain new experiences in life. They are exposed to alcohol around them, their curiosity is aroused, and they drink.
3. A third reason is that teenagers are growing up and they think that drinking is an 'adult' thing to do. This is especially so because they are not of the legal age to drink and drinking is something that makes them feel as if they were grown up.

4. Teenagers also drink because they are influenced by advertisements in the media. These ads are very sophisticated and make it appear that to be successful and popular they must drink.

Notice that these answers build on each other. The student used the answer for the "list" question to organize the answer for the "discuss" question.

UNDERSTANDING DIFFERENCES

1. Show that you understand the difference between listing and discussing by answering the following questions.
   a) List three environmental issues that teenagers need to be concerned about.
   b) Discuss three environmental issues that teenagers need to be concerned about.
2. Share your answers to these two questions with a partner and show him or her how your second answer showed more detail than your first one.

How can you know what is expected of you? The chart on page 336 outlines three levels of comprehension that require the use of different skills. Knowing when and how to apply these skills will help you answer questions – and gain more from your reading.

LEVELS OF COMPREHENSION			
If the question is at this level	*then* you will need to apply thes skills	*because* the answer implies that you will answer	this involves
Literal	You must be able to: • give details • find specific facts • follow directions • list things in order	as if you were reading: "on the lines"	giving facts
Interpretive	You must be able to: • show cause and effect • give the main idea or theme • infer time, place, mood • classify • infer motives • compare and/or contrast	as if you were reading: "between the lines"	assimilating, putting together and interpreting facts
Evaluative	You must be able to: • make judgments • evaluate	as if you were reading: "beyond the lines"	giving your opinion by evaluating and judging facts and ideas

Figure 20-1
Sometimes you'll find yourself using aspects of the different levels of comprehension at the same time.

READING ON THE LINES

When you read "on the line," you read literally – looking for the facts. To answer questions at this level, you need to read, to listen, and to answer questions that involve:

- giving details
- finding and listing facts
- following directions
- listing facts in order

This level of comprehension is referred to as the literal level.

WOODTICK

Joy Kogawa

The spring day the teen on his bike slanted his caucasian eyes
At my eight year old beautiful daughter
And taunted gibberish
I was eight years old and the Japs were
Enemies of Canada and the big white boys
And their golden haired sisters who
Lived in the ghost town of Slocan
Were walking together, crowding me
Off the path of the mountain, me running
Into the forest to escape
Into the pine brown and green lush dark
And getting lost and fearing woodticks
Which burrowed into your scalp beneath
Thick black hair follicles and could only be
Dug out by a doctor with hot needles –
Fearing sudden slips caused by melting snow
And steep ravines and the thick silence of
Steaming woods and cobwebs, so listening
For the guiding sound of their laughter
To lead me back to the path and
Following from a safe distance unseen
Till near the foot of the mountain
Then running past faster than their laughter
Home, vowing never to go again to the mountain
Alone – and Deidre whispers to walk faster
Though I tell her there are no
Woodticks in Saskatoon.

ACTIVITY 2 **READING "ON THE LINE"**

After reading the poem, "Woodtick" on page 337 answer the following questions in your notebook:

1. What happened on the spring day when the poet and her eight-year-old daughter were out walking? This incident caused the poet to remember a childhood experience. Describe the poet's experience as an eight-year-old.

2. Think about what you did to answer question 1. Did you apply the skills suggested in the chart on page 336?

3. Create your own question about a fact or detail from the poem.

4. Form groups of three and answer the following questions:

a) Compare your responses to questions 1 and 2.
b) Ask each other the questions you developed in question 3. The person who created the question could evaluate the other two answers.

READING BETWEEN THE LINES

To read "between the lines" means that you interpret the facts. It requires more than simply reading or listening. You must put the facts together and show relationships. This level of comprehension is referred to as the interpretive level.

Notice that at the first level of comprehension – reading "on the lines" – you can answer questions directly from the text that you are reading. At the second level of comprehension, you must read for information and then answer by using facts from the text in addition to facts and ideas from your own store of knowledge.

The interpretive level – reading "between the lines" – asks you for more than facts. It asks you to use the facts to show relationships. The chart on page 339 contains some key words that show you how to go beyond a statement of facts to read "between the lines."

READING "BETWEEN THE LINES"

1. Using the poem "Woodtick" answer the following question in your notebook.

   In what period of time did each of the incidents that frightened the eight-year-olds occur? Be sure to support your answer using words from the poem. Here is an example of an answer for the second incident mentioned:

   "The second incident mentioned took place at the time of the Second World War. The poet describes being eight years old when 'the Japs were enemies of Canada.'"

   Notice that the student who wrote this answer had to pull facts from the poem and use his or her knowledge of history to infer the answer: this statement refers to the Second World War and the historical events of that time.

2. In groups of three or four, compare your answers to question 1.

Figure 20-2 When you read "between the lines" you are interpreting the facts.

READING "BETWEEN THE LINES"

A question about ....

cause and effect	asks you to	explain why something happens by interpreting preceding facts main idea or theme asks you to summarize briefly, usually in a sentence, what the reading is about
time	asks you to	infer when something occurred
place	asks you to	infer where something occurred
mood	asks you to	infer the feeling or feelings the reader responds to
classify	asks you to	put things in order
infer motives	asks you to	show why something occurred
compare	asks you to	show how things are alike
contrast	asks you to	show how things are different
compare and contrast	asks you to	show both similarities and differences
discuss	asks you to	support a statement with facts and ideas
analyze	asks you to	examine closely and look at all the details

ACTIVITY 4

MORE READING "BETWEEN THE LINES"

1. Further explore the interpretative level of comprehension by responding to the following questions based on "Woodtick." Your answers must show that you are reading "between the lines."

a) Where did the incidents take place?
b) What is the mood of the poem? What specific lines in the poem have the strongest impact on you? Why?
c) What is each of the eight-year-old girls afraid of? Compare the sources of the fear.
d) What do you think the main idea of "Woodtick" is?

2. Choose a partner and compare your answers to these questions. Explain to each other how you developed your responses. Refer to the chart on page 339 to review the skills which you applied to read "between the lines."

3. Create a question at the interpretive level based on this poem.

4. In groups of two or three, answer each other's questions and compare each other's answers. Think about how the answers required you to apply skills at the interpretive level.

READING BEYOND THE LINES

Reading "beyond the lines" – the critical level of comprehension – is the most difficult and complex level. At this level, you use facts, synthesize by putting them together, and then evaluate or judge them. You make decisions about the text that are not contained within it.

Here are the skills you use at this level:

- evaluating
- speculating
- proving
- making judgments

At this level, you form opinions about what you have read and you support your opinion by using facts and relationships presented in the text.

READING "BEYOND THE LINES"

1. Kogawa, the poet, describes two incidents of racial prejudice – one she experienced as an eight year old and the other she experienced with her eight-year-old daughter. Do you think the poet was affected by the way she was treated? What do you think she is afraid of for her daughter? Do you think the poet is talking about something beyond her own experiences? State your opinion and provide facts to support your stand on these questions.

THE MAN WHO FINDS HIS SON HAS BECOME A THIEF

Raymond Souster

Coming into the store at first angry
at the accusation, believing
the word of his boy who has told him,
I didn't steal anything, honest...

Then becoming calmer, seeing that anger
won't help in the business, listening patiently
as the other's evidence unfolds, so painfully slow.

Then seeing gradually that evidence
almost as if slowly tightening around the neck
of his son, at first circumstantial, then gathering damage,
until there's present guilt's sure odour seeping
into the mind, laying its poison.

Suddenly feeling
sick and alone and afraid, as if
an unseen hand had slapped him in the face
or no reason whatsoever; wanting to get out
nto the street, the night, the darkness, anywhere to hide
e pain that must show to these strangers, the fear.

st be like this.
d not be otherwise.

ACTIVITY 6 READING AT ALL LEVELS OF COMPREHENSION

1. Read "The Man Who Thinks His Son Has Become a Thief " on page 341. Then form groups of three members and talk about the poem. Use these questions as a guide as you think about this poem:

    a) What was the mood of the man when he entered the store? (literal)
    b) What picture is created in your mind by the line "then seeing gradually ... of his son"? (interpretive)
    c) What is "circumstantial evidence"? (literal) Suggest a piece of circumstantial evidence the store owner might give the father. (interpretive)
    d) Why did the father want to get out of the store? (critical)
    e) What is the meaning of these lines:

        "It must be this.
        It could hardly be otherwise."
        (literal and interpretive)

    f) How would you have reacted if a brother or sister, or perhaps a friend, were caught stealing? (interpretive) Compare your reaction to that of the father in this poem. (interpretive)

END THOUGHTS

In this unit you have looked at the skills needed to answer questions. You examined three levels of comprehension or understanding. The first level is reading "on the lines" to answer factual questions. The second level is reading "between the lines" to answer questions by putting facts and ideas together. The third level is reading "beyond the lines" to answer questions by making judgments or evaluations. If you know what kind of question you are answering, and if you know what skills to apply to this question, you are more likely to write an effective answer.

UNIT 21

★ ★ ★ ★ ★ ★ ★

LEARNING SKILLS

- ★ ORGANIZATION
- ★ TIME MANAGEMENT
- ★ MEMORY
- ★ CATEGORIZATION
- ★ CUE CARDS
- ★ THINKING SKILLS
- ★ PERSONAL LEARNING STYLES

A RESOURCE UNIT

INTRODUCTION

Everyone needs to practise. Through practice you succeed. Musicians in a rock concert didn't learn their craft by accident – most likely they've spent many hours in a basement, driving other people mad with their practice. The athlete standing on the victory podium is backed up with years of tedious and meticulous practice. The Grey Cup in the Canadian Football League is won more on the practice field and in the locker room than during the actual game.

This unit is about practice – practice to help you succeed in school. In this unit, you will be asked to think about learning skills involving organization, time management, memory, thinking skills, and personal learning styles. If you learn these skills and then practise them, you will be on your way to a more successful school career. And all of these skills will be of help to you when you leave school.

ORGANIZATION

If you're organized you're more likely to succeed in school. Having a well-organized notebook for each subject and a proper place to study at home are two important aspects of being an organized student.

A Notebook System: It's been said that a student is only as good as his

DEVELOPING YOUR OWN NOTEBOOK SYSTEM

Follow these suggestions to develop your own system of notebooks for all of your school subjects.

- Have a three-ring binder for each subject.
- Have dividers between sections of the subject. For example, you could have divided sections for each unit, for returned tests, for course outlines, for records of evaluation, and for blank paper.
- Put the date on notes, hand-outs, and assignments.
- Keep notes in order according to date.
- Correct all wrong answers on tests when they are returned and place them with the unit or section they test.
- Use point form for most of your notes. Use clear headings and list your points underneath. Don't use sentences and paragraphs.
- Keep neat notes. This may mean recopying some of them.
- Highlight headings and key words in your notes during your regular review time.
- Have a section for extra paper, both lined and unlined. Don't put loose paper in your binder.
- Have a homework/assignment sheet in a special place in the binder.

DEVELOPING YOUR OWN PLACE TO STUDY

Here are a series of suggestions on how to create your own environment in which to do homework, work on assignments, and study.

1. Make a chart in your notebook similar to Figure 21-1 and list your suggestions in point form. This will help you to decide what you have and what you need.

Figure 21-1 Different people have different study needs.

A STUDY PLACE OF MY OWN			
Suggestions	What I Have	What I Need	Comments

2. Think about each item and write down your conclusions in your chart. Here are some examples of items that you might include in your chart:

- desk or table to work on
- desk lamp on the work surface
- straight chair
- bulletin board
- drawer where you store ruler, pens, pencils, extra paper, coloured markers, a highlighter, some paper clips and a stapler
- door you can close
- regular time to study

TIME MANAGEMENT

If you use your time well you're more likely to succeed in school than those who are disorganized in the management of their time. Having a system to record deadlines for assignments and the dates of tests will allow you to plan your time. If you're prepared for tests and on time with assignments, you'll decrease the stress that you feel about school. Reducing your stress level will increase your self-confidence in all subject areas and all aspects of school life.

WHERE DOES MY TIME GO?							
	Monday	Tuesday	Wednesday	Thursday	Friday	Saturday	Sunday
7:00-8:00							
8:00-9:00							
10:00-11:00							
11:00-12:00							
12:00-1:00							
1:00-2:00							
2:00-3:00							
3:00-4:00							
4:00-5:00							
5:00-6:00							
6:00-7:00							
7:00-8:00							
8:00-9:00							
9:00-10:00							
10:00-11:00							
11:00-7:00							

Figure 21-2 Keep track of all your activities for a week.

A SUMMARY OF MY TIME

Activity	Hours Each Day (24 Hours)	Total Hours Per Week
Sleeping		
Eating		
Classes		
School activities		
Household duties		
Out-of-school recreation		
Fitness activities		
Job		
Studying		
Time with friends		
Television viewing		
Hobbies		
Other		

Figure 21-3 What activities take up most of your time?

ACTIVITY 4 STRENGTHS AND WEAKNESSES

2. Use these questions to extend your thinking about your time use:

   a) What is your prime time for studying? When are you most alert and able to concentrate on a difficult learning task?
   b) Where is the best place for you to study with the fewest distractions?
   c) How much sleep do you need to be alert?
   d) What distracts you most easily from study?
   e) What excuses do you most often use to avoid study?
   f) What priorities in your life are being neglected?
   g) How much time per week do you allow for relaxation away from study?
   h) How long are your study breaks and how do you pace them?
   i) What rewards do you give yourself for the completion of study tasks?

3. Use your answers to questions 1 and 2 to think about the strengths and weaknesses of your time use. Use the following headings to organize your answer and make at least four points under each heading:

   - the greatest strengths of my time use
   - the weaknesses of my time use – what I have to work on
   - how I will improve my use of time

Two Helpful Systems: When you begin to manage your time, you need a system to help you get organized and keep organized. You could, for example, make notes for yourself, but this system has a disadvantage: you could lose your notes. There's also the danger that you'll spend as much time looking for your notes as you do keeping yourself organized.

Two very helpful management systems are the weekly planner and the calendar. A weekly planner is one way to keep a record of homework requirements as well as long-range assignments such as test days, reports, essays, art work, and lab reports. You can make a sheet for each subject like the example in Figure 21-4 (p. 350) to put in the front of your binder.

A WEEKLY PLANNER

Week of ____________ to ____________. Name ____________

Monday
1. ____________
2. ____________
3. ____________
4. ____________
5. ____________

Tuesday
1. ____________
2. ____________
3. ____________

Date	Assignment/Test	Due Date	Complete	Evaluation

Figure 21-4 Use your weekly planner to anticipate assignments and commitments.

THE WEEKLY PLANNER VERSUS THE CALENDAR

1. Find a monthly calendar that has spaces in which you could write

REMEMBERING WITH CATEGORIES

1. Go to a unit in any subject that you've finished and for which you have included information about the unit in your notebook.
2. Make a list of words that you need to remember from that unit.
3. Think of the categories that the words fall into. They could be names, terms dealing with what you are reading, or new vocabulary.
4. Make a list of the words under the category headings. When you have about fifteen, find a partner. Time yourselves for two minutes and learn the words under your partner's categories.
5. Write the words on another page and have your partner check them.
6. Discuss how well this system of remembering works for each of you.
7. Make a list of five areas where you could use this system. Don't restrict your ideas for application to this English course only.

CUE CARDS

There are many different systems for developing your memory. A shopping list, for example, can be used as a memory supplement. Your notes are another memory system. The cue card is a system that performs two functions:

- it helps you learn difficult material
- it helps you review from time to time

Figure 21-5 Cue cards

Question Side:

Dana Shimrat English, Unit 5

Q: What is a good way of remembering a list of names?

Answer Side:

A: Categorizing

As you can see from the example in Figure 21-5, cue cards are very simple to use. Follow these guidelines when making your own cue cards:

- Use ordinary recipe cards.
- On one side write a question. Make it clear and precise. On the same side of the card write your name and the course and unit at the top. This way the questions won't get mixed up with the answers.
- On the other side of the card write the answer.
- Don't waste cards on questions and answers that you can remember easily.
- Write only one question per card, although it could be a question with several points in the answer, for example, listing the names of the main characters in a book you are reading.
- You can ask more complex questions as well. For example, what is the theme of the story you read in Unit 1?

Ways to Use Cards: Let's say that you have made a set of cards from your notes two or three days before a unit test. This is a good idea, because the actual making of the cards will be a serious review activity if you have chosen to make cards for items that you expect to find hard to remember.

- Put an elastic around the cards and carry them in your pocket. You can ask yourself the questions on the school bus or almost anywhere.
- Work with a friend by asking the questions on each other's deck of cue cards.
- Play card games with the cards. Shuffle and deal them. Count the cards that you can answer correctly.
- Play a game with several people in a group. Give the person on your left your pack of cue cards so they can quiz you when your time comes. If this is a regular classroom practice to review for tests, you may have to limit the number of questions to three or four per turn in order to give everyone a chance to learn.
- As the year goes by file your cards by unit. When examination time approaches, review your whole course using one of the methods suggested above.

MAKING CUE CARDS

1. Choose a unit or chapter that you'll be tested on soon. Read your notes on the material.
2. Use a highlighter or a red pen to highlight in your notes key headings and points. This could include new words and definitions of terms that you're using.
3. Get a package of recipe cards or cut up stiff paper into card-sized pieces.
4. Go back over the highlighted items and form questions from the points. Put the questions and answers on the cards or paper.
5. Have someone you trust check your questions and answers.
6. Use your cards for review by going over them several times during the days before the test.
7. Consider your results:
   - Did the system help?
   - Did you feel more confident going into the test?
   - Were you relaxed?
   - Will you use cue cards again? When? For what purpose?
   - Will you use them in all your courses?

THINKING SKILLS

Although some people can think about two things at once, most of us need to focus our mind on one specific task in order to think clearly and fully. If you want to be a clear thinker, you need to learn to concentrate – and you need to practise!

Problem Solving: There are many ways of approaching a problem in order to solve it. The problem may be complex – perhaps involving a decision about your personal life, your family, or your school work. No problem is isolated, and the more you think about a problem, the more you realize there are many factors involved. One way of dealing with a problem is to think clearly and fully about all the factors related to that issue. A useful problem-solving strategy is to LAF (List All Factors) after you've thought and talked about the issue with others.

ACTIVITY 10

LAFING

1. Listing all the factors involved in a problem requires practice. Here are some suggested problems with which you could practice:

   - skipping classes
   - trying to join a team
   - deciding to help with a volunteer program
   - deciding to hold an after school job
   - choosing a trade or career
   - doing homework
   - talking to a counsellor about a personal problem
   - asking for a date
   - going to a movie

2. Try the following steps to practise LAFing.

   a) Choose a problem.
   b) Work in a small group.
   c) Discuss your problem. Try to concentrate and think about all aspects of the problem.
   d) List all the factors related to the problem.
   e) Share your list with your group.
   f) Repeat the process with a different problem.

MORE LAFS

1. Make a list of issues or problems that concern you and your friends now. They may have to do with any aspect of your life.
2. Select the one that is a really hot issue with you right now.
3. Think clearly. Concentrate. Discipline your mind to think about this issue only. List all factors.
4. Draw a conclusion, make a choice, or come to a decision regarding your problem.
5. Plan what you'll do or say to carry out your decision.

PERSONAL LEARNING STYLES

Different people learn better under different social conditions. Some people like to be around others when they learn. Others like to be alone. Some people need quiet while others like some noise such as a radio playing. A few people work best when it's noisy. These questions will help you think about your personal learning style.

- Do you like to work independently and alone?
- Do you like to talk with a friend?
- Do you need the teacher close by to help you?

Once you understand how best you learn, apply this information to the tasks that you are asked to do at school. If you understand what's best for you in many different learning situations, you can make good choices both in class and out of it.

QUESTIONNAIRE

The questionnaire in Figure 21-6 will help you to identify the conditions that you prefer when you are working on school assignments or studying.

1. Read all of the statements in Figure 21-6 and think about them.
2. In your notebook, write down "yes," "no," or "maybe" for each statement in the questionnaire. You'll need this information for Activity 13.

SOCIAL CONDITIONS FOR LEARNING

Alone:

1. I am self-motivated.
2. I like to work alone on most tasks.
3. I like to read the material myself.
4. I am a very independent and responsible person.
5. I don't like working with a partner – I prefer to work alone.
6. Groups waste a lot of time and I can learn more alone.

Figure 21-6 Which statements in each category apply to you?

Peer Pairs:

7. I like to work with a friend on tasks at school.
8. I need to work with someone else in order to clarify the task.
9. When I work with a partner I have greater success.
10. Talking about a task helps me to think clearly and feel confident.
11. I feel lonely just doing my own work and need others close by.

Small Groups:

12. I feel relaxed speaking within a small group.
13. I like to work with a group of five or six people on certain tasks.
14. I find that working with a group teaches me about other people.
15. I feel uncomfortable in a whole class and prefer not to answer questions.
16. I am too self-conscious to speak or perform in front of a class.

Whole Class:

17. I prefer to discuss things as part of a whole class.
18. I learn more as part of a whole class than I do by myself.
19. I feel comfortable in a class and prefer it to group work.

With the Teacher:

20. I need very specific instructions from the teacher on every task.
21. I prefer the teacher nearby when I am working.
22. When I go to the library, I ask the librarian to help me.
23. I like the teacher to explain the task clearly and then let me do it on my own.
24 . I like to check with the teacher regularly on my progress.

SUMMARY OF SOCIAL FACTORS

1. Write this title in a section of your notebook: "My Learning Profile: Social Preferences." Then use the headings in the questionnaire in Figure 21-6 (for example, "Alone") as sub-headings.
2. Under the appropriate sub-headings, list the sentences that best describe you. You may want to change the wording of the statements in the questionnaire to more accurately describe your feelings. Your chart might look something like the example in Figure 21-7.

Figure 21-7 Does your learning profile look like this?

MY LEARNING PROFILE:
SOCIAL PREFERENCES

Alone:
I like to work alone on most tasks.
I like to read most material by myself (except science).

Peer Pairs:
Talking about some tasks helps me to think about the problem more clearly (especially in math class).

HOW I LEARN BEST

1. Look at the chart in Figure 21-8 on page 360. Write the headings in your notebook.
2. Under "Type of Work" list some tasks that you're often required to complete in school.
3. Under "Social Factors" write one of the following:
    - alone
    - peer pair
    - small group
    - whole class
    - with the teacher
4. Under "Comments," explain your choice of social factor.

HOW I LEARN BEST		
Type of Task	Social Factors	Comments
Read a novel	Alone	I take it home and read before going to sleep at night.
Answer a math question	Peer pair	I like to talk to a friend about the problems so I can think out loud and get some feedback.

Figure 21-8 You might find that each type of task requires a different social factor.

END THOUGHTS

In this unit, you've thought about some basic learning skills. You've learned how to organize your notebooks and your time. You've also learned ways to memorize information by increasing your memory power. You've also learned about LAFs, a way to increase your thinking skills. Finally, you've studied your own personal learning style and examined the social conditions that you prefer when you are learning.

But the information in this unit is just the beginning. You can use all of it to help improve your success in school. But success in school isn't the real goal of this unit. If you learn to use these skills, you'll master them for life. And you'll find them helpful not only in your personal life but in your job as well.

All learning skills are mastered through practice. The more you practice them, the easier they become, until they become an automatic aspect of your daily life. So, as they say out on the practice field: One more time around the track!

INDEX OF INFO-BOXES

CREDITS

Every reasonable effort has been made to find copyright holders of the preceding material. The publishers would be pleased to have any errors or omissions brought to their attention.

Unit 1

"The Magic In Your Name" by Conrad King from *Nova* by Olive S. Niles, Jerry Walker, and J. Jaap Tuinman. Copyright © 1981, 1977 by Scott, Foresman and Company. Reprinted by permission.

"I Am..." by Collette Lascombe from *Notes Plus*, September 1985. Copyright 1985 by the National Council of Teachers of English. Reprinted with permission.

"Long, Long After School" from *The Rebellion of Young David and Other Stories* by Ernest Buckler. Used by permission of the Canadian Publishers, McClelland and Stewart, Toronto.

"Report Card Writing" by Pat Sadowy from *Bridges 4*. Prentice-Hall, Canada.

Unit 2

"Public can fight back with Crime Stoppers" by Gary Taljit. Reprinted with permission from the *Star Phoenix*.

"The Execution" by Alden Nowlan. Reprinted by permission of the Estate of Alden Nowlan.

Unit 3

"Indians and Animal Activists Duel at Europe's Parliament" by Edward Greenspon. Reprinted by permission of *The Globe and Mail*.

"*Bobby Clobber: Radio Helmet*." Reprinted by permission of Air Farce Productions Inc.

"Canadian Fishery Agents Fire Warning Shots at U.S. Trawler." Reprinted by permission of The Associated Press.

"Hunger" from *Black Boy* by Richard Wright. Copyright 1937, 1942, 1944, 1945 by Richard Wright. Reprinted by permission of Harper + Row, Publishers, Inc.

"To Save the Rainforests of Brazil." Reprinted by permission of *The Globe and Mail*.

Unit 4

"The Trade Off" by Paula Mitchell. Reprinted by permission of the author.

Haiku from *A Few Flies and I: Haiku by Issa*. Reprinted by permission of Pantheon Books. Copyright © Jean Merrill.

Unit 5

"Deke's First Car" by Gary Hyland. Excerpt from the poem "The Old Ladies" reprinted from *Just Off Main* by Gary Hyland (Thistledown Press, 1982) with permission.

"Speed of the Cheetah, Roar of the Lion" by Harry Harrison. © 1975 by Mercury Press, Inc. Reprinted from *The Magazine of Fantasy and Science Fiction*.

Unit 6

"Odd jobs help youngsters polish their financial skills" by Tony Van Alphen. Reprinted by permission of The Canadian Press.

"The Road Not Taken" by Robert Frost. Copyright 1916 by Holt, Rinehart and Winston and renewed 1944 by Robert Frost. Reprinted from *The Poetry of Robert Frost* edited by Edward Connery Lathem, by permission of Henry Holt and Company, Inc.

"An Eye on the Future" by Jerald G. Bachman. Reprinted with permission from *Psychology Today Magazine*. Copyright © 1987 (PT Partners, L.P.)

Unit 7
"Fashion" is part 3 of "Pieces of String" from *Dancing for Men*, by Robley Wilson, Jr, reprinted by permission of the University of Pittsburgh Press. © 1983 by Robley Wilson, Jr.
"Deke" by Gary Hyland. Excerpt from the poem "The Old Ladies" reprinted from *Just Off Main* by Gary Hyland (Thistledown Press, 1982) with permission.

Unit 8
"Programming for Profit" by Merrill Panitt from *TV Guide: The First 25 Years*. © 1978 Triangle Publication, Inc. All Rights Reserved.

Unit 9
"Healthy Hearty Taste" from *The Edible Woman* by Margaret Atwood. Used by permission of the Canadian Publishers, McClelland and Stewart, Toronto.

Unit 10
"In the Shadows" by Tina Kirkeby. Reprinted by permission of the author.
"The Cardboard Room" by Teresa Pitman. Reprinted by permission of the author.

Unit 11
"I Got Lost," "It's a Sin," "The Colour of Your Skin," and "Three Words – You Got Job?" from *The Immigrant Years* by Barry Broadfoot. Reprinted by permission of the author.
"Spelling" by G.J. Terpstra. Reprinted by permission of the author.
"Heritage" by Wayne Keon from *Many Voices: An Anthology of Contemporary Canadian Indian Poetry*. J.J. Douglas Ltd.
"Mixed Blood" by Mireille Sioui. Reprinted by permission of the author.
"We Must Have Dreams" by John Amagoalik. Reprinted by permission of the author.

Unit 12
"Arrival" from *Digging Up the Mountains* by Neil Bissoondath © 1985. Reprinted by permission of Macmillan of Canada, A Division of Canada Publishing Corporation.

Unit 16
"A Secret Lost in the Water" by Roch Carrier from *The Hockey Sweater and Other Stories*, translated by Sheila Fischman. (Toronto: House of Anansi Press, 1979). Reprinted by permission.

Unit 17
"Your Listening Profile" by Lyman K. Steil. *The Toastmaster*, July 1987.
"Set Up Your Listening Ladder" by Jane Kvasnica. *The Toastmaster*, July 1987.

Unit 20
"Woodtick" by Joy Kogawa from *A Choice of Dreams*. Used by permission of The Canadian Publishers, McClelland and Stewart, Toronto.
"The Man Who Finds His Son Has Become a Thief" from *Collected Poems of Raymond Souster* by permission of Oberon Press.

PHOTO CREDITS

1-0 Athlete Information Bureau
1-2 *Saturday Evening Post*, March 17, 1956
1-3 "The Far Side" cartoon by Gary Larson is reprinted by permission of Chronicle Features, San Francisco, California
1-5 "For Better or For Worse" cartoon by Lynn Johnson. United Features Syndicate, Inc.

2-0 Julian Murray
2-2 NYT Pictures
2-3 Zach Hauser
2-5 Julian Murray

3-0 Stephanie Hollyman/UNICEF
3-1 Universal Press Syndicate
3-2 © 1988, *Bloom County*. Washington Post Writers Group. Reprinted with permission
3-3 Reprinted with special permission of King Features Syndicate, Inc.
3-4 Stephanie Hollyman/UNICEF

4-0 Neil Newton, Canadian Museum of Contemporary Photography/National Museums of Canada
4-1 Neil Newton, Canadian Museum of Contemporary Photography/National Museums of Canada
4-2 United Features Syndicate, Inc.

5-0 Marg Lyons
5-7 Hugh Howden, Trevor Petrow
5-8 Norris – *The Vancouver Sun*
5-9 Mr. and Mrs. McCormick
5-11 Marg Lyons
5-12 Laura H. Chapman
5-13 Marg Lyons
5-14 Canapress

6-0 Saskatchewan Government Photograph
6-1 United Features Syndicate, Inc.
6-2 Saskatchewan Government Photograph
6-3 Cathy Bellesisles
6-4 Cathy Bellesisles
6-6 Saskatchewan Government Photograph

7-0 *Louis XIV* by Rigaud, Musée du Louvre
7-1 Fred Smith
7-2 *Louis XIV* by Rigaud, Musée du Louvre
7-3 Colleen Wilson
7-4 Norris – *The Vancouver Sun*
7-5 *Long Branch, New Jersey*. Winslow Homer. American, 1836-1910. Oil on Canvas. 16 x 21 3/4 in. Hayden Collection, Courtesy, Museum of Fine Arts, Boston.
7-6 The Leather Ranch
7-7 Wilhelm Verhulst
7-8 Marg Lyons
7-9 Marg Lyons
7-10 The Ontario Ministry of Tourism and Recreation

8-0 Lorie Sikura
8-1 United Features Syndicate, Inc.
8-2a Lorie Sikura

8-2b CTV/Settler Film Productions, Inc.
8-2c Athlete Information Bureau
8-3a Athlete Information Bureau
8-3b Children's Television Workshop
8-3c CTV
8-4 United Features Syndicate, Inc.

9-0 MacLaren Advertising
9-1 MacLaren Advertising
9-2 Apple Canada Inc.
9-3 The Cancer Society
9-4 DDB Needham Worldwide Advertising Ltd.
9-5 Tourism British Columbia
9-6 Yamaha Motor Canada Ltd.
9-7 Castrol Canada Inc.
9-8 Paco Electronics
9-9 MacLaren Advertising
9-10 MacLaren Advertising

10-0 Jacket illustration by Amy Hill from *The Victim* by Saul Bellow. Copyright © 1988 by Viking Penguin Inc. All rights reserved. Reprinted by permission of Viking Penguin, a division of Penguin books USA, Inc.
10-1 By permission of Johnny Hart and NAS, Inc.
10-3 Jacket illustration by Amy Hill from *The Victim* by Saul Bellow. Copyright © 1988 by Viking Penguin Inc. All rights reserved. Reprinted by permission of Viking Penguin, a division of Penguin books USA, Inc.

11-0 Taken from *Fields* © 1976 William Kurelek published by Tundra Books.
11-1 Cathy Bellesisles
11-2 Taken from *Fields* © 1976 William Kurelek published by Tundra Books.
11-3 Cathy Bellesisles
11-4 Cathy Bellesisles
11-5 Cathy Bellesisles
11-6 Inglis Sheldon-Williams, *The Landmark*.Collection of the Mackenzie Art Gallery, Gift of Mr. Norman Mackenzie.
11-7 Alootook Ipellie

12-0 Ontario Science Centre
12-1 David Yee
12-2 The Ontario Ministry of Tourism and Recreation
12-3 The Ontario Ministry of Tourism and Recreation
12-4a Ontario Science Centre
12-4b Ontario Science Centre
12-4c Cathy Bellesisles

16-2 Wilhelm Verhulst

17-1 J.Walter Thompson on behalf of Adams Brands

18-1 *Regina Leader-Post*
18-2a Reprinted with permission – The Toronto Star Syndicate
18-2b Reprinted with permission – The Toronto Star Syndicate
18-3 Reprinted with permission – The Toronto Star Syndicate
18-4 Reprinted with permission – The Toronto Star Syndicate
18-5 Len Norris – *The Vancouver Sun*
18-6 Vahan Shirvanian
18-7 Vahan Shirvanian